The Making of Florida's Universities

UNIVERSITY PRESS OF FLORIDA

Florida A&M University, Tallahassee
Florida Atlantic University, Boca Raton
Florida Gulf Coast University, Ft. Myers
Florida International University, Miami
Florida State University, Tallahassee
New College of Florida, Sarasota
University of Central Florida, Orlando
University of Florida, Gainesville
University of North Florida, Jacksonville
University of South Florida, Tampa
University of West Florida, Pensacola

The Making of Florida's Universities

Public Higher Education at the Turn of the Twentieth Century

CARL VAN NESS

University Press of Florida
Gainesville · Tallahassee · Tampa · Boca Raton
Pensacola · Orlando · Miami · Jacksonville · Ft. Myers · Sarasota

Copyright 2023 by Carl Van Ness
All rights reserved
Published in the United States of America

28 27 26 25 24 23   6 5 4 3 2 1

Library of Congress Cataloging-in-Publication Data
Names: Van Ness, Carl, author.
Title: The making of Florida's universities : public higher education at
    the turn of the twentieth century / Carl Van Ness.
Description: 1. | Gainesville : University Press of Florida, 2023. |
    Includes bibliographical references and index.
Identifiers: LCCN 2022052917 (print) | LCCN 2022052918 (ebook) | ISBN
    9780813069753 (hardback) | ISBN 9780813070537 (pdf)
Subjects: LCSH: Public universities and colleges—Florida—History. |
    Education, Higher—Florida—History. | BISAC: EDUCATION / Schools /
    Levels / Higher | HISTORY / United States / State & Local / South (AL,
    AR, FL, GA, KY, LA, MS, NC, SC, TN, VA, WV)
Classification: LCC LB2328.6 .V36 2023 (print) | LCC LB2328.6 (ebook) |
    DDC 389.759—dc23/eng/20221123
LC record available at https://lccn.loc.gov/2022052917
LC ebook record available at https://lccn.loc.gov/2022052918

The University Press of Florida is the scholarly publishing agency for the State University System
of Florida, comprising Florida A&M University, Florida Atlantic University, Florida Gulf Coast
University, Florida International University, Florida State University, New College of Florida,
University of Central Florida, University of Florida, University of North Florida, University of
South Florida, and University of West Florida.

University Press of Florida
2046 NE Waldo Road
Suite 2100
Gainesville, FL 32609
http://upress.ufl.edu

To Laurel
For Sharon and Spencer

Contents

List of Figures ix
Preface xi
Acknowledgments xv
Introduction 1

Part I. Before Buckman

1. Public Education in Redemption Florida 11
2. A Curse Rather Than a Blessing 26
3. Turmoil at Lake City 42
4. The Revolutions of 1904 57

Part II. Buckman

5. The Buckman Revolution 69
6. The Immediate Aftermath of Buckman 78
7. The Agony of Andrew Sledd 94
8. The Fallout from Florida's Sledd Affair 108

Part III. After Buckman

9. The Quandary of the Normal School 120
10. Budget Battles 132
11. The Ordeal of Nathan Young 146
12. President Murphree's Final Battle 161

Postscript: More Revolutions and Then the Counterrevolution 173
Notes 187
Sources 211
Index 217

Figures

1. East Florida Seminary cadet Warren McNair, age thirteen, 1903   8
2. Statue of Albert Murphree at the University of Florida   33
3. Statue of Albert Murphree at Florida State University   34
4. Campus of the Florida Agricultural College, circa 1890   39
5. Flagler Gymnasium at the University of Florida, Lake City, 1901   41
6. "A Company of Volunteers," 1897   45
7. Student Ida Morgan at the University of Florida, 1903   54
8. Student Ida Morgan at Florida State College, 1904   54
9. Postcard of the University of Florida, Lake City   79
10. Mailer distributed by the City of Gainesville, 1905   87
11. The University of Florida, Gainesville, circa 1906   96
12. Carnegie Library at Florida Agricultural and Mechanical College   147
13. Architect's depiction of proposed administrative and classroom complex at the University of Florida   163
14. The University of Florida Auditorium, circa 1925   172

Preface

As with many histories, this one involves conflict. Central to this history is the Buckman Act of 1905, a state law that upended and completely revamped Florida's system, if we can call it that, of higher education. Commentators of its day frequently referred to the act as a revolution. Doubtless, the Buckman Act was a watershed event, and the prepositional phrases "before Buckman" and "after Buckman" will appear frequently in this text. The act was intended to eliminate two conflicts that were undermining public education in Florida: conflicts between Florida's schools of higher learning and conflicts between those schools and Florida's public high schools. Regarding those purposes, the act was very successful as it lessened the former and eliminated the latter. However, the act engendered new conflicts: over where Florida's public colleges and universities would be located, who would head them, and, most significantly, who would manage the affairs of higher education.

Governance is crucial to this story. No one person or group determines the affairs of a state university system, and all the relevant actors respond and react to one another in a multitude of ways. In an ideal academic world, which has never existed anywhere, the actors would interact in positive ways to achieve common and desirable goals. When the actors are at constant loggerheads, though, the system and its constituents suffer the consequences. In the two decades after Buckman, there was an almost constant battle between the Florida Board of Education and the Florida Board of Control, an entity created by the Buckman Act, to determine how much control over higher education the latter would have. Caught between these two contentious poles of authority were the beleaguered presidents of the University of Florida, the Florida State College for Women, and Florida A&M College.

The Buckman Act was passed in the Progressive Era under a progressive governor. Scholars have viewed it as an attempt to reform a system sorely in need of change. The progressive aspects of the act are indisputable, as was evident from the reaction of conservative educators when it was passed. However, there were also facets of the act that mystified progressive educators. Furthermore, if the act was intended to improve higher education, it can be reasonably argued that it failed that purpose. Briefly put, Florida's system of higher education made little progress in the Progressive Era. In that regard, Florida's history is a subversion of the standard histories of modern higher education, which often convey to their readers a sense of upward and onward progress. More often, those histories have focused on the nation's largest and most forward-looking institutions. In the public sphere, Michigan, Wisconsin, and California often serve as historical proxies for other state university systems. The three were paragons of progressive education and models for how other public colleges should operate. Sadly, though, most state universities had histories that were far more precarious and arduous than those golden three. This was particularly true in the South. Much of this story will be familiar to any student of southern higher education: the proliferation of inferior schools, racial tensions, gender divisions, the lack of articulation between secondary and tertiary education, and the extreme poverty in which the region's universities emerged.

Not all was gloom and doom in early twentieth-century Florida. Secondary education made great strides, the state's college campuses grew, and enrollments flourished. Florida dealt with its plague of substandard colleges by simply removing them, a solution that other southern states did not pursue. However, educational progress in Florida required years of contention and supplication before political leaders would relent, change course, and allocate even minimally adequate funds. This was nowhere more evident than at the Florida Agricultural and Mechanical College, where, after decades of neglect, the Board of Education attempted to terminate all higher education for African Americans. This draconian attack spurred a dramatic student revolt that was more guerrilla warfare than protest. Before it was over, several campus buildings were put to the torch. From the actual ashes of the uprising's apparent defeat, though, rose a new and better Florida A&M.

This history covers the years leading up to and the twenty-two years following Buckman. It would be difficult to put a precise date on when higher education in Florida began. Something akin to a public college came into being in the last fifteen years of the nineteenth century, coinciding with the establishment of Florida's first private colleges, Rollins College and Stetson University. That the State of Florida did not possess a single college for the first thirty-five years of its existence is unprecedented in the history of the nation. Florida can claim other dubious distinctions in the history of American higher education. It was the last of the former Confederate states to open its land grant college (1884) and one of the last states in the lower forty-eight to establish a state university (1903), even managing to beat out the territories of Arizona (1885), New Mexico (1889) and Oklahoma (1890). It is the only state in modern history to abandon and relocate the campus of its state university.

The story ends in 1927. Although not exactly a watershed year in American history, it was in Florida. Two years ahead of the American stock market crash of 1929, Florida's economy experienced its own crash as land values plummeted, banks failed, and frozen oranges dropped from trees. The year 1927 was tumultuous in Florida for everyone and everything, including the state universities. It is also a convenient year to end, as a central character and a principal voice in this story, Albert Alexander Murphree, died on December 20, 1927. Murphree presided at Florida State College from 1897 to 1909 and at the University of Florida from 1909 until his death. Finally, 1927 marked the culmination of the twenty-two-year conflict between the Florida Board of Control and the Florida Board of Education. Governance issues and conflicts did not end in 1927, but they took on a different character with new actors after that year. Today, we are still debating the issue of higher education governance in Florida, and we are likely to do so for decades to come.

Acknowledgments

It would be difficult to state exactly when I began to write a book. For thirty-eight years I labored as an archivist at the University of Florida's George A. Smathers Libraries. A considerable portion of that time was spent in the University of Florida Archives. There I was introduced to two central actors in my narrative, Andrew Sledd and Albert Murphree, who served consecutively as presidents of the University of Florida from 1904 to 1927. My interest in Andrew Sledd and his brief time in Florida led to the publication of an article in the Winter 2009 *Florida Historical Quarterly*, and it was then that the idea of a book first crossed my mind. Portions of that article appear in this book with the *Quarterly*'s permission. Seven more years of research were followed by a much-needed sabbatical to write the first of many drafts. This was followed by a travel grant to do further research at the State Library and Archives of Florida. Both the sabbatical and the travel grant were essential, and I am indebted to my former employer for its support. It was not until 2021, though, that I felt comfortable submitting a complete manuscript to the University Press of Florida for review.

I find myself in the strange position of being an archivist who has written a book that was only made possible by the work of other archivists. Colleges and universities tend to be conscientious about preserving their histories. Sometimes, though, nature intervenes to impede the work of archivists. In the case of Florida, heat, humidity, hurricanes, and hordes of insects do not lend themselves to document preservation. This history relied heavily on the records of the one public university in Florida that managed to preserve a substantial body of its early records, the University of Florida. For that I can thank the tireless efforts of the university's first appointed historian, Samuel L. Proctor, and the archivists who followed him. As one of those archivists, I had the privilege of working with Sam Proctor, and it was a great honor to be named the University of Florida's second historian.

When I arrived at the University of Florida in 1983 as a graduate student in Latin American history, I had no plans to enter the archival profession. However, a series of serendipitous events landed me in the special collections unit of the Libraries, and I loved the work. For that I thank the university archivist at the time, Carla Summers, who hired and tutored me. Over the years, I shared time and workspaces with some incredible coworkers. A special acknowledgment goes to everyone, past and present, in the Department of Special and Area Studies Collections. The P. K. Yonge Library of Florida History is an important part of that department, and it provided many of the resources cited in this book including the papers of P. K. Yonge, who served on the Florida Board of Control for more than twenty-five years. My position in the Libraries brought me into contact with others who would influence my work, including Michael Gannon, who always had an encouraging word when I saw him. The State Library and Archives of Florida also proved to be a treasure trove of information. A collegial thank-you goes out to the staff there.

Having never submitted a book manuscript for publication, I had no expectations as to the process involved or the assistance that might be provided by a scholarly press. Now that I have gone through the process, I can attest to the diligence and professionalism of the University Press of Florida. The Press was also a fountain of encouragement. Special recognition goes to Senior Acquisitions Editor Sian Hunter, who reviewed bits and pieces of an early draft, encouraged me to finish the manuscript, and then counseled me until the manuscript was publishable.

A final thank-you goes to my "editor," Ida Altman. Her eager and loving support pushed me to the finish line.

Introduction

The Historical Foundations of Public Higher Education

The history of American public higher education in the nineteenth and early twentieth centuries rests on three institutional pillars: the state university, the land grant college, and the state normal school. In each state, the three pillars are represented in at least one but more often several existing universities. In Michigan, for example, the University of Michigan is the oldest of that state's public colleges and traces its beginning to a territorial charter in 1817; Michigan State University is the land grant college founded in 1855; and Eastern Michigan University began as the Michigan State Normal School in 1849. In most states, though, the pillars are not as distinctly represented. In fact, there is no classic historical path for public higher education, and there may be as many paths as there are states; every state's history of higher education seems to be unique. Florida's story is one of the more interesting and certainly one of the most painful.[1]

If there is no single path to contemporary public higher education, the nation's state universities nonetheless have managed to arrive at common destinations. All but the smallest states have more than one state university, and each university offers degrees in a variety of fields and disciplines. One school might be more oriented to the liberal and fine arts and another geared toward applied and theoretical sciences, but they all offer at least a core curriculum that covers dozens of additional subject areas. What is often obscured is the origin of a particular institution. It is of no concern to students currently enrolled at Arizona State University or Eastern Washington University that their alma maters began as normal schools; a student at either school will find a wide variety of course offerings.

Of the three institutional pillars, the state normal school has received scant attention from historians of higher education.[2] Normal schools were organized to provide coursework and practical training to teachers.

They hark back to sixteenth-century European traditions where apprentice teachers worked alongside veteran teachers in model demonstration schools. These model schools also served as social laboratories that established standards for teaching. In the United States, model, or laboratory, schools were often attached to normal schools, but local public schools would sometimes conduct their own normal programs. The "county normal" affixed to a public secondary school was a popular way for rural school districts to train teachers in the late nineteenth and early twentieth centuries.

Normal schools served a variety of teaching and institutional needs. Some, like the county normal schools, catered to grammar schools, whereas others covered the entire gamut of primary and secondary education. Normal schools could also be public or private. Private normal schools flourished in the nineteenth century and rapidly disappeared in the twentieth century. Framingham State University in Massachusetts, established in 1839, is the nation's oldest public university that began as a normal school. Normal schools in the nineteenth century were typically stand-alone institutions. By the end of that century, though, it had become common to attach normal schools to both public and private universities. Even so, normal schools were below college grade, and the normal school's licentiate of instruction, or LI, was inferior to the bachelor's degree.

The dearth of history on the normal school is unfortunate because in obscuring its history we also obscure an important part of the history of women. Women have long made up a large majority of the students taking classes in education. By the early 1900s, it was unusual to find a man teaching in a grammar school, and women were beginning to dominate secondary education as well. Women also found employment in the normal schools, whereas they were routinely excluded from the faculties of the colleges. The absence of discussion regarding the normal school is even more amazing given the extent to which it appears in the historical record. Historians cannot complain about a lack of archival documents. In Florida, and elsewhere, the normal school figured heavily in the correspondence and reports of nineteenth- and twentieth-century educators.

In the South, there is an additional institutional pillar to be discussed, and that is what is usually referred to as the "historically Black college or university," or HBCU. Race, of course, is an unavoidable subject in any history of the region and perhaps nowhere more so than in a history of education. A critical blow against segregation was delivered in 1954, when the United States Supreme Court ruled in *Brown v Board of Education* that the concept of "separate but equal" invoked in *Plessy v Ferguson* had yielded manifest disparities in the delivery of education to white and Black children in the South. Decades of Jim Crow education left many institutional legacies, including the Florida Agricultural and Mechanical University, Florida's only historically Black public university.

Florida's Pillars

Florida's pillars rest figuratively on the campuses of the three oldest state universities—Florida State University, the University of Florida, and the Florida Agricultural and Mechanical University. Each school invokes its own historical narrative. Yet, buried on the sites of six ghost campuses are forgotten narratives. Ghost campuses are common in the United States, but most are the remains of failed private colleges. Hundreds dot the nation's map, and each year seems to add another ghost or two. It is rare, though, for public colleges to fail, and Florida is certainly unique in counting six such ghosts. These ghosts cannot be ignored. They are an integral part of this history, and they beckon us to paths taken and not taken. To better understand Florida's interesting and complex history, the following is a brief synopsis of Florida's earliest public institutions of higher learning and the legislative acts associated with their establishment and disbandment.[3]

In literature and legend, ghosts are often the victims of murder, injustice, or mayhem. The slayer of four of Florida's ghost schools is the Buckman Act of 1905. Whether the deeds of Buckman were foul or fair, murders or mercy killings, is a subject for this book. The Buckman Act abolished—that is the word used in the act—seven institutions of higher learning and created, in their stead, a state university for white men and a state college for white women. Lawmakers and educators presumed that two of the eradicated institutions would revive in the form of the new schools. That prediction proved to be only half-accurate as the pre-Buckman Florida State College in Tallahassee did become the Florida State College for Women and is now Florida State University. However, the University of Florida, which had been in Lake City, is now in Gainesville.

Florida's first state-funded schools were the East Florida Seminary and the West Florida Seminary. It is from these two schools that the University of Florida and Florida State University derive their current founding dates. The University of Florida settled on 1853, the year the East Florida Seminary opened its doors, whereas Florida State looks to 1851, the charter date for both seminaries. Of the two seminaries, the West Florida Seminary became the Florida State College and lives on as Florida State University; the East Florida Seminary campus is now occupied by the First United Methodist Church of Gainesville and an adjacent city park.

What were the seminaries? The seminaries emerged from federal land grants given to seventeen states created between 1796 and 1861. Land in the form of townships—a surveying unit that measured 46,080 acres—was set aside in each territory to support education. Proceeds from the sale of the land were used to create endowments to fund the construction of schools and to hire instructors. Each territory received a land grant to establish a common school fund for basic education and another grant for schools at a higher level, often referred to as seminaries. The seminary grants did not specify the character of the schools to be created, but most territorial governments used the opportunities to endow colleges. Congress provided the Territory of Florida with two townships to support a seminary in 1823 and two more townships when Florida became a state in 1845. However, the additional townships came with a stipulation that two seminaries be established, one east and one west of the Suwannee River. The territorial grants were actualized after statehood when the state legislature passed the Seminary Act of 1851. Ocala was chosen as the first site for the East Florida Seminary. The state legislature created the first ghost campus in 1866, when the charter was transferred to Gainesville after the Civil War. The West Florida Seminary opened in Tallahassee in 1857.

If the additional townships appear to have been strokes of fortune, subsequent history suggests that the state would have been better off with just one seminary. The additional school created unnecessary and unhealthy competition and diverted the state from efforts to create a state university. When it was suggested in the 1870s that the schools be consolidated, it was discovered that the federal and state laws creating them would have to be repealed first. The Buckman Act avoided that problem by allocating the seminary funds to the two new schools created by the act, which were conveniently located east and west of the Suwannee River.

In 2012, the nation marked the sesquicentennial of the passage of the Morrill Act of 1862. Much was written and said then about the significance of the law, and there is a substantial body of work and a wide range of opinions on just how great an impact it had on higher education. In brief, though, the act created another gift of land to be sold for the creation of educational endowments. This act differed from the seminary acts in several ways. First, the lands of the seminary acts were in the states receiving the grants, whereas Morrill Act lands might be located anywhere in the nation and often came from the vast and still contested regions of the West. The amount of land granted to a state was based on the number of congressmen from that state and thus varied significantly. Finally, the Morrill Act grants were not restricted to newly created states but were available to all states and territories.

Unlike the seminary acts, the Morrill Act set some rules on how the monies were to be spent. For one, they could not be used on capital projects or to acquire land. Land grant schools were also required to provide instruction in agriculture and engineering. The law further advocated that these courses be taught alongside the traditional liberal arts. Otherwise, though, the act gave no guidance as to how the money should be spent, nor did it mandate the creation of new or separate colleges. The Morrill Act was strengthened and expanded by a string of subsequent acts, including the Second Morrill Act of 1890.

Florida, in 1862, was not the beneficiary of any federal largesse as Florida and ten other states were at war with the government that was handing out the free land. When the war ended, the eleven former Confederate states were permitted to secure their land grants. Florida chartered its land grant college in 1870 under the name the Florida Agricultural College. Two attempts were made during Reconstruction to establish the college, and both failed. The first try was made, oddly, in Gainesville. Lands from the Florida Railroad, which passed through Gainesville, were to be used for the campus; Gainesville offered a cash incentive as well. Nothing came of that venture, not even a ghost campus, and another potential campus was found in Eau Gallie, part of present-day Melbourne. The offer came from William Henry Gleason. Gleason was a native of Eau Claire, Wisconsin, who arrived in Florida after the war. He was one of many northerners with ready cash who came south to speculate in lands cheapened by postwar economic conditions. Gleason and his sons, William and George, invested heavily along Florida's central and southern Atlantic coast. Gleason was also a prominent member of Florida's Republican Party and served as lieutenant governor in the Reconstruction government.

Gleason reasoned that an agricultural college in Florida should be located with the "design of establishing a nursery of semi-tropical plants." "Florida is the only State in the Union possessed of a semi-tropical climate and the only one where a botanical experimental garden for the acclimatization of tropical plants can be successfully established," he argued. Gleason offered 2,320 acres that included a campus stretched along the banks of the Indian River.[4] The state accepted Gleason's proposal in 1875, and a flurry of activity followed. The campus was surveyed and cleared, a road leading up to the campus was laid, a single building was constructed of coquina, and a pamphlet advertising the anticipated opening of the college was distributed in 1877. That year also marked the end of Reconstruction and the advent of southern Redemption, and Florida's Redeemers wanted nothing to do with the lands offered by the carpetbagger Gleason. The years immediately following 1877 provide few clues as to what transpired, but future state superintendent of public instruction William Nicholas Sheats later remarked, "Verily, verily, Florida had a white elephant on her hands in the shape of an Agricultural College for a long time before she learned what to do with it."[5] Fourteen years after its charter, the college opened in 1884 in upland and inland Lake City. In 1903, the college was renamed the University of Florida. It completed two academic years as the University of Florida before it was abolished by the Buckman Act.

The ghost of the Eau Gallie campus presents an intriguing historical "what if." One can imagine and dream about a University of Florida two miles from some of the nation's most scenic beaches. Talk about your Suntan U! Alas, it was not meant to be.

Forty years after it became a state in 1845, Florida had no public school to train its teachers, even though the seminaries were mandated to provide teacher training. This was clearly stated in the first sentence of their 1851 charter. By the 1880s, though, both seminaries were comfortable in their unintended roles as regional preparatory schools. The Florida Constitution of 1885 remedied the situation by mandating the creation of at least one and no more than two normal schools. Two schools opened in 1887, one in DeFuniak Springs as the State Normal School for White Students and the other in Tallahassee as the State Normal School for Colored Students.

Shortly after its creation, the State Normal School for Colored Students became the recipient of federal funds from the Second Morrill Act of 1890. It added the word "Industrial" to its name and began to provide vocational training. This action was necessitated by a clause in the Second Morrill Act requiring states that forbade admission of Black students to their designated land grant colleges to split the annual federal appropriation with a school for African American students. The Buckman Act abolished the State Normal School in DeFuniak Springs but left intact the State Normal and Industrial School. It is now Florida Agricultural and Mechanical University.

To meet the demand for teachers in South Florida, the state legislature voted in 1901 to provide funds for the St. Petersburg Normal and Industrial School, a local public school in what was then Hillsborough County. The Buckman Act terminated state funding to the St. Petersburg Normal and Industrial School, but the school survived into the 1920s as a county vocational and normal school. The Buckman Act also abolished two other schools, the South Florida Military Institute in Bartow and the Florida Agricultural Institute in Kissimmee. The South Florida Military Institute was founded as a private military academy, and there is some question as to when it truly became a state school. Its founder and principal was Evander M. Law, a renowned commander in Lee's Army of Virginia. It was Law's brigade that unsuccessfully assaulted the Union army's left flank at Little Round Top on the second day of the Battle of Gettysburg. Like many Confederate officers, Law took to schooling after the war. Shortly after the school opened, the state began to fund scholarships for it, and this became the school's primary source of income. In 1903, the Institute became a college and received the right to confer the bachelor's degree even though two of its six faculty members did not possess the very degree being awarded to its graduates. Fortunately, only two such classes graduated before the Buckman Act brought its history to a close. The Florida Agricultural Institute in Osceola County was chartered in 1903, and it is unclear what its purpose was intended to be. It was not given the power to award degrees, only certificates for completed courses. The Institute, had it opened, would have replicated much of the agricultural work being done at the University of Florida, only in a climate and environment more congenial to citrus production and cattle farming. As the campus was never completed, it does not even qualify as a ghost. It merits mention simply to highlight further the odd situation that Florida faced in 1905 and the need for radical action.[6]

The state schools before Buckman were creatures of southern Redemption. In their curricula and clientele, they had one foot embedded in an antebellum plantation past while the other foot lurched toward modernity and capitalism. Geographically, the schools were situated primarily in the areas settled before the Civil War. The men—boys, really—at three of the six state schools for white students attended classes under military discipline. They were hardly military schools, though, as the military component amounted to little more than parades and occasional rifle practice. Oddly and sadly, in the years before Buckman, women had more educational choices than in most southern states; after Buckman, they would enjoy fewer. Looming

Figure 1. Cadet Warren McNair was thirteen when he entered the East Florida Seminary at Gainesville in 1903. McNair was from the nearby town of Archer. University Archives Photograph Collection, George A. Smathers Libraries, University of Florida.

over every aspect of public education, from grammar to graduate school, was the race question and the inferior quality of education available to African American students.

Such was the state of higher education in Florida before the Buckman Act brought it all to an end. The proliferation of state-supported schools in the nineteenth century yielded largely negative results. Instead of becoming institutions with statewide appeal, they catered largely to local clienteles. They also attracted high school–age students and even younger. The image of East Florida Seminary cadet Warren McNair, age thirteen, illustrates the problem. The schools were also a tremendous drain on the state's limited resources and prevented any serious consideration of developing a state university. Still, it must be said that the schools were a success in one manner; they attracted students and therefore filled a social need. But this success only exacerbated the problem. Counties without state schools looked with envy on those that had theirs, and pressures intensified to create new ones. By the end of the nineteenth century, the state schools were not only a detriment to tertiary education, but they were also having a toxic effect on Florida's emerging system of public high schools, high schools that were competing indirectly and sometimes directly with the state schools.

I

Before Buckman

1

Public Education in Redemption Florida

The confusing array of state schools that existed in late nineteenth-century Florida was typical of the South. Most offered instruction at the secondary level, if that, but often advertised themselves as colleges. Andrew Sledd estimated that 90 percent of southern colleges were sham institutions guilty of producing "intellectual infants." The college of the South had only one purpose, he stated, "to *graduate* men, not educate them—make them masters of degrees, not masters of themselves." Many, like Florida's seminaries, predated the Civil War. After the war, southern state governments frequently interceded to prop up or acquire failing private schools, which further added to the public burden. The Morrill Act prompted the creation of more schools. Six of the former Confederate states opted to use their land grant funds to create new colleges rather than designate an existing school. South Carolina, North Carolina, and Mississippi initially declared their state universities as the land grant recipients, only to bow to pressures from agrarian interests to create separate agricultural colleges. The dictates of southern apartheid led to the creation of separate colleges for African Americans—today's HBCUs—but few received state funding. In short, the South had no shortage of schools calling themselves colleges, but few that were.[1]

Redemption-era politics and the social doctrines of Jim Crow shaped all aspects of public education in the South. Poverty, racism, and extreme fiscal conservatism condemned large parts of the southern citizenry to generations of ignorance and illiteracy. Rural antipathy to compulsory education and school taxes frustrated urban enthusiasm for school improvements and made any level of educational progress difficult. Political candidates running for statewide office typically avoided the divide between urban and rural voters by giving counties considerable autonomy on educational matters. Within this political and social milieu, there arose a variety of positions on public education. At one extreme were hard-line conservatives who resisted any attempt to provide more than a rudimentary education for the children of either race. Advocates for economic development, on the other hand, saw education as a prerequisite for growth and industrialization. Between the two, there was ample room for debate and conflict, particularly regarding secondary and higher education. Representative of the divergent pedagogical and political stances in Redemption Florida were those of State Superintendent of Public Education William N. Sheats and Tom McBeath, editor of the *Florida School Exponent*, the journal of the Florida State Teachers Association.

No single person shaped educational policy in late nineteenth-century Florida more than William Nicholas Sheats. Sheats served as superintendent of public instruction for Alachua County from 1880 to 1892 and then as state superintendent of public instruction from 1893 to 1905. He was defeated in the Democratic primary of 1904, the first of the so-called white primaries, but returned as superintendent in the election of 1912. He remained in office until his death in 1922. He first came to the public's attention, though, as a delegate from Alachua County to the Florida constitutional convention of 1885. Sheats's persistent efforts at the convention on behalf of education prompted journalist John Temple Graves to label him the "school crank."[2]

The Constitution of 1885 marked the consolidation of single-party rule in Florida through the imposition of a poll tax that disenfranchised poor Black and white voters. With fewer and fewer African Americans on the voting rolls, opponents of the Democratic Party were pushed to the margins of Florida politics. Overall, the Constitution of 1885 was a reactionary document that effectively served as a brake on the burgeoning alliance of white and African American political independents. The genesis of the constitution's article on education, on the other hand, marked a rare moment at the convention when independents, populists, Republicans, and urban Democrats came together to thwart a conservative agenda. Among the delegates at the convention was Thomas Van Renssalaer Gibbs, one of a handful of African Americans. Gibbs was the son of Jonathan C. Gibbs, who served as secretary of state in Florida's Reconstruction government from 1868 to 1873 and then briefly as state superintendent of public instruction before his sudden death in 1874. He had also been a delegate to Florida's 1868 constitutional convention. The junior Gibbs was a teacher and lawyer in Jacksonville and one of the few remaining Blacks in the Florida House in 1885. His outspokenness at the convention impelled the *Florida Times-Union* to brand him as "tonguey." He had, undoubtedly, a lot to say while witnessing Florida's reactionaries brazenly hammer the final nails into the coffin of African American suffrage. Although few in number, the African American delegation at the convention arrived well-prepared to push for education reforms and played a significant role in the outcome.[3]

As Sheats would freely admit, Article 12 of the Constitution of 1885 borrowed from the Constitution of 1868 and the education laws passed during Reconstruction. Article 12, section 1, required the legislature to create a uniform system of public schools. Section 6 established a one-mill state property tax to support public education, and section 7 required each county to impose a property tax of 3 to 5 mills to support local schools. Section 12 prevented white and Black children from attending the same schools, making de jure what had been de facto. Section 14 required the state legislature at its next session to create "such Normal Schools, not to exceed two, as the interests of public education may demand."[4] Subsequent to the convention, Representative Gibbs initiated the legislation that would create the constitutionally mandated normal schools, one for white teachers and another for Black teachers. Although he had hoped the school for African Americans would be located in Jacksonville, Gibbs took a position as professor of mathematics at the State Normal School for Colored Students when it opened in Tallahassee in 1887.[5]

Section 2 of Article 12 changed the position of state superintendent from an appointed position to an elected one. Section 3 provided for the Florida Board of Education, which included the superintendent, the secretary of state, the state treasurer, the attorney general, and the governor. It was, simply, an extension of executive power. Florida was unusual among the states in having an elected cabinet, although it was not technically a cabinet since the officials did not serve at the pleasure of the governor. Florida's cabinet members commanded far greater power than in other states and, collectively, were more powerful than Florida's governor. Governors in Florida were limited to a single four-year term, whereas the cabinet officers could serve multiple terms and often ran unopposed. In the years that followed the ratification of the 1885 constitution, the state expanded the number of ex officio executive boards to a total of thirty by 1940, including the State Board of Health, the State Board of Conservation, and the Budget Commission. Some, like the Board of Education and the Budget Commission, consisted solely of executive officers, whereas others contained both elected and appointed members. These boards operated under an authority system whereby one executive officer exerted greater influence than the others. In the case of the Board of Education, that officer would be the superintendent of public instruction. Overall, the network of administrative boards created a unique "collegial executive" that diffused power and responsibilities.[6]

Article 12 of the constitution did not address the missions and governance of the existing state schools, of which there were three in 1885, the two seminaries and the Florida Agricultural College. A proposal at the convention to create a board of trustees to govern the schools failed. Instead, the three schools would continue to operate independently to pursue their distinctive missions under their respective boards. The constitution did place the newly established normal schools under the direction and supervision of the Board of Education but gave neither the superintendent nor the Board of Education specific roles in the management of the other state schools. Instead, the Board of Education was only allowed "such supervision of the schools of higher grade as the law shall allow." In the absence of such law, the state schools would operate independently for the next twenty years. The superintendent would always include a section on the state schools in his reports, but he could only make suggestions regarding their appropriations and operations.[7]

Sheats and the other school cranks had already gained the upper hand by the time the constitutional convention took place. Immigration to Florida would play a role in their ascendency. The newcomers to the state clamored for better schools at all levels, kindergarten through college. Superintendent of Public Instruction Albert J. Russell noted a year before the convention that "we are inviting and drawing our increasing population . . . almost solely from the States in our own country, most of whom are, and have been, accustomed to the privileges of fine public schools." Russell's observations were echoed by educationalist George Gary Bush, who remarked, "The adherents of the new order were sure to win, but their success was greatly promoted by the addition to their numbers of a large body of settlers from other States, who brought with them broad views of the importance to the State of affording the opportunity for the highest intellectual training."[8]

Central Florida became a hub for the newcomers. One of the first areas settled was along Lake Monroe, where Henry Shelton Sanford, American ambassador to Belgium in the Lincoln administration, purchased extensive acreage on the lake's south side. Sanford promoted citrus cultivation and encouraged the emigration of hundreds of Swedes to take up farming. Some did; others opted for bourgeois pursuits in Sanford's namesake town. Sanford's own businesses were largely failures, but other investors who followed had more success. By 1885, the City of Sanford was part of a cord of thriving communities in what politicians now refer to as the "I-4 corridor," a key battleground in recent state and national elections. In the late nineteenth century, the trains of the Plant System Railroad connected the towns, and the region became the center of the state's citrus industry. The corridor also produced a string of denominational colleges. The phenomenon of "college belts" following the path of railroad development was quite common in the United States. Florida's college belt was also its citrus belt.[9]

Just as the Redeemers were relocating the Florida Agricultural College from Eau Gallie to Lake City, the first denominational colleges appeared in Central Florida. Stetson University, named after hatter and benefactor John B. Stetson, began as the DeLand Academy in 1883 and was granted a college charter by the state legislature in 1887. Stetson had a Baptist affiliation, but the Methodists were also active in the region. In the same year that the DeLand Academy opened, the South Florida Institute opened in Orlando. After several permutations and location changes it eventually became Florida Southern College in Lakeland. Catholics entered the picture with the establishment of St. Leo College near Dade City in 1889. The distinction of being the first private four-year college in Florida, though, goes to Rollins College, founded in 1885 in Winter Park by Congregationalists and financially supported by Chicago entrepreneur Alonzo Rollins.

African Americans also moved into the region. Many found work in the fields and groves as agricultural laborers, but others worked independently as farmers and shopkeepers. They formed communities of their own, including Eatonville, one of the few self-governing Black townships in the nation. Eatonville was home to the Robert Hungerford Normal and Industrial School founded in 1897 by Tuskegee alumni Russell and Mary C. Calhoun and funded by a variety of donors including Tuskegee's president, Booker T. Washington. Its principal benefactors, though, were northern philanthropists. The school was situated on a 160-acre site donated by E. C. Hungerford of Chester, Connecticut, who also owned a winter home near Eatonville. In addition to local students, Hungerford attracted students from across the state. Private until 1950, the school was transferred to the Orange County School Board that year and was shuttered in 2010. Its derelict ghost campus was still intact as of 2018. Daytona Beach is the eastern terminus of Interstate 4 and the site of Bethune-Cookman University, founded in 1904 by Mary McLeod Bethune as the Daytona Literary and

Industrial Training School for Negro Girls. In 1923, it merged with Jacksonville's Cookman Institute, founded in 1872 by the Methodist Church, and was renamed Bethune-Cookman College in 1931.

Jacksonville was the true heart of African American educational activity after the Civil War. Initially focused on freed slaves of both genders and all ages, several of the schools founded in Jacksonville played a critical role in the development of HBCUs in Florida. What is today Edward Waters University has its origins in 1866 as a school for freed slaves established by missionaries of the African Methodist Episcopal Church. It was followed by the Edwin M. Stanton School, founded in 1868. Although it would never become a college, its influence in the early twentieth century was equally profound. Under the tutelage of James Weldon Johnson, the school rapidly expanded its high school curriculum and eventually became Florida's first senior high school for Black students. Johnson's brother, J. Rosamond Johnson, taught music at nearby Florida Baptist Academy, where he set to music the poem James wrote entitled "Lift Every Voice and Sing." Florida Baptist Academy evolved to become present-day Florida Memorial University in Miami Gardens. The school was uprooted twice during its history by white intimidation and threats of violence. It began as the Florida Baptist Institute in Live Oak in 1879, but several of its faculty fled to Jacksonville in 1892, when shots were fired into the school. The school in Jacksonville moved to St. Augustine in 1918 and was renamed the Florida Normal and Industrial Institute, which, like Hungerford, patterned its curriculum on that of Tuskegee. When racial tensions in the 1960s threatened that school's safety, it moved to its current campus in Miami Gardens.

In 1892, William Sheats became the beneficiary of his own reforms when he became the first elected state superintendent of public instruction. Sheats took the opportunity in his first official report as state superintendent to expound on the history of public education in a sixty-page treatise entitled "History of the Origins and Growth of Public Schools in Florida." He felt it necessary to do so because official records were "difficult to obtain and becoming more so every year." His history begins with an assessment of antebellum attitudes that states, "It can be said thirty years after it is dead, that the institution of slavery was not conducive to the growth of free education." He noted that, prior to the Civil War, only Gadsden and Franklin Counties provided local resources for public schools. Public monies elsewhere in the state went to private schools. "So, in the midst of some form of public school operation, there was virtually no public school system," concluded Sheats's commentary on the antebellum period.[10]

A frank confession by an elected official in the Redemption era that slavery had been an impediment to educational progress was not unusual. Southern educators frequently linked postwar opposition to public education to prewar aristocratic aversions to manual labor. What was more unorthodox, though, was Sheats's view on Reconstruction. He began with the admission that Florida's pre-Reconstruction constitution of 1865 made no provision for public education. He excused the inaction and argued that it stemmed from the fear that the "odious doctrine of co-education of the races" would be forced upon the white population. This was a baseless contention as the framers of the constitution of 1865 acted under the assumption that the conciliatory policies of President Andrew Johnson would prevail and, therefore, school integration would not have been considered. Sheats moved on to Reconstruction and stated, "To be a just and impartial historian, it must be admitted that no effective legislation contemplating the establishment of a uniform system of public school supported by taxation was secured until the adoption of the Constitution of 1868, and the enactment of the school law compiled by State Superintendent C. Thurston Chase."[11]

Sheats's history summoned the standard horrors of Reconstruction—carpetbagging, race mixing, and corruption—intermingled with adulatory assessments of the individual Reconstruction superintendents including the one African American, Jonathan Gibbs, of whom Sheats remarked, "He is reputed to have been a man of integrity, culture, an orator, and quite a gentleman." As Sheats saw it, a legacy of support for public education was the one redeeming feature of an otherwise disastrous Reconstruction. Sheats also invoked the standard Redemption canard that the South would have arrived at the same destination on its own terms if only the North had not forced the needed reforms on a defeated and resistant population. As proof, he cited a number of accomplishments by the superintendents who followed Reconstruction. Yet he openly acknowledged that only a coalition of dissident forces, which he helped lead, defeated conservative opposition to the educational platform of the constitutional convention of 1885.[12]

Sheats's history also omitted the many accomplishments of the Reconstruction governments as well as a discussion of the role played by the Freedmen's Bureau. He could also have noted that the work of the Freedmen's Bureau benefited both races. By the end of Reconstruction, 137 schools for African Americans had been built. Eighty-seven of those were constructed with federal funds; the remainder were funded by northern philanthropists and benevolent societies. In lieu of the two counties with public schools before the war, there were eighteen in 1877 serving both Black and white children.[13]

Sheats would always be an oddity in Florida's Democratic Party. Early in his career, he had been a member of the populist Farmers Alliance, and his acceptance of the Democratic nomination for state superintendent in 1892 was part of a campaign to pull Alliance men into the Democratic Party. However, Sheats never embraced the extreme racial rhetoric of other southern populists turned Democrats, such as Tom Watson, Ben "Pitchfork" Tillman, and Sidney Catts. Sheats would walk a thin political line throughout his career. While he criticized his fellow southern statesmen for their refusal to support public education, he also upheld their core social values. This was most evident in the question of race and the education of African Americans. Sheats fought to maintain strict racial boundaries in education and endorsed vocational education for African Americans. In his day, though, he received both rebukes from whites and praise from Blacks. W. E. B. Du Bois referred to him as "an unusually broadminded man" for his insistence that African American teachers be given the same training opportunities as white teachers, while conservative whites thought him too liberal in this regard and attacked him for his association with Black educators.[14]

Sheats's 1894 report also took up the matter of the state schools and their histories. He noted several recommendations by previous superintendents to merge some or all of the schools, and he recounted the two aborted attempts to establish the land grant college during Reconstruction. Curiously, of the years between the abandonment of Eau Gallie and the decision to relocate the school to Lake City, Sheats stated that it was "not necessary to record here" what happened—curious because the historical record provides few clues as to why Lake City was chosen and why it took seven years to decide. He also made a derisive comment about an ill-fated attempt—an *ignis fatuus,* as he termed it—to create a state university at the West Florida Seminary. Sheats had kind words for the denominational colleges and the private normal schools. He was especially enthusiastic about the Jasper Normal Institute and the Independent Normal School at White Springs, noting that the two schools produced far more public school teachers than the state schools. He could not, however, disguise his disappointment in the state-supported schools, which had been the recipient of "munificent gifts" but had not "fully measured up to the limits of its possibilities nor wholly met the demands of public expectations."[15]

Sheats's principal concern as state superintendent was not the state's colleges, of course, but the disquieting array of local public schools. In the 1890s, the school calendar varied considerably from county to county. Some rural counties offered only a few months, typically in the fall, whereas a few urban counties held classes in the fall, winter, and spring. For Black students, the school year was typically shorter than for whites. Some counties failed to provide any level of graded education for either race and tossed students of various ages into common classrooms. Elsewhere, graded schools terminated anywhere between the fifth and tenth grades. As late as 1905, the percentages of white students attending school beyond the fifth grade ranged from a high of 36 percent (Citrus County) to a low of 2 percent (Santa Rosa County.)[16] By Sheats's estimation, there was only one bona fide senior high school in the entire state, Duval High School in Jacksonville. Parents who wanted to extend a child's education beyond what was available in the local public school system had only two options. The first option was to pay tuition at a private academy, and the second was one of the state schools. Everywhere, though, the dearth of teachers and the inferior quality of their training hampered the cause of education in Florida. This was where Sheats centered his efforts.

As state superintendent, Sheats brought a degree of integrity to a teacher certification system corrupted by favoritism and outright fraud. In 1893, he crafted legislation that would completely revamp Florida's rules, procedures, and examinations for teacher certification. The law was enacted on June 8, 1893, and amended in the 1895 legislative session. Sheats based his approach on the education laws of New York and Indiana as well as his experiences as school superintendent in Alachua County. The act provided for a two-tier system of certification, one for county certification and one for the state. Both tiers had three grades, and there were six grades that a teacher could attain, the first-grade state certificate being the highest and the county third grade the lowest. Certification was based solely on examination. Sheats rejected certification upon graduation from a normal school or college but acknowledged that other states allowed it.[17] Simply put, Sheats had little faith in Florida's public and private colleges, nor did he have any means of assessing the worthiness of their degrees.

Rather than grandmother the 561 teachers holding state certificates in 1893 into the new grading system, all had to take the new exams. Sample questions for the first-grade state certificate were distributed, and only seventeen opted to take the examination in 1894. Of that number, seven passed. Among the seven was William S. Cawthon, who would succeed Sheats as state superintendent in 1922. The remainder opted for the county examinations. Two hundred eighty teachers secured county first-grade positions, with the rest settling for second- and third-grade certificates. Several teachers failed altogether. The senior class of the State Normal School in DeFuniak Springs also took the county examination. The results confirmed Sheats's misgivings about the quality of teacher training in Florida; only two students passed the exam.[18]

Despite Sheats's efforts, the two-tiered system of examination was still prone to fraud and incompetence at the county level. County examiners often lacked the educational background needed to grade the exams. Some were "party tools" who doled out certificates as political favors. Cheating was common. County examiners had the discretion to alter the examinations by voiding questions they considered too hard. Wilbert A. Little, an instructor at the Jasper Normal Institute, described one unnamed county as a "certificate mecca" where incompetent teachers were routinely certified. As a corrective measure, Little advocated eliminating county examination boards and replacing them with regional boards under the supervision of the state superintendent.[19]

Summer schools were an indispensable facet of teacher training throughout the nation. Practicing teachers spent a month or so of their summer breaks in coursework that would prepare them for examinations or qualify them for specific subject assignments. Tuition-based summer schools were held at the private normal schools, but Florida's public summer schools had been suspended long before Sheats took office in 1893. To revive the program, Sheats first had to convince the Peabody Education Fund to restore funding to the state. George Peabody, a Massachusetts financier and philanthropist, established the fund in 1867. Until the creation of the Rockefeller-backed General Education Board in 1902, it was the largest northern philanthropy working to improve education in the South. The Peabody Fund had terminated grants to Florida because the state had failed to provide its required share of the costs. Five racially segregated summer schools were held in 1894 in Marianna, Monticello, Gainesville, Ocala, and Bartow. Sheats reported that 505 white teachers and 428 Black teachers attended the summer schools that year.[20]

Within two years of his election, Superintendent Sheats had radically moved the needle of educational reform in a positive and progressive direction. The needle would have shifted further but for the conservatism of other education leaders. As editor of the *Florida School Exponent*, the official organ of the Florida State Teachers Association, Tom McBeath voiced strong opinions on the quality of education in Florida, opinions that were not always in line with those of his colleague and friend William Sheats. McBeath was also one of the seven who passed the 1894 state certificate exam. He held several professional positions over the years, including a short stretch at the East Florida Seminary, before ending his time in Florida as principal of Gainesville High School. He served as Sheats's secretary during his first term as superintendent and then challenged Sheats for the office in 1900. Sheats and McBeath shared a number of views on educational improvement, but they also had profound disagreements. Although far more conservative than Sheats, McBeath was, by the criteria of his time and region, an educational reformer. That time was rapidly passing, though.[21]

McBeath's views on public education harked back to an earlier time in the nation when parents were discouraged from prolonging their children's formal education, lest they become dependent on the family and the state. By McBeath's increasingly outdated standards, Florida's public schools in the 1890s "were the equal of the best."[22] Given what we know about the condition of public education in late nineteenth-century Florida, the assertion seems preposterous. McBeath's contentious views on compulsory education and child labor laws were indicative of his overall philosophy. He opposed both. In McBeath's case, the opposition to compulsory education was not a tactical position, as it was for Sheats and others, but a deeply held conviction. As late as 1907, McBeath remarked: "We know the statement will raise . . . a regular rafter-raising howl, but it is true, and we are going to say it: *The schools are responsible for more dwarfed manhood and womanhood than are the factories.*"[23] In his opinion, 75 percent of the children needed only a basic grammar education before learning a useful trade and entering the workforce. Accordingly, he resisted the expansion of high school education and categorically rejected the idea that public high schools should prepare college-bound students. If these sentiments now seem strange for an officer of the State Teachers Association, they were sadly common when he penned them. By the advent of the twentieth century, though, progressive educational theories began to filter into the South, and McBeath would spend his last years in Florida cast in the role of a reactionary flamethrower. He left Florida soon after the Buckman Act for a position in Mississippi, where his views were still in vogue.

In a speech before the Florida Press Association in the winter of 1897, McBeath alerted his audience to a forthcoming *Exponent* article on the "delicate" and "difficult" subject of Florida's state schools.[24] There were six state schools at the time. They included the two seminaries, the Florida Agricultural College, the State Normal School in DeFuniak Springs, and the state's most recent acquisition, the South Florida Military Institute. McBeath did not, however, comment on the State Normal and Industrial School for Colored Students. In Jim Crow Florida, the pedagogical needs of African American teachers were not suitable subject matter for the *Exponent*. African American teachers established a parallel Florida State Teachers Association with its own journal, the *Florida Teachers Bulletin*. McBeath's article appeared in the May 1897 *Exponent*, and he felt no need to restrain his remarks. He began his jeremiad by stating that Florida was "sadly behind even the most backward of our sister [southern] states."[25] McBeath offered no path to improvement, or even an explanation as to how Florida's system of higher education came to be, but only a litany of the schools' woes. In a later editorial, McBeath suggested consolidation of the state schools as the only logical remedy.[26]

He began his exposition with the two seminaries: "Whatever the two seminaries may have been, or may have been meant to be, they are now practically nothing more than respectable high schools for their respective counties; indeed, it is hardly proper to call them high schools, since the majority of pupils in attendance are pursuing, for the most part, simply the ordinary grammar school studies." His critique of the white State Normal School was largely the same: "The State Normal School at DeFuniak Springs is a Normal in name only. Its work is distinctively elementary and secondary, largely elementary. It has no chair of pedagogy nor model practice-school. At most it could be called nothing more than a high school with a grammar-school attachment." He went on to dismiss the normal school's Panhandle location as an excuse for its failure and as proof noted that most teachers opted to attend private schools and pay a high rate of tuition rather than the tuition-free State Normal. The South Florida Military Institute was next in line for assessment, and he questioned its status as a state school: "It is merely a private enterprise to which the State donates annually $6,400 in consideration of the board and tuition of some thirty odd boys who could, without a cent's cost to the State, get identically the same training at some of the regular State institutions."[27]

McBeath reserved his final comments for the state's land grant college, the Florida Agricultural College: "The State Agricultural College is exceedingly unfortunate either in its location or in its management. An institution that might and should have been the glory and pride of the State, it has almost from the very beginning, been a shame and a reproach to the whole commonwealth. Almost from the day of its establishment down to the present writing, it has been prominently before the public only through the noise and clamor of its disgraceful wranglings. Like a Central American republic, it manifests its continued existence chiefly through its periodic revolutions."[28]

McBeath's reproach to the state's land grant college differed substantially from his critique of the other four schools. Whereas the others were condemned for being parochial in their patronage, far below their intended grades, and for being a drain on state resources, the college's shortcomings stemmed from internal problems and conflicts. Again, he offered no explanation for why these periodic revolutions happened; he simply noted that the issue prevented the college from achieving its potential. Despite its problems, McBeath argued that the college could and should be the foundation for a state university.

While the *Exponent* decried the failures of the state's public institutions of higher learning, it would, over the years, heap lavish praise on what was then Florida's largest private college, Stetson University. The motivations for that praise are unclear, but, it should be noted, Stetson was a frequent advertiser in the *Exponent*. The *Exponent* supplemented the advertisements with free publicity in the form of feature articles on the school's physical charms and the quality of its faculty and curriculum. Later, when the competition with both public and private colleges stiffened, the *Exponent*'s fawning adulation of Stetson became more pronounced. It reached a pinnacle of obsequiousness in a 1907 article describing a visit to the campus: "We . . . came away thoroughly convinced that not only is this Florida's great school, but that it is some day destined to be the great University of the South, if not the entire Union."[29]

Whatever their disagreements on other education matters, McBeath and Sheats found common ground in the problem of the state schools. While Sheats duly noted the suggestions of McBeath and others for consolidation of the state schools, he considered their existence a fait accompli by the time he entered office in 1893. At the 1885 convention, though, Sheats favored making the land grant college the state university and having the seminaries serve as preparatory schools with a common governing board for all three schools. Governor Francis P. Fleming made a similar proposal in his 1891 address to the state legislature, but the legislature failed to act on it.[30] Sheats's biennial report for 1899–1900 included a section entitled "A Mistake in the Outset" in which he argued that it had been a mistake to create "so many schools aspiring to college rank." He went on to say,

"The State Superintendent has been warned that he is treading on dangerous ground even in suggesting that a mistake has been made." But, he reassured his readers, "No school now enjoying the distinction of being a State institution need be abandoned. Each might be co-ordinated with the general system . . . and continue to do high school work, which each for the most part is doing at the present." In his 1902 report, though, Sheats finally acquiesced to the idea of consolidation.[31]

As he approached reelection to a fourth term as state superintendent in 1904, Sheats had garnered considerable support for his persistent and resolute adherence to stricter standards for public schools and their teachers. Inevitably, though, he made a number of enemies. His combativeness and a touchy disposition—he really was a bit of a crank—did not win him additional friends. McBeath stated that Sheats was "too suspicious of his friends and under-officers" and was "bossy" as an administrator. Adversaries called him a "vindictive old parasite" and a "consummate old hypocrite," among other things. Furthermore, Sheats left himself open to accusations of being soft on the race question by his insistence on proper training for African American teachers. The election of 1904 would be the first in which the Democratic Party chose its candidates in a spring primary rather than a state party convention. The Democratic primary also excluded African American voters, and those votes would likely have gone to Sheats.[32]

His opponent in the 1904 primary was his successor as superintendent of public instruction for Alachua County, William H. Holloway. Holloway's political backer was State Senator H. H. McCreary, editor of the *Gainesville Sun*, who had been the recent object of Sheats's wrath. McCreary had sponsored two bills that Sheats considered destructive to public education. The first was a bill that would have weakened teacher certification, and the second was a textbook bill that would have made textbook purchasers vulnerable to kickbacks from publishers and distributors. Sheats used his influence to kill both bills. Holloway's campaign centered on Sheats's involvement in a speech given by Tuskegee president Booker T. Washington in Gainesville in 1902. Holloway claimed to have a copy of a damning invitation to Washington, written by Sheats, indicating that Washington would speak before an integrated audience at Gainesville High School. Sheats was eventually able to procure the actual invitation from President Washington, which did not suggest the attendance of both races, and then demanded that Holloway produce his version. Holloway refused, but the accusations had already done their damage, and Holloway easily won the primary. Sheats then petitioned the Executive Committee of the Florida

Democratic Party to investigate Holloway's conduct, and the Executive Committee found sufficient grounds to deny Holloway the nomination. However, the committee declined to make Sheats the nominee and gave the nomination to J. Emmett Wolfe of Pensacola. In the fall general election, Holloway won as an independent, while Wolfe largely avoided the campaign.[33]

Sheats would make one final comment on the problem of the state schools before leaving office. After citing his earlier reports on the subject, Sheats concluded his last biennial report with the following declaration: "In view of these repeated utterances, supported by statistics, suggesting the wisdom of consolidation rather than multiplication in the number of state-supported schools for higher education, and considering the fact that my term of service is so soon to expire, I believe it inexpedient to say more on this subject and that my duty is fully performed."[34] Someone else would have to come up with a satisfactory solution.

2

A Curse Rather Than a Blessing

If the antiquated views of Tom McBeath and others continued to hold sway at the turn of the twentieth century, it was largely because they reflected existing economic and social realities. School attendance exemplified the problem. Enrollments increased steadily in the early twentieth century, but the percentage of attendance declined. For many young Floridians, urban and rural, white and Black, there was little to be gained by staying in school. The demand for education came largely from an emergent middle class, but their numbers could not keep pace with the demand for juvenile labor in the fields and factories. The laissez-faire economic policies of conservatives served as an additional brake on educational progress, but progressive and populist politicians threatened the conservatives' political dominance in the first decades of the twentieth century. Convulsive as it was, positive change was evident in the field of education.

The changes were more apparent at the grammar school level than in secondary education; higher education was still in its infancy. The difficulties in secondary and tertiary education were, to some degree, related to the state schools. McBeath's blistering attack on the state schools pointed to the problem without suggesting a remedy. Localism pervaded the system, and the state schools had little incentive to branch out to distant constituencies. It would have been difficult even if they had wanted to do so. The state schools were tucked away in hard-to-access insular towns, and Florida's peculiar geography and lack of public conveyance did not help matters. Site selectors for the schools had avoided the state's population centers in Jacksonville, Pensacola, and Tampa, which relied, instead, on local taxes to create Florida's first senior high schools. The urban high schools taught at essentially the same grade levels as the state schools but without their emphases on rhetoric, forensics, and classical languages and minus the military trappings. Fundamentally, localism reflected the reality of Redemption politics and the diffusion of power to Florida's rural counties.

The lack of a political center or any coherent program for development and improvement at the state level impeded the creation of secondary and tertiary schools. Each county had tremendous latitude in school funding, and each county could campaign to have a state school established within its boundaries.

Nationwide, the Morrill Act of 1862 prompted the creation of new public universities. In the former Confederacy, Arkansas utilized its land grant funds to create the University of Arkansas, and Louisiana combined its seminary and Morrill endowments to create what is now Louisiana State University. (Tulane was, at that time, the University of Louisiana; it was not privatized until 1884.) As evidenced by both Sheats's and McBeath's remarks, there was support in Florida for making the land grant college the state university. But even without the status of a state university, the college in Lake City created an existential dilemma for the other state schools. Each would have to decide if it was content to remain a preparatory school catering to the middle-class children of a local community or instead broaden its curriculum and clientele to serve a greater need. One school in particular, the West Florida Seminary, was intent on challenging the Florida Agricultural College as an institution of higher learning. The current academic and athletic rivalry between the Florida State University and the University of Florida has its roots in that challenge.

African Americans were largely excluded from the discussion of public higher education. In 1900, there were no publicly funded senior high schools for Black students, and the better grammar and secondary schools were supported through religious organizations and northern philanthropy. The sole state school was the State Normal School for Colored Students in Tallahassee. That school would face its own existential crisis after the implementation of the Second Morrill Act of 1890. Would it remain an institution devoted to the education and training of teachers, or would it be forcibly reoriented as a vocational training facility serving the needs of an economy dominated by white business interests?

The Florida State Normal School for Colored Students Becomes the State Normal and Industrial School

The presidents and faculty at the school that would eventually become Florida Agricultural and Mechanical University labored in a hostile environment unknown to their white counterparts. Florida A&M began its history in 1887 as the Florida State Normal School for Colored Students at a site called College Hill before moving to its present location on what had been Highwood, the plantation of territorial governor William Pope Duval. The school's main building was, in fact, the plantation mansion.[1] As the only state school for African Americans, it was apparent early on that the Florida State Normal School for Colored Students would be required to serve purposes far beyond its original charter as a normal school. Moreover, it had to do so under the governance of white officials whose perceptions of what constituted a proper education for African Americans clashed with the genuine needs and desires of its students and faculty.

The person initially chosen to lead the State Normal School for Colored Students was Thomas deSaille Tucker. Tucker was an accomplished man with an interesting background. He was born in Sierra Leone, a nation populated by displaced Africans sent there from various regions of the British Empire as well as Africans liberated from slave ships after the abolition of the slave trade in 1807. He came to the United States when he was twelve and was educated at Oberlin College in Ohio, the first racially integrated college in the United States, where he earned both bachelor's and master's degrees. He also received a law degree from Straight University in New Orleans and was practicing law in Pensacola when he received his appointment as the school's principal. His faculty included the "tonguey" Thomas Gibbs, also an Oberlin graduate, and science professor Thomas W. Talley, who would later have a distinguished career at Fisk University.[2]

The school had been in existence for only three years when its mission and purpose were dramatically altered by the Second Morrill Act. The Second Morrill Act attempted to correct one of the deficiencies of the first act by providing twenty-five thousand dollars annually to each state. For states such as Florida, which received the smaller endowments, this would have significantly boosted annual income. However, the act also required states that denied admission to African Americans to split the proceeds with a designated school for African Americans. The State Normal School for Colored Students was the chosen recipient in Florida.

The stipulation, introduced by Senator James Pugh of Alabama, did not require the schools for Blacks to be colleges. In fact, there was an assumption by both southern and northern congressmen that the schools would almost certainly be below college grade. The stipulation had an unanticipated positive outcome. Schools outside the South that did not admit Blacks in 1890 chose to integrate rather than divide the appropriation. Of course, the stipulation had an anticipated negative outcome for the existing southern land grant colleges. They would receive only half the funds that other land grant schools received.³ For the State Normal and Industrial School, as it was renamed, the requirements of the Morrill Act presented a dilemma and the beginning of academic mission creep. The school's original and principal mission was to serve Florida's African American teachers. The Morrill Act brought a new and ill-defined mission with meager finances to support it. The need for more and better-trained teachers in Florida's African American communities was clear. Moreover, the curriculum for teachers included coursework that prepared students for other professions open to African Americans, such as law, the ministry, and medicine.

The land grant curriculum, however, lacked relevance to African American students who were prevented from entering the professions associated with it. There was no job market for African American engineers even if the school had had the faculty and equipment to train them. In the context of racial apartheid, the "mechanic arts" for African Americans were replaced with training in specific trades. Instead of engineers and chemists, the Black land grant schools produced carpenters, bricklayers, and cobblers. The school's agricultural component had, at least, marginal application for Florida's Black farmers and more so after the passage of the Smith-Lever Act of 1914. That act established a national network of county extension agents, Black and white, who advised local farmers on better methods of crop cultivation and animal husbandry.

The State Normal and Industrial School had far less autonomy than its white counterpart in Lake City. Although there was periodic grousing about the lack of actual agricultural training at the Florida Agricultural College, that college had considerable freedom to spend its federal funding in the manner it deemed most useful. Furthermore, the liberal arts and sciences were never subordinated to engineering and agriculture at the Florida Agricultural College. The intent of the Morrill Act was not to create trade schools but to broaden educational possibilities for working-class and farming families. In the South, though, Morrill Act funds were used as a cudgel to restrict educational opportunities for African Americans. As Florida A&M president Nathan Young remarked in 1923, there was "a well-defined movement . . . throughout the South to *sub-standardize* the few State-supported Colleges for Negroes by devoting them solely or mainly to vocational training with the evident purpose of making the Negro a permanent economic asset to the white South, with but small regard to his own group welfare—to educate him narrowly as a Negro, not *broadly* as a man and a citizen."⁴

As exemplars of the vocational approach, the Tuskegee Institute in

Alabama and the Hampton Institute in Virginia were held up by southern and northern white educators, as well as some Black educators, as models for African American land grant schools. Robert Curtis Ogden, a northern businessman who helped establish Hampton and a member of Rockefeller's General Education Board, toured the South in 1901 and touted the merits of Tuskegee and Hampton. Ogden's views were not shared by Thomas Tucker, who boldly emphasized the literary program in his school's catalogue and consigned what he called the "incidental industries" to students who found the standard curriculum too difficult. In doing so, Tucker was following a well-established policy for white students. This policy also put him in the crosshairs of his white superiors, and he found himself fighting a rearguard action in a racial conflict that he was certain to lose. Growing tired of Tucker's recalcitrance, Superintendent Sheats dismissed him in 1901 and chose Nathan Benjamin Young, who had served as head of the normal departments at Tuskegee and the Georgia State Industrial College for Colored Youth, as Tucker's replacement.[5]

As a Young biographer wrote, "The selection of Young to replace Tucker was interesting and ironic in view of the fact that both Tucker and Young shared relatively the same philosophical values and the same Oberlin liberal arts training." Young, though, attempted to balance academics and practical training, in part to appease his white supervisors but also because he saw the value of both. Despite being told by President Washington at Tuskegee that academics would never be a priority there, he stayed on for six years. Young remained on amicable terms with Washington after he left Tuskegee while also maintaining a relationship with Washington's ideological adversary W. E. B. Du Bois at Atlanta University, with whom Young was more pedagogically aligned. Young's tightrope walk between vocational and liberal arts education would continue until his forced departure in 1923. In the interval, he struggled to maintain the school with minimal financial support from the state. In the last budget allocation before the Buckman Act, the State Normal and Industrial School received only $2,640 from state appropriations, about a tenth of what it received from federal funds. By comparison, the State Normal School in DeFuniak Springs took in $28,280 from the state in the same period. This disparity in funding was not evident when the two normal schools opened in 1887. It was not until after the Morrill funds began to arrive that the gap appeared, a clear indication that Florida had simply decided to use the Second Morrill Act as a rationale to defund higher education for African Americans.[6]

The West Florida Seminary Becomes the Florida State College

Both state seminaries began as private academies before they received state charters in the 1850s. The change in status did not correspond to any change in the schools' clientele or the coursework. The students came almost exclusively from the wealthier families in their respective counties, and there was a curricular emphasis on what the children of enslavers required to succeed in their roles in southern society. Although both seminaries tried to ignore their legislative mandates, the fortunate outcome of their mandate to provide teacher training was that it required them to be coeducational. That was atypical for southern academies; most were either girls' or boys' schools. For the boys, there was often a heavy dose of military discipline and a modest amount of actual martial instruction. The antebellum West Florida Seminary included a military component for its boys, and much was made of the cadets' participation in a minor skirmish at the close of the Civil War.[7]

Despite the University of Florida's insistence that it began when a local academy in Ocala was granted the state's first seminary charter in 1853, the East Florida Seminary would never be anything more than a regional preparatory school. The history of the West Florida Seminary, on the other hand, is far more complicated, in large part because it had to contend with the *ignis fatuus* mentioned in Sheats's 1894 history. Literally translated from the Latin, *ignis fatuus* means "foolish fire." Sheats used the phrase to refer to a foolish and deceptive hope. The source of this deceptive hope was the Reverend John Kost, MD, DD, LLD, his library of three thousand volumes, and a "large and valuable collection of Natural History and Museum of Geological specimens," many of which were pulled from Florida phosphate mines.

Kost and his library and museum arrived in Tallahassee in the early 1880s where he established a medical college. According to Peter Henry Rolfs, who taught at the Florida Agricultural College and later headed the agricultural units at the University of Florida, Kost had a "bizarre" reputation and was more "adventurer than scientist." In 1883, he persuaded the legislature to award him a charter for a state university as well as the lofty title of chancellor. The Florida University was organized with two colleges, a medical college and a literary college. The latter was the West Florida Seminary, magically transformed from a local school to a college. Three other planned colleges failed to materialize. It was, according to State

Superintendent Albert Russell, a "private and philanthropic enterprise," as the legislature did not appropriate funds for the Florida University. The project ended before it truly began, but not before Kost and his museum had moved to the Florida Agricultural College in Lake City along with the deceptive hope of a Florida University. The medical college, still claiming to be part of the Florida University, moved to Jacksonville, where it had a brief existence and turned out a handful of graduates. Kost and his museum, meanwhile, showed up in Tiffin, Ohio, where he persuaded the trustees of Heidelberg College to appoint him president. Kost lost that post in 1891 after a conflict with his faculty. History does not record his subsequent career but does record the fate of his museum and library. The museum had suffered considerable damage after leaving Florida, and the library was auctioned after his death.[8]

The legacy of this episode is that the West Florida Seminary began to consider itself as a bona fide college and, accordingly, created another college department in 1887. The seminary's catalogues describe three departments: a preparatory department, a high school, and the college. The college curriculum stressed classical studies and included advanced classes in both Latin and Greek. The announcement of a college department at the West Florida Seminary provoked an emphatic retort from the East Florida Seminary, which stated in its catalogue that "it was a SCHOOL, not a COLLEGE" with coursework designed "to prepare boys and young men for admission into university classes."[9] McBeath did not consider the West Florida Seminary a college in 1897; he was uncertain whether it even qualified as a high school. In his biennial reports, Sheats, too, failed to draw any distinctions between the two seminaries. Nonetheless, the West Florida Seminary appointed its first president, George M. Edgar, in 1887 and awarded its first bachelor's degrees to seven students in 1891. Matters, though, took a decisive and positive turn after Albert Alexander Murphree assumed the presidency in 1897.

Murphree had all the attributes of a successful academic leader of the early twentieth century, and his lengthy tenures at both Florida State, 1897–1909, and the University of Florida, 1909–27, helped shape both institutions. He achieved iconic status at the University of Florida when a statue was raised in his honor in 1946. The imposing figure of Murphree in academic garb presides eternally in the campus historic district. His outstretched open hand has also been an enticement to generations of University of Florida students. On many postgame Sunday mornings, the teetotaling Murphree will have a beer container in his hand. Murphree

Figure 2. The statue of University of Florida president Albert Murphree, photographed shortly after a memorial dedication ceremony in 1946. The statue was created by Paul Manship, who also created the iconic *Prometheus* sculpture at the Rockefeller Center skate rink. University Archives Photograph Collection, George A. Smathers Libraries, University of Florida.

makes a less dramatic statuary appearance at Florida State, where his hands appropriately hold what appears to be a campus plan.

Murphree was an astute administrator and a student of academic trends and innovations. He was not a scholar, holding only a bachelor's degree when he became the seminary president. Later he would earn a master's degree from the University of Nashville. His lack of academic credentials did not prove a hindrance. His faculties at both Florida State and the University of Florida respected and supported him; the students loved him.

Figure 3. Statue of Albert Murphree at Florida State University. The statue is located near the building named for his wife, Jennie Henderson Murphree. FSU Photography Services.

Murphree was, by nature, pragmatic and diplomatic. He was not a risk taker, nor was he adversarial. He was opportunistic, but usually in a positive way. In other words, he had the ability to recognize needs, and he found ways to fill them. He also recognized the limits of his authority and was willing to compromise if it served his immediate purpose. Most important, though, he understood how to make his resource allocators happy. It also helped that those resource allocators were within walking distance much of the year, and he certainly didn't hurt his situation when he married Jennie Henderson, the daughter of Colonel John A. Henderson, president of the seminary's board of trustees and an influential political and business leader.

One of the first steps Murphree took as seminary president was to enhance the school's mandated normal program. Rather than see it as a distraction or a burden, he saw it as an opportunity. The state clearly needed more teachers. Enrollment figures for academic year 1901–2 showed 65 normal students in Murphree's Teacher Training School as compared to 111 at the State Normal School in DeFuniak Springs.[10] Murphree also realized that the school's ultimate survival required a new identity; it could no longer be an academy funded by the state. Moreover, by 1900 the word "seminary" had become associated with the training of theologians, and a new name was required. The school's board of trustees cautiously opted for Florida State College in 1901. The choice of college, rather than university, reflected the school's emphasis on the liberal arts. Even so, the name change was more aspirational than real.

In keeping with the school's new status, Murphree eliminated the primary grades altogether and established a minimum entrance age of twelve for the high school. The first catalogue of the Florida State College shows there were three grades in the high school department and four grades in the college, with far more students in the former than the latter. There were improvements to the faculty as well. None of the faculty in 1897 held a doctorate, and most had only a bachelor's degree. By 1903, Murphree had recruited PhDs to teach classics, English, and the physical sciences. The course offerings were brought up to date with the addition of a bachelor of science degree, courses in the social sciences, and an emphasis on the living languages rather than the dead ones. Murphree also expanded course offerings outside the standard college and high school curricula to include music, oratory, and business. In its final catalogue, issued in 1904, the college listed the following departments and their respective enrollments:

College Department	118
Normal Department	46
Preparatory Department	153
Music Department	72
Oratory Department	60
Commercial Department	24

There was considerable duplication of enrollment among the different departments. Total enrollment in 1904 was 318, far higher than at the other state schools. College-level enrollment was only slightly below that of the land grant college. Of the state schools, only the Florida State College had monetary assets beyond those from federal grants and state appropriations. The 1904 catalogue states the college had a net worth of $175,000, which included the proceeds from the Westcott Estate. The latter was not, in fact, in the college's possession. Florida Supreme Court Justice James D. Westcott bequeathed properties and stocks to a trust managed by George Lewis. The estate yielded approximately $2,500 annually.[11] Although the Florida State College was still a work in progress when the Buckman Act was passed, it was already a rival of the land grant college in more ways than academic.

Their football teams met on the gridiron several times between 1901 and 1905. The last matchup was in 1904, and Florida State came out the winner. There would be a fifty-four-year interval between that contest and the next.

Florida State's continued existence in Tallahassee is in no small measure thanks to the determination of Albert Murphree. His reforms enhanced the school's reputation and effectively guaranteed its survival. Florida State's rival at Lake City, on the other hand, lacked that steady executive hand.

The Florida Agricultural College Becomes the University of Florida

Florida was the last of the former Confederate states to make use of its land grant funds, and the events leading up to the college's opening were far from promising. In addition to the conflicts over locating the campus, there were also problems involving the sale of its assigned land scrip. The Florida Agricultural College was chartered in 1870, but it took four years of haggling between the state and the brokers handling the land transaction before Florida received its grant funds in 1874. The proceeds were invested in one hundred $1,000 State of Florida Thirty Year Gold Bonds. Florida's endowment income was as small as a land grant endowment could possibly be. Florida received the minimum number of acres, 90,000 (30,000 times its three members of Congress in 1860), and it sold the land after land values plummeted following the "Panic of '73." For most years, the annual return on the bonds came to $9,107.[12]

It bears noting that both the Reconstruction and Redemption superintendents of public instruction agreed that it would be folly to open a third state school when, in their opinion, the state already had one school too many. Reflecting on the possible establishment of an agricultural college in 1871, Superintendent Charles Beecher noted that both state and federal law required two seminaries. "Now, it may be doubtful whether, at the present stage of development and program, Florida can maintain one institution worthy of being called a college, or a university," he stated, "but it is beyond a doubt that she cannot support three." He then added, "If the grants of Congress, aforesaid, necessitate the attempt to sustain two seminaries and an agricultural college, those grants will be a curse rather than a blessing." He went on to suggest that the seminary and Morrill funds be combined to support a university.[13]

The first superintendent in the Redemption era was William P. Haisley. Haisley's report for 1878 paints an equally grim picture. He began by asking why the seminaries had not established normal departments as they were required to do before launching into an attack on the agricultural college: "Agricultural colleges, as such, even when supported by endowments of from three to nine hundred thousand dollars [as opposed to Florida's one hundred thousand dollars] . . . have proved to be failures. Any amount of testimony from the most distinguished educators could be presented, to prove that but few students have been induced to attend these institutions." He concluded his comments by suggesting that the state use the Morrill and seminary funds to provide scholarships to teachers to attend the seminaries. If this proved impractical, he suggested sequestering the funds until their endowments were sufficient to establish a state university, with normal and agricultural departments attached, and in that way comply with the existing laws. In response to Haisley's proposal, the state legislature passed a joint resolution to Congress requesting permission to merge the seminary, agricultural college, and common school funds. Congress never replied, and the state waited six years before acting. On the positive side, the delay created a substantial cash reserve as the endowment income accrued.[14]

Although the state legislature had some influence on the choice for the college's site, the final decision rested with the college's board of trustees. Regardless of what the United States Congress might have decided, the state legislature and the board of trustees had options that would have prevented the opening of a third school. There was nothing to prevent the legislature from mandating the agricultural college be located at one of the seminaries or, at least, in the same town as one of the seminaries. That almost happened when the college was first awarded to Gainesville in 1874. In 1883, Gainesville would again recommend itself but also suggested the legislature divide the Morrill fund between the two seminaries. Tallahassee also made a bid with the idea of combining the agricultural college with the West Florida Seminary and Kost's Florida University. In the end, though, localism prevailed, and the board of trustees did exactly what successive superintendents implored them not to do and created a third campus in Lake City. Lake City sweetened the pot with $15,000 in cash.[15]

In 1884, thirty-nine years after its admission to the Union, the State of Florida admitted its first student to a publicly funded college. From its beginning, the Florida Agricultural College resembled what people then and now would consider a college. It had the standard four-year curriculum leading to the bachelor's degree. It had a campus with more than one academic building, and it had a student population that extended beyond the county line. The minimum age for freshmen was fifteen, which was low, but not unusually low for a southern land grant college. Southern colleges had lower admission ages than other regions, and, nationwide, admission standards for land grant schools tended to be lower than for state universities. The age requirement at the Florida Agricultural College was two to three years higher than the seminaries.[16]

For the first ten years of its existence, the Florida Agricultural College was restricted to white males; women were admitted in 1894. Tellingly, not a single student in the college's first class was able to pass the entrance examination; all had to spend at least one year in a preparatory class. The absence of anything resembling a high school in any county in 1884 meant that a preparatory department would be a requirement for some time. The first class to graduate from a public college in Florida was the Class of 1889. It had the distinction of being one of two college classes to graduate in Florida as Rollins College also matriculated its first class that year.

The board of trustees selected Ashley Davis Hurt, a Virginian, as the college's first president. Hurt, who served in the Confederate Department of the Navy, stayed for only one semester. He left no archival record of his time in Florida save for one long and pessimistic letter to his wife. In it, Hurt joined the chorus of voices advocating consolidation with another school, in this case the West Florida Seminary in Tallahassee, a town that Hurt described in glowing terms:

> I cannot describe [Tallahassee] to you properly, for it is a changing picture at every turn, but, I believe, there are few prettier landscapes in the world than the environs of Tallahassee. The college ought certainly to have been placed here, and Lake City only got it by offering $15,000, while Tallahassee offered 200 acres of beautiful land, her seminary and her good will. They simply made a big mistake, and result will be that the Ag. College of Florida will be absolutely nothing. I know I am in a swamped boat, but it is too late to do anything but try to get to land. The trouble is, there is no money ahead for the college to draw on, and I'm afraid the Legislature will not appropriate any. The different sections of Florida hate each other like the Devil, and the day is distant when one section will vote an appropriation that will benefit another.[17]

By contrast, the superintendent of public instruction's first report on the college was glowingly optimistic. Superintendent Russell stated that the trustees of the college were "determined to found a school in which liberal culture and practical education shall proceed together." He listed

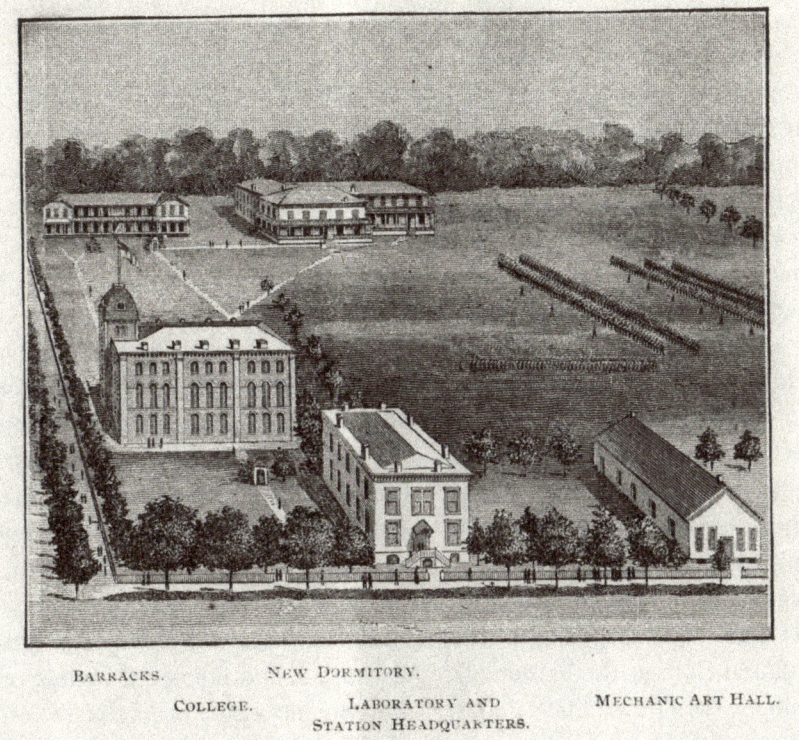

BARRACKS.
COLLEGE. NEW DORMITORY.
LABORATORY AND STATION HEADQUARTERS. MECHANIC ART HALL.

Figure 4. Illustration of the campus of the Florida Agricultural College from the college's 1890 catalogue. George A. Smathers Libraries, University of Florida.

six courses of study: classical, literary, philosophical, scientific, mechanical, and agricultural. Of the latter, special attention would be paid to the "cultivation, propagation, and marketing of those fruits which are making Florida celebrated throughout the world." The ultimate benefit, though, was to the state. Not only would its young men now be educated in their own "native genial climate," hundreds from less fortunate states would be enticed to Florida to do the same.[18]

Russell's second report in 1886 built on the enthusiasm of the first report. The report noted that the "large and valuable collection of Natural History and Museum of Geological specimens, the property of Rev. Dr. J. Kost, has been transferred to this college, and a library of 3,000 volumes will soon follow." If they did, they were not there long, as Kost soon moved to Ohio. The 1886 report also called for the creation of a commercial department that would stress practical skills needed in modern business and government organizations such as telegraphy, stenography, and accounting. Russell's comments on the need for this department reflect the changing attitudes of southern whites toward practical education. He began with a quote from a speech by Atticus G. Haygood, president of Emory College, who spoke of a student who expressed mocking pleasure at leaving Emory before it, too, introduced vocational studies: "But his sneer is noteworthy because it is an echo. It gives semi-articulate voice to bad sentiment so prevalent among our white people who can live without working with their hands—a sentiment that breeds discontent and a certain shame in those who labor with their hands [and] it is part of the curse of slavery upon white people."[19]

Alexander Quarles Holladay succeeded the quickly departed Ashley Hurt as president. In his 1886 report to the superintendent, Holladay took up the matter of the school's name. Holladay traveled throughout the state recruiting prospective students, and he found that students and their parents were confused about the name. People were under the impression that the purpose of the college was "to instruct boys in hoeing, ploughing, seeding, etc." He suggested the University of Florida and State Agricultural College as an alternative, a suggestion that Superintendent Russell endorsed. At times, the college was unofficially advertised as the Florida State Agricultural College, the Florida State Agricultural and Industrial College or, simply, the Florida State College.[20] Enrollments at the college were very low the first four years. There were only 38 students in 1886 and 60 in 1888. There was a suspicious jump in enrollment to 160 in 1889, but it plummeted to 103 the next year. A clue to why was provided in the 1890 report by President F. L. Kern—the college's fourth president in six years—which referred to a better class of students after the elimination of the lowest grade of cadets and the removal of students of "immoral character." He then added, "A wholesome moral atmosphere now pervades the college, and all are striving to attain to a higher standard of excellence."[21]

In 1889, the Florida Agricultural Experiment Station was established after passage of another federal grant, the Hatch Act of 1888, which provided funds specifically for agricultural research. Florida presented both opportunities and obstacles for agricultural research. Unlike Eau Gallie, Lake City is too far north to qualify as a semitropical environment. Neither its soil nor its climate could support the many crops grown in peninsular Florida. Consequently, the college opened temporary substations in different agricultural zones of the state, including stations in South Florida at Ft. Myers and Miami.

Figure 5. Flagler Gymnasium at the University of Florida, Lake City, 1901. University Archives Photograph Collection, George A. Smathers Libraries, University of Florida.

Just before its demise in 1905, there was a promising flurry of activity at the college. The school's physical plant doubled with the addition of three significant brick-and-mortar buildings. The first was a gymnasium with an indoor swimming pool. The building was endowed by railroader Henry Flagler, who also purchased equipment for the gym. It was the first endowed structure at a public college in Florida, but the circumstances surrounding the gift do not paint an uplifting picture of benevolence. The donation for the building was made as partial payment to the Florida legislature for having changed the state's divorce laws. Flagler's second wife had been committed to an asylum for the mentally ill in New York, and neither New York nor Florida allowed someone to divorce a mentally incapacitated spouse. In 1901, Florida changed its law, Flagler got his divorce and married his third wife, and the college received its gymnasium. The law was repealed in the next legislative session.[22] Enrollments were down slightly in the final years, but that was largely due to tightened admission requirements, the termination of coeducation, and the elimination of all but one year of the preparatory department. Finally, the college was granted the authority to change its name to the University of Florida in 1903. In the public record, everything seemed to be going well, or as well as might be expected given the school's exceedingly low budget. Under the surface, though, the college seethed with internal and external dissension and resentments, and more than once the discord erupted to the surface for all to see.

3

Turmoil at Lake City

The origins of the Florida Agricultural College's "periodic revolutions" are as mysterious today as they were in Tom McBeath's day. McBeath suggested that the problems arose from either the college's location, Lake City, or the management. It may well have been both. There were times when even the college presidents could only speculate as to who or what was behind a particular attack. Yet, the incidents were frequent and known to many people. The *Gainesville Sun* took particular delight in airing the dirty laundry of the East Florida Seminary's nearby rival.

Some of the internal strife at Lake City stemmed from tensions between the college president and the director of the agricultural experiment station after the passage of the Hatch Act in 1887. Florida was not alone in this regard.[1] The Hatch Act created a second axis of authority at land grant colleges by providing funds specifically for the stations. The stations managed their own lands and personnel and were required to make reports to the US Department of Agriculture. Questions concerning the stations' relationships to their parent institutions took years to resolve. Given this uncertainty, disputes between station directors and college presidents were inevitable. Another bone of contention between stations and their colleges was over classroom instruction. In theory, station personnel conducted research, and the faculty of the college were responsible for teaching. In practice, most land grant colleges could ill afford to hire agricultural instructors, and station personnel were often pressed into classroom service.

Although tensions between the agricultural staff and the college administration were evident at the Florida Agricultural College, much of the conflict there emanated from the typical discord endemic to all nineteenth-century colleges, namely, town-gown disputes and faculty-president battles. What was not typical, though, was the frequency of conflict and the tendency of town leaders to inject themselves into what were distinctly gown matters. In short, the college community in Lake City was a viral stew of personal grievances and group infighting. The result of this situation was a high turnover at the top; seven men presided at the college during its brief twenty-year history. Presidents were often at the flashpoint of conflict and were its frequent casualty. One, Wilbur F. Yocum, served six years, but he had two separate terms, and the first ended after a series of disputes with the station director. No other president served more than four years. The poisonous atmosphere yielded one more casualty: the University of Florida is no longer in Lake City. Although there were other factors involved in the decision to relocate the university, there was a perception at the time that the school would never succeed as long as it remained there.

The earliest recorded upheaval occurred in January 1893 and involved an argument over a parcel of experiment station land that President Yocum wished to use for nonstation purposes. Station Director James DePass angrily confronted the president on the campus grounds to express his outrage with the decision, and the two men were soon exchanging blows in public view.[2] The incident came before the board of trustees for resolution. After hearing the arguments of both parties, the board found that Yocum had acted in good faith but had erred in his decision to use station land for general college purposes. The *Florida Times-Union* covered the hearings, as did the *Gainesville Sun*. The *Sun* described the hearings as a "stormy session" where "disorder prevailed." Superintendent Sheats, who presided over the board, declared himself "thoroughly disgusted" and added, "Your institution here will never amount to a baubee as long as it is run as it is." Yocum tendered his resignation, but the board declined it. "Every member . . . appealed to him personally," the *Sun* continued in its eloquent style: "Some of it was like tributes to the dead, or flowers for the slain—and would have been 'beautiful' if it had not made folks who knew 'tired.' There was a general love-feast—almost tears." In the end, Yocum reconsidered his decision and stayed. However, the dispute between the two executives had not been settled, and Yocum's authority had been undermined by the board's support for DePass. The *Sun* speculated that DePass had some hold on the board and argued that the board's unwillingness to support its president was "a set-back from which it will take years to recover." In truth, it never would.[3]

Shortly after the January hearings, the state legislature reorganized the college's governing board and gave the board more independence.[4] The state superintendent no longer served on the board, and the governor appointed new members with more political clout. Among them were William Dudley Chipley, a railroad developer in West Florida and a former mayor of Pensacola. He would later serve in the Florida Senate. Another board member was Frank Harris, publisher and editor of the *Ocala Banner*, who would serve on the board until the end. Later trustees included George Wilson, publisher of Florida's paper-of-record, the *Florida Times-Union* of Jacksonville, and Charles A. Carson, superintendent of public instruction for Osceola County and later its state senator. At its first meeting in June, the new board asked President Yocum and Director DePass to make arguments for or against abolishing the position of station director and replacing it with a joint director/president appointment.[5]

The conflict between the president and the director was resolved at the board's meeting on July 11, when it was decided to jettison DePass and the station director position. Yocum also stepped down as president but retained his faculty post as professor of mental and moral philosophy. The removal of the station director did not go unnoticed in Washington. Five years after the decision was made, Alfred Charles True, director of the Office of Experiment Stations, complained to the college's board about the commingling of Hatch and Morrill funds. True listed a number of problems at the Florida station including low pay, high staff turnover, and the poor quality of station lands. His principal complaint, though, involved the misuse of station funds and, specifically, the use of Hatch money to pay for half of the president's salary. Board president E. L. Stringer apologetically replied that the merger had less to do with saving money and more to do with reducing jealousy. He feared separating them again for the same reasons.[6] The matter was not resolved until 1905, when President Andrew Sledd appointed Peter Henry Rolfs as the station director.

After eliminating the position of station director, the board then considered who should succeed Yocum and DePass as joint president/director. The search focused on two nominees, Frederick Pasco, principal of Duval High School and a cousin of US Senator Samuel Pasco, and Oscar Clute, president of the Michigan State Agricultural College, now Michigan State University. The board voted 4–3 for Clute and divided his $2,500 salary equally between Morrill and Hatch funds.[7] Oscar Clute was a native of New York and had been a teacher in Michigan when he entered Michigan State University's forerunner in 1859. He graduated in 1862 and served briefly in the Union army in Howlett's Engineers. After the war, he decided on a life in the ministry and spent the next twenty-two years as a Unitarian minister in New Jersey, Iowa, and California. He came back to Michigan State in 1889 and served as president of his alma mater for four years before coming to Florida. The day after the board offered the presidency to Clute, it would

Figure 6. "A Company of Volunteers," 1897. Whereas men at the Florida Agricultural College were required to undertake military training and wear uniforms, women attending the college could volunteer for a similar unit. Edward Orville Powers Collection, George A. Smathers Libraries, University of Florida.

make two significant changes to the college. First, it created the commercial department that President Holladay had proposed in 1886. The department offered courses in bookkeeping, penmanship, stenography, typing, and telegraphy, but did not award degrees. Classes were funded by student fees, and students received certificates for each course completed. The second board decision was to make the college coeducational.[8]

At the board's April 1894 meeting, Clute made recommendations for how coursework should be organized in a coeducational environment. He suggested a separate curriculum for women that substituted modern languages and domestic science for courses in mathematics and science. All courses were opened to women, but women were advised to take the special women's course as it was "intended to fit them for those duties which usually fall to the lot of women—the duties of the home, of the Church, and of society."[9] Reaction to the women's curriculum was mixed. In fact, the college's first woman graduate, Daisy Rogers, received her degree in engineering in 1895. Even more telling was the reaction to the college's mandatory military requirement for male students. Some of the women entering the college could not see why they should be treated differently than the men and requested similar privileges. President Clute agreed to the creation of a company of women volunteers who also wore uniforms and drilled. Women also organized their own literary society, which they named The Clutonians in honor of the president.[10]

A separate dormitory for women had to be constructed. Until then, the women boarded in town. Clute also recommended the hiring of a "mature well-trained, experienced woman Professor in the Faculty who, in addition to her duties as Professor, will be a friend and counselor for the women students." Helen Ingram from Jacksonville was recruited as professor of history and English and de facto dean of women. Clute advised that the position of professor of modern languages also go to a woman and then decided that one of the languages needed to be Spanish: "Our near proximity to the people of Mexico, Central America, and the West Indies, and the rapidly increasing commercial and social relations between these countries and own, led us to believe that instruction in the Spanish tongue should become an important part of our College work."[11] Instead of hiring one woman to teach modern languages at a salary of $1,100, he hired Cordele Mooring to teach French and German for $750 and "Senorita Aurora Mena" to teach Spanish for $350. Mena was Cuban, and she had been a Spanish tutor to several prominent families in Key West. She was also active in the Cuban independence movement and wrote a highly sensationalized first-person account of the Cuban struggle. She did so, "Inspired by the desire of giving to this country, whose whole people show so much sympathy for my suffering land, a more intimate knowledge of the truth concerning the misfortunes of the noble Cuban people, and the cruelty and injustice of a despotic and tyrannical government."[12] She later returned to Cuba to promote public education and became a leader in the Cuban suffragist movement. Señorita Mena was not the only Spanish speaker at the college as students from Cuba and Puerto Rico were often enrolled.

Enrollment jumped from 83 in academic year 1892–93 to 187 in 1893–94, with women adding 54 to the student rolls. The new business school also contributed to the increase. Clute reported few disciplinary issues and no expulsions in his first year. He also noted, "The young women by their careful attention to duty and by their excellent standing in class work have proven themselves most admirable members of the College." Clute urged the state to generate new revenue sources to finance the college. He suggested a severance tax on phosphate as well as the sale of public lands in South Florida to supplement the college's endowment. Clute also noted that the lands assigned to the experiment station were unsuitable as they sloped too much to retain water and suggested the purchase of adjacent properties. Academic year 1894–95 showed a further increase in enrollment, with 201 students, of whom 123 were in college courses.[13] Overall, the college appeared to be heading in a positive direction, and the four years of Clute's administration had been an oasis of tranquility. But that was simply the proverbial calm before the storm.

The first indication that something might be amiss occurred on January 29, 1897, when the president's official residence burned to the ground. It was later determined to be an act of arson. The board posted a $250 reward for information, but the person or persons behind the attack, and their motivations, remained a mystery. Then, on June 15, the board received a petition from several Lake City residents to discuss "certain rumors against Dr. Clute." The board agreed to meet with the delegation and listened to the charges. The petitioners, though, failed to provide any evidence or testimony, and the allegations were not entered into the minutes. Despite the accusations, the board renewed Clute's contract for another year.[14]

The attacks on Clute intensified, and calls were made for his resignation. Instead, the board instructed Clute's accusers, who now numbered twenty-two, to submit any charges they had against Clute along with testimony. The board appointed an investigatory subcommittee, and the charges were delivered the next morning. The local delegation also brought testimony against Professor of Mechanical Engineering Henry C. Powers. The charges began by stating Clute "was unfitted for the position from immorality and indecency—in that he appeared to be addicted to an unnatural and abominable practice and vice." The vice was not named, but the subsequent testimony clearly indicated that Clute was thought to be gay. Powers was accused of "continuously visiting [a] negro whore-house in Lake City."[15]

The testimony came in the form of signed affidavits, but none of Clute's accusers gave in-person testimony. In all, he was alleged to have made "indecent overtures" on seven occasions. Most of these overtures occurred on public transportation, three on coastal steamers in the Ft. Myers area and two on railroad coaches, including a purported dalliance with an African American porter. The other two cases occurred at a troop encampment in Tallahassee and a hotel in Jacksonville. In all, sixteen witnesses claimed to have been either approached by Clute or had seen what they perceived to be a sexual advance. In several cases, there were multiple witnesses. They also accused him of allowing students to visit a local pool hall. The last accusation, although far from damning, was sworn to by members of the community, as was the allegation against Professor Powers. Clute was not in Lake City during the proceedings, and there is no record of a response.[16]

Peter Henry Rolfs, who was on the faculty during Clute's tenure, would claim thirty-eight years later that Clute was the victim of a "whisperphone" attack.[17] Was Clute the casualty of a rumor mill? Given the number of witnesses, it is hard to imagine that the attack lacked substance. Still, there are questions that cast doubt on the testimony. None of the incidents, save the poolroom accusation and the charges against Powers, occurred in Lake City, and all took place between 1893 and 1895, two to four years before the investigation. Furthermore, none of the witnesses came before the board or any other state or local official with the accusations. Instead, the witnesses, *none of whom resided in Lake City*, somehow made themselves known to people there, and citizens of Lake City then brought the charges to the board. Finally, the records of the board indicate that Clute did not tender an immediate resignation, but he remained as president, in absentia, for the remainder of his term. Such leniency was not normally accorded to people accused of what was then considered sexual deviancy, and it is possible the board had doubts about the veracity of the testimony. After leaving Florida, Clute returned to California and the ministry. He died five years later in a soldiers' home.

Clute's departure prompted yet another presidential search. The position was first offered to William Sheats, who pondered the offer and then declined. After interviewing several candidates, including Horace Stockbridge of Americus, Georgia, the board was unable to come to a consensus. They then asked Wilbur Yocum to return as president. Yocum had left the college shortly after Clute took office to become professor of psychology and pedagogy at the East Florida Seminary. He later served as principal of Bartow's high school and was superintendent of public instruction for Polk County when he received the call to return to Lake City. Stockbridge was appointed professor of agriculture and became the de facto head of the Experiment Station.[18]

Horace E. Stockbridge had a long career in agriculture. He attended the Massachusetts Agricultural College and earned his bachelors in 1878. He did graduate work at Göttingen in Germany and received his doctorate there in 1884. He spent the next four years in Japan, where he was professor of chemistry and geology at the Japanese Imperial College. He returned to the United States in 1889 and served briefly as the director of the agricultural experiment station at Purdue before being offered the presidency at the newly established North Dakota Agricultural College. As president there he hired the first faculty, created a campus plan, and helped design its first buildings. He lost his position in 1893 after becoming embroiled in a political struggle between Governor Eli Shortridge and the college trustees. That led him to Georgia and Florida, where he became a promoter of southern agriculture in the pages of *Southern Ruralist* and *Southern Farmland*

and Dairy. He was also an accomplished scientist with several publications based on groundbreaking work in plant diseases.[19] After the Clute episode, the board of trustees may have been hesitant to take their chances on another land grant president from outside the South, particularly one with a recent history of political involvement. For his part, Stockbridge may have taken the post at Lake City with the idea that he might one day ascend to the position of president or, if the two positions were to be separated, station director. He was certainly qualified for either position. Over the next ten years, though, the board would come to regret his appointment.

The twentieth century began on a promising note for higher education in Florida. The election of William Sherman Jennings as governor in 1900 brought a new political conviction to the Florida executive office. Jennings, a cousin of William Jennings Bryan, and his successor, Napoleon Bonaparte Broward, were both activist governors who used the limited powers of their office to promote needed changes. The ascendency of progressive and populist politicians in the South marked a shift in fiscal policy and a loosening of the economic reins held by the conservatives. Until the Jennings administration, Florida's financial contribution to its largest public college was negligible, and to make ends meet the college was compelled to carry a substantial debt. From 1884 to 1900, the college subsisted almost exclusively on the funds provided by the two Morrill Acts and the Hatch Act, and, as previously noted, the temptation to misuse Hatch Act money for general purposes had been simply too great to resist. Beginning in 1901, the first year of the Jennings administration, there was a dramatic increase in the college's state appropriation. From $9,150 in the biennium prior to Jennings it rose to over $60,000 in the next two bienniums. The other state schools showed increases as well, but not on the scale of the agricultural college. Most of the increases went to brick-and-mortar in the form of three modern structures, a science building, a dormitory, and the state's contribution to the Flagler Gymnasium.[20]

Yet another college president entered in 1901, Thomas Hardy Taliaferro, who was elected by the board on June 6, 1901. At the same board meeting, outgoing president Yocum accused Horace Stockbridge of using college agricultural equipment for his personal gain. The board investigated the matter, but Stockbridge was reappointed. There is nothing in the records to indicate that Stockbridge factored into Yocum's departure or that there was any dissatisfaction with Yocum's management. On the contrary, his second three-year term is notable for the absence of public embarrassments. He returned to the faculty as professor of Latin and Greek.[21]

Thomas Hardy Taliaferro was a product of Johns Hopkins University, the nation's pioneering graduate university. He received his PhD there in 1896 and taught at Pennsylvania State University before getting the post at Florida. Taliaferro (pronounced Tollifer) came from one of the South's most distinguished families. Taliaferros were prominent in Virginia during colonial and antebellum days and served in both houses of Congress. A Taliaferro commanded Confederate forces in Florida. Taliaferro's uncle—Uncle Jimmie in his letters—was James Taliaferro, US senator from Florida. One can only assume that the Taliaferro name was not a hindrance in his appointment. Four issues would dominate Taliaferro's brief, but busy, administration. The first was a conflict with Horace Stockbridge; the second was the successful effort to rename the college the University of Florida; the third was a decision to end coeducation at the university, and the last was a faculty revolt that resulted in his resignation. Taliaferro was a young and ambitious executive. He was only thirty when he got the call, and he certainly had vision and a sense of purpose. He may have lacked the maturity he needed for the office, though, and he clearly overestimated his executive power.[22]

The first issue came to the fore in June 1902, when the board terminated Stockbridge's services. The circumstances surrounding the decision were not explained, and it is unclear whether they were related to the charge brought by Yocum the year before. Regardless, it was not an amicable departure. Soon after Stockbridge was allowed the "privilege" of presenting his resignation, Taliaferro informed trustee and State Senator Charles Carson of the following: "I understand that the Doctor [Stockbridge] says he is going to make all the trouble possible for the Board and myself and it would be well for you to be on the lookout for anything that may turn up. I do not think he can do more than stir up a little excitement through a few of his unthinking friends who have been deceived by his specious arguments." Taliaferro failed to name either his unthinking friends or his specious arguments. But Stockbridge did stir up some excitement, and he remained in the state long enough to cause trouble for Taliaferro and Taliaferro's successor as well.[23]

Stockbridge may have been more trouble on the outside than he was as a member of the faculty. Freed of his academic responsibilities, Stockbridge launched a campaign to transfer all or part of the land grant funds to another institution with him as the head. Taliaferro speculated that Stockbridge was behind a bill proposed in the 1903 session to divert funds for the Farmers' Institute from the college to another institution. The Farmers'

Institutes were an early form of agricultural extension whereby farmers were introduced to innovations emanating from the land grant colleges via traveling exhibits and colloquia. States that sponsored Institutes shared the costs with the federal government. Stockbridge had organized the first Institute in Florida when he was at the college, and Taliaferro wanted the money for the Institutes to continue to come to the college. If that was not possible, he wanted the bill killed altogether rather than have the money go to an organization that Stockbridge influenced.[24]

Taliaferro also guessed that Stockbridge was behind the move in the state legislature to create an agricultural school in Kissimmee. Taliaferro wrote to Senator W. A. Blount urging him to oppose the bill, which was, in Taliaferro's opinion, "an entering wedge introduced by some of our enemies to divorce from the University its agricultural interests." He went on to add, "I think the chances are good that there is an intention to place Dr. Stockbridge there and while I do not wish to do that gentleman any harm, I consider that it would be a curse to the State to have him have any further connection with it." Taliaferro and his allies were unable to prevent the passage of the act creating the Florida Agricultural Institute, but the Buckman Act prevented its actual opening. There is no record of who was to preside at the doomed institute.[25]

The second issue was the college's problematic name and the state's lack of a genuine public university. Once again, Florida found itself trailing the rest of the nation. Many states founded their state universities, on paper at least, during territorial days. In 1903, the territories of Arizona, New Mexico, and Oklahoma already had their respective universities. The decision by the West Florida Seminary to rebrand as the Florida State College in 1901 put the Agricultural College at a name disadvantage. To up the ante, the land grant college sought to remake itself as a university. But, unlike the seminaries, its charter did not grant it the authority to do so on its own. Instead, the college would have to seek the approval of the state legislature. The trick would be to do it without attracting a lot of attention. On April 9, 1903, the trustees gave their approval for a bill to change the name. The bill was sent to the House Committee on Education on April 21, passed both houses on April 25, and was signed by Governor Jennings on April 30.[26] The navigator for the bill's passage was a college trustee, State Senator Charles Carson. Questions must have been raised early on about the legitimacy of a name change as Taliaferro wrote to Carson to convince him that other states had done this. The bill passed "with flying colors," but not before it had provoked opposition from Florida State.[27] Murphree would later explain why Florida State chose not to use the word "university" in its name and took the opportunity to take a swipe at his rival: "The more pretentious name is not assumed by the college owing to the fact that it does not wish to misrepresent its resources and purposes. Should it become in fact a university, its charter grants ample powers for the assumption of the more pretentious title."[28]

The name change was followed by one of the more mysterious episodes in the history of higher education in Florida, the decision by the University of Florida's trustees to terminate coeducation and revert to an all-male school. The plan, as Taliaferro understood it, was for both the university and Florida State to mutually agree to restrict enrollment by gender. On June 16, 1903, the board of trustees for the University of Florida requested a meeting with its counterpart at Florida State to discuss the question of coeducation. The trustees of Florida State subsequently rejected the proposal offered by the university, and the trustees of the university then decided, "after thoroughly discussing the matter," to unilaterally end coeducation and to dismiss its female faculty as well. This episode raises two fundamental questions: would the Florida State College have seriously entertained a proposal to become a women's college, and why would the University of Florida, having its proposal rejected by Florida State, act alone?[29]

Would it have been in the best interests of Florida State to restrict its college enrollment to women? An argument can be made in the affirmative, and it is conceivable that its board would have considered the possibility. The University of Florida, with its emphasis on the applied sciences, had an advantage over Florida State in its appeal to some male students. Its disadvantage had been its name and the perception that it did not offer a broad liberal arts program. With the name change and the concurrent creation of a College of Liberal Arts, its appeal to both men and women was strengthened. The university made one more change in 1903 that would broaden its appeal to men; it ended military discipline. Military instruction would still be compulsory and would remain so until 1969, but men were no longer required to wear their cadet uniforms every day and were no longer subjected to military rules and regulations. Under the circumstances, some at Florida State may have felt that the university had gained a decisive and perhaps permanent advantage. By mutually ending coeducation, Florida State would have ensured itself a share of the market for college students. Nationwide, female enrollment was increasing dramatically and at a much higher rate than male enrollment.[30] Regardless, Florida State declined the opportunity to become a women's college in 1903 only to be forced into doing so in 1905. In the meantime, the University of Florida acted alone, and President Taliaferro was left to deal with the consequences.

Taliaferro's letters indicate that he was surprised at the board's decision and hoped the board would reverse itself. In a letter to English professor Augusta Barnes, Taliaferro explained the situation after offering her a temporary position in the preparatory department: "I hope however, before the summer is over to do better than that. In regard to Tallahassee, it is still co-educational as they refused to meet our propositions. I am as much surprised as you are that we should drop the girls in spite of their refusal, for my understanding of the case was that it depended upon Tallahassee's cooperation."[31] A more ominous message came from State Senator W. K. Jackson. Senator Jackson had been a key supporter of the name change bill and had two sons at the university. "I had intended to send my daughter back with them," he said, "but since coeducation has been abolished in the university will have to send her somewhere else, and now think I will send the Boys with her. I am of the opinion that abolishing coeducation is the Death Knell of the institution." Taliaferro replied that the decision was an act of the board and that he was "unable to express an opinion on the matter."[32]

Jackson's statement that the decision to end coeducation would be the death knell of the university should not be construed as simple hyperbole. Enrollments were the bane of every college president's existence in the late nineteenth and early twentieth centuries. Funding and enrollments went hand in hand, and the correlation between the two produced a perhaps inevitable tendency to take on students who were not college material. Presidents understood, too, that most politicians did not look at enrollment data closely and were prone to stop with the total annual headcount. If two-thirds of the freshmen class failed to return for their sophomore year, as was often the case, most legislators were not going to notice. Why, then, would the trustees do anything that would automatically decrease the school's enrollment?

The obvious reason for gender segregation is that it would have ended the ongoing and growing rivalry between the University of Florida and Florida State. By 1903, it was evident to many more people than William Sheats and Tom McBeath that the status quo in higher education was no longer sustainable and that corrective measures were inevitable. It was also evident that the overall situation was getting worse, not better. In 1903 the quasi-public South Florida Military Institute became the South Florida Military College and began issuing state-approved bachelor's degrees to its teenage cadets. The year 1903 was also when the state legislature created the

Figures 7 and 8. Ida Morgan (*far right in figure 7 and center in figure 8*) was a student at the University of Florida when it opted to eliminate coeducation in 1903. She transferred to Florida State College and played basketball for both schools. Morgan Family Collection, George A. Smathers Libraries, University of Florida.

last of the state schools, the Florida Agricultural Institute, and there were constant calls for more.[33] The sad situation described by McBeath in 1897 had now reached the level of farce and was spiraling out of control.

Although change seemed imminent, no one could predict what that change would look like. Florida's academic landscape seemed to offer an infinite number of possibilities. However, one thing seemed certain: there would be a minimum of two colleges for white students, and the state would be hard-pressed to adequately fund one. Two coeducational colleges would be locked in perpetual conflict, fighting for both students and dollars, and neither would prosper. Gender segregation was an obvious way to reduce the conflict. By unilaterally making the decision to restrict enrollment to men, the trustees may have gambled that the state legislature would see the method to their madness when change finally happened. If so, they succeeded, as gender segregation became a defining feature of the Buckman Act. Finally, the decision was not irreversible. If change was delayed indefinitely, the trustees could always welcome the women back. In fact, only a year after the decision, Taliaferro recommended to the board that "young women of fixed purpose and mature mind" be admitted.[34]

As commencement day for 1903 approached, President Taliaferro was optimistic about his career and his school's future. The trustees' problematic decision to end coeducation was still a month in the future. He was now the president of the state university, and the budget situation was steadily improving. A new science building was under construction and would be ready in the fall, and the Flagler Gymnasium would be dedicated at the commencement ceremonies. Sadly, though, Henry Flagler was unable to attend. Florida congressman Robert W. Davis was the scheduled commencement speaker, and Davis had asked Taliaferro for information on the school's history. Taliaferro suggested he avoid the past in his speech and, instead, look forward:

> I have been trying to get some data for you which would be really useful, but the records, excepting in the near past, are so incomplete and so hard to get at, that I have been far from successful. . . . As a matter of fact, a great deal of the past should be buried in oblivion, for it represented simply a series of squabbles, political and otherwise. I think that your theme could well be extended to take in the future of the institution, now that we have our name changed, and, I trust, a brilliant future before us.[35]

Taliaferro could not have imagined then that another "squabble," a revolt by half of his faculty, was on the horizon and that it would bring his brief days in Florida to an end.

4

The Revolutions of 1904

The year 1903 ended on a portentous note with yet another campus fire at Lake City. This one consumed what had been the women's dormitory, which included an apartment for the president and his wife. The apartment replaced the president's residence destroyed in 1897. The fire occurred during the Christmas holidays, and the only students on campus were several Cubans who had been unable to return home. The wooden dormitory burned in less than twenty minutes. It was replaced by a modern brick facility financed in part by the insurance on the wooden dormitory. It housed students for only one year before the university moved to Gainesville.[1]

Enmity between President Taliaferro and his adversaries on the faculty came out in the open in April 1904, but it had been simmering almost from the day Taliaferro arrived. Both parties in the dispute agreed upon that. Taliaferro referred to the rebel faculty as "a remnant of the old regime" whose disloyalty to him and the board was long-standing. He added: "I have kept them only because of the fact that the Board was anxious for me to do so in the hope of making them loyal. I never expected to succeed and results have proven that I was correct in the main."[2] The remnant composed roughly half of his faculty. Just as Taliaferro had hesitated to act against the men who opposed him, they, too, held back from attacking the president. As one explained it: "The unfortunate history of the Institution during some preceding periods, especially during the administration of President Clute, by which public confidence in its future was to some degree shattered, constrained the members of the Faculty to exercise all possible patience and forbearance with the President's behavior."[3]

The series of events that ultimately led to the trustees' intervention began with a letter of complaint circulated by the professor of mechanical engineering, Nicholas H. Cox, and signed by eight members of the faculty. Cox later testified that he had told Taliaferro on April 9 of his intentions to come before the board with complaints against him and "thought it best to carry with [him] some endorsement in writing from the faculty." When Taliaferro heard of his petition, the president suspended him and told him to leave campus.[4] Taliaferro described the events quite differently and spoke of town conspirators as well as faculty: "The immediate cause is that I trapped one of a number and found him to be disloyal, gave him three days in which to reconsider, begging him to be loyal and straight for the sake of the institution. . . . I found that same night that with the aid and encouragement of other members of the clique in town and at the University he was circulating a letter among the faculty. . . . I consulted members of the Board in Jacksonville and called for his suspension immediately, as insubordinate. Then the clique met secretly, as they have been doing for some time past, and promulgated the letter which you received."[5]

In his correspondence to the board, Taliaferro insisted that the board sustain his actions and referred to promises made when he accepted the position. Instead, the board scheduled a hearing on the matter for June 21, two months hence. Taliaferro protested the delay and, once again, appealed for support: "I do so for the sake of the Institution as well as my own sake, since the University will never prosper until the said authority is vested in the President of the University and acted upon by the Board without reservation." Then, in an allusion to the Yocum-DePass incident ten years prior, he added, "Contrary action in the distant past is to a large extent the cause of the present delicate situation at the University."[6]

Prior to the June hearing, the board requested that the signatories to the protest letter provide written testimony as to why they had signed. This was included in the board minutes as Exhibit D. The existence of Exhibit D provides a unique record of one of the college's periodic revolutions. We know the names of the disaffected professors as well as their specific grievances. Some gave very brief remarks, whereas others provided lengthy commentary supplemented with gossip and insinuation. Reading the extensive comments of Professor Cox, who had been on the faculty since 1896, one gets a sense of the corrosive campus and community environment that prevailed in Lake City.

Although Taliaferro painted the dissidents as the "old regime," several had been at the university for fewer than six years. The group included the two instructors in the commercial department and two from the sciences. Four of the dissidents had appointments in the Agricultural Experiment Station, which might be an indication of unresolved tensions between the station and the president. If so, it was not mentioned in the testimony. Two names stand out in the list. One is H. K. Miller, professor of chemistry, who, as assistant station director, became the head of the station after the departure of Stockbridge. The second name is H. Harold Hume. Hume, a Canadian, would have a long and distinguished career as an agriculturalist in both academia and in the private sector. He would return to the University of Florida in the 1930s and would end his career there as provost of agriculture. Hume had already notified the president and the board several weeks before the revolt that he was leaving for another position, and he left with Taliaferro's good graces. Consequently, Hume had nothing personal to gain by supporting the resistance.

The list of complaints against Taliaferro was long, but most fall into four categories. They considered him to be unprofessional in his personal conduct; he was morally weak; student discipline had disintegrated under his administration; and he insulted the faculty on numerous occasions. Under the first category, the most common complaint was his alleged profanity. "*More* than simply D—n," is how Cox put it. He was also "inconsistent and untruthful." Hume argued that he governed by expediency, not right or wrong. His moral failings were largely related to alcohol, that is, he was not temperate, himself, and he vocally opposed the temperance movement. He was also "ungentlemanly" in his conduct with women, and, according to Cox, a rumor had "long been current" that Taliaferro and a friend had been seen "drinking beer with a couple of colored women late one night on the steps of the Chemistry laboratory." The one rumor manages to embrace several early twentieth-century southern social taboos: public alcohol consumption, sexual impropriety, and race mixing.[7]

The complaint that Taliaferro was lax in discipline can be attributed largely to his decision to end military regulations. Cox noted that Taliaferro's laxity would have been acceptable for older college men but not for the boys who attended the university. This, of course, evaded the real issue in that Taliaferro was striving to bring the university up to modern admission standards by ending the recruitment of underage students. Taliaferro's personal relationship with the student body, which the dissidents deemed too familiar, was also a factor. The early 1900s marked a transition in student-faculty relations. Older faculty fought to maintain strict boundaries with their students, while younger faculty, like Taliaferro and Murphree, saw themselves as mentors and sought more personal contact with the students rather than less. As a harbinger of things to come, there were also complaints about the athletic program and the types of students it attracted. The final category involved perceived insults from Taliaferro to his faculty. There are no specific examples given of these insults, but Taliaferro's own comments to the board reveal an obvious contempt for his unlettered faculty, many of whom lacked the academic credentials required of a modern university.[8]

Initially, Taliaferro refused to respond to charges he considered "puerile." He arrived at the hearings with two legal representatives and read a statement, which was filed as Exhibit E. Unlike the statements from his accusers, his did not survive. Only one faculty member testified on Taliaferro's behalf, history professor Melville C. Marion, who was as much a part of the old regime as any of the dissidents. The *et tu, Brute?* moment for Taliaferro may have been the resignation of English professor James Marion Farr on the same day as the hearings. Taliaferro had hired Farr and considered him a friend. Both were avid tennis players, and the two had laid out a clay tennis court on the campus and played each other regularly. They also gave tennis lessons to curious students who had never seen a tennis court or handled a racket. Farr had not signed the petition, but testimony from mathematics professor Robert Borger indicated that Farr had also grown dissatisfied with Taliaferro and had initiated another petition the year before.[9] Taliaferro submitted his resignation on the afternoon of the hearings, and the board accepted it "with full confidence ... in Dr. Taliaferro's personal integrity and honor."[10] The dissidents also wrote their resignations, but the board took no action. Their fates were left to Taliaferro's successor.

The June hearings were probably pro forma as the trustees had been investigating a possible successor to Taliaferro for almost a month before the board met. In this case, the board had not actively sought out a candidate but had been approached by Bishop Warren A. Candler about a possible opening. A power in the Methodist Church, South, and a former president of Emory College, Candler was also the brother of Asa Candler, head of the Coca-Cola Company. In a letter to trustee Charles Carson, who had been a student at Emory when Candler was president, Candler intimated that his son-in-law, Andrew Sledd, might be a suitable candidate if a position were available. Sledd had been a member of the Emory faculty, and he had recently completed his doctorate at Yale. Candler's inquiry set off a series of letters between Sledd and the trustees.[11]

The focus of their discussion was whether Sledd was orthodox on the vital question of race. Sledd's orthodoxy had been called into question in 1902, when he taught at Emory. In an article penned for the *Atlantic Monthly* entitled "The Negro: Another View," Sledd condemned the lawlessness of the South and those who participated in racial vigilantism. "There is nothing," he asserted, "in a white skin *or a black* to nullify the essential rights of man as man." He went on to assert that the South had no prerogative on matters of race. "The negro question is a national one; as much so as the question of tariff," Sledd argued. For a white southerner to assert that anyone outside the region should have a say on matters of race relations was tantamount to treason.[12] Sledd intended the article to be a springboard for a broader conversation on race. Instead, the article engendered a wave of white hostility and denunciation. The Sledd Affair, as it came to be called, led to Sledd's forced resignation from Emory's faculty. His expulsion, in turn, exposed the lack of academic freedom in the South on matters of race and brought Emory and southern academe into disrepute among colleges outside the region.[13] At some point in the board's inquiry, Sledd convinced the trustees that his views on race were not, in fact, heretical. His cause was also aided by an endorsement from another Emory graduate, Nathan Philemon Bryan. Bryan, who was Carson's brother-in-law, was an influential member of Napoleon Bonaparte Broward's inner circle, and Broward had just won Florida's first Democratic gubernatorial primary election and was the presumptive governor-elect.[14]

The *Atlantic Monthly* article was to some extent a diversion from Sledd's chosen crusade. He saw himself, first and foremost, as a champion for educational improvement. "The fundamental problem that confronts the South," he wrote, "is an educational one." Sledd lamented the poverty of southern colleges, their weak academic standards, and their intellectual dishonesty, and hoped that one would rise above the rest to initiate the "intellectual regeneration of the South."[15] In contrast to the pragmatic and diplomatic Albert Murphree, Sledd was idealistic and uncompromising. A supporter referred to him as "a typical Virginian gentleman of the old school, high minded, frank and fearless." His fearlessness was rooted in his religious convictions. "Necessity requires no moral compromise," a student of his remembered him saying: "A man never actually *has* to do but two things: die and face the judgement of a righteous God." Klein Graham, who served as Sledd's bookkeeper at the University of Florida, thought the student and faculty "were out of step with him and his religious ideals."[16] Florida, though, was certainly a good testing ground for Sledd's evangelical approach to educational reform.

While the board pondered a possible change at the top and whether Sledd was a proper adherent to southern racial norms, Sledd, himself, questioned the wisdom of accepting a position that had bedeviled every person who held it. For an assessment of the situation, Sledd called on a family acquaintance in Lake City, L. E. Robertson. Robertson wrote back with a sober description of what the university needed most: "During its years of existence, it has had its ups and downs, its seasons of prosperity and adversity. The trouble has been, it seems, to get a proper man at the head of the faculty, and that is the trouble at this time." He then added, "The present President of the faculty has held his position for three years, and from the indications now, has been a decided failure."[17] After interviewing two other candidates, the board met on July 7 and offered the presidency to Sledd. The board also received an unexpected application from William Sheats, who had just lost his position as superintendent to William Holloway in the Democratic primary. Sheats was certainly well respected by the trustees as he had been offered the presidency in 1898. However, the circumstances in 1904 were different, and Sheats's selection could have placed the university in the crosshairs of his political opposition.[18]

Sledd paid a visit to Lake City shortly after his election and met with the outgoing president, the trustees, and members of the community. After departing Lake City, Sledd received an emotional letter from Taliaferro warning him of certain individuals in the town and on the faculty. "Rumors are flying thick and fast in town," Taliaferro wrote, "[and] it is said that you promised the malcontents and others to do just what the best people of town wished you to do. (Do not be fooled by them regarding the best element in the town.)" He then went on to give his assessments of the three professors who had remained neutral during the faculty revolt—E. R. Wharton, Yocum, and Farr—calling each a "snake in the grass" for pretending "to a friendship they never felt." Finally, he cautioned Sledd about specific townspeople, and among them was L. E. Robertson.[19] Taliaferro followed with a second letter that was much calmer and free of the vitriol of the first: "It was not my intention when writing you to give you a case of the blue devils or to make you thoughtful, in the sense of being anxious regarding the situation here. My desire was simply to warn you against the many pitfalls that exist here, as they do in every institution in a small town, when the said institution is new and has begun growing. Personally, I should have been glad to have someone warn me when I came here."[20]

During this time, Sledd kept an account of his life entitled "Autobiography of a Southern Schoolmaster," which reads more like a journal than an actual memoir. The manuscript ends, regrettably, in 1905, just after the Buckman Act was passed. Nonetheless, it provides a one-year snapshot of the travails of a southern college president in a small town. His first entry after arriving in Lake City noted that he "found the institution in a chaotic condition, consequent upon one of its periodic upheavals."[21] The situation may have been chaotic, but it gave Sledd an opportunity to do what Taliaferro had so ham-handedly attempted, that is, to remove some academic deadweight and radically transform the faculty culture. In addition to the faculty who had resigned, there was also the position of professor of modern languages that Taliaferro had not filled after the departure of the women faculty. Furthermore, Sledd made it clear that he was under no obligation to renew anyone's contract, dissident or loyal.

His first mission was to convince James Marion Farr to return. The board had already asked Farr to withdraw his resignation, but Farr needed some assurances from Sledd before he agreed to return. Sledd then turned his attention to other faculty positions. In letters to potential recruits, Sledd was honest in his appraisal of where the university stood. But he laid out a vision of what the university could become and the opportunity it provided to younger professors. The following excerpt from a letter to Karl Schmidt, whom he hired as the mathematics professor, is typical:

> Our Institution here is in a transition stage and I look forward to great progress and prosperity during the course of the next few years, if we can be wise and discreet in our conduct of the school. Up to two years ago, the Institution was known as the Florida Agricultural College, when the Legislature changed our name to the University of Florida, with the idea that we should as rapidly as possible develop into an actual university. At present we are a hybrid, part Preparatory school, part college, part technical school and part—a small part—university, and it is our task to make of this hybrid (if you will allow me to mix my figures) a homogeneous and vigorous institution along university lines. Rather a difficult task, as you will perceive.[22]

Schmidt was Sledd's fifth hire, and not all the malcontents were replaced. Surprisingly, Professor Cox, who had instigated the petition against Taliaferro, retained his position. His lasting contribution to the University of Florida came a year later when he surveyed the 517 acres donated by Gainesville to acquire the university.[23] Sledd also filled the position of history professor even though the incumbent was not among the disaffected faculty. Melville Marion, who also headed the preparatory department, occupied the chair of history, and his highest degree was a bachelor of literature from Central University of Kentucky. When informed of the decision, Marion requested leave for the remainder of the year with pay. When Sledd refused his request, Marion invaded his office and began in "very discourteous terms" to verbally attack him. Sledd went to the door, opened it, and commanded him to leave. As he exited, Marion shook his finger in Sledd's face and called him a liar. Feeling that his honor had been impugned, Sledd struck him and a brief fight ensued.

Sledd apologized to the board for "forgetting himself as to strike Professor Marion," but he considered his actions "not only justifiable but necessary." Both combatants were southerners, and Marion clearly understood that he crossed a regional line of honor when he uttered the word "liar." The board's entry on the incident is amusing. After investigating what it referred to as the "unpleasantness," the board declared "the provocation fully justified Dr. Sledd in ordering Prof. Marion from the office." The record was later amended with the phrase "and the subsequent action" written in pencil. The incident did not go unnoticed. It was reported in the *Gainesville Sun*, and Sledd wanted to sue the paper for defamation. As head of the preparatory department since 1896, Marion had deep ties in the community as the prep school was composed mostly of local boys. Marion did not leave Lake City after the incident but would foment trouble as yet another member of the notorious "clique in town."[24]

As a Methodist lay clergyman, Sledd was careful to avoid denominational preferences in his faculty selections. On August 9, 1904, before he had completed his hiring, he proudly reported that his selection included two Congregationalists, a Lutheran, a Friend, an Episcopalian, but only one Methodist. Although he preferred regional candidates, none were Floridians or had any personal or political ties with Florida. In his autobiography he commented, "Judging from my experience on that occasion and since the principle of selection seems to have been a novel one, and not altogether approved in the State."[25] The political repercussions of his selection process soon became evident. One of the applicants he snubbed was Williams Sheats. After being rejected for the post of president, Sheats demanded that Sledd appoint him professor of mathematics. When Sledd demurred, Sheats made political threats. To counteract those threats, Sledd called upon Napoleon Bonaparte Broward at his home in Jacksonville and requested his support. Broward assured Sledd that the university would be politically independent under his administration and encouraged him to hire the best men available. While in Jacksonville, Sledd conferred with Broward's closest advisers, the Bryan brothers William and Nathan. Nathan Bryan had a particular interest in educational reforms, and his meeting with Sledd began an association that would endure until Sledd's forced resignation in 1909.[26]

The conflict between Sledd and Sheats was ironic as they shared many of the same values. Sheats had been a rare voice in Tallahassee for educational progress, and both men valued educational standards, although Sheats was less strident on the subject than Sledd. They shared similar views on racial matters, and Sheats's invitation to Booker T. Washington to speak in Florida in 1903 cost him the 1904 election. This had not escaped the attention of Sledd, who remarked that Sheats's defeat was "brought about largely by the malicious and mendacious agitation of the 'negro question,' and the usual frantic assertion that Mr. Sheats was unorthodox in the particular."[27]

By academic year 1905–6, the University of Florida's teaching faculty numbered thirteen, ten of whom held doctorates. It was, by any standard of the day, an excellent faculty, one that compared favorably with those of northern schools. Sledd would rightly claim that the percentage of PhDs on his faculty exceeded that of other state universities in the Gulf region. In a letter to the parent of a prospective student who was considering the University of Georgia, Sledd noted that Florida had nine PhDs and Georgia only four.[28] Among those Sledd recruited were several who would have long careers at Florida including John Benton in engineering, Charles Langley Crow in modern languages, and Edward Flint in chemistry. After convincing Farr to stay as professor of English, he also made him vice president. Farr would serve in that capacity for more than thirty years.

Just as the quality of the faculty improved so, too, did the standards for student admission and matriculation. Shortly after his arrival, Sledd received permission from the trustees to raise admission requirements to roughly the eleventh grade. The decision would eventually compel local school districts to elevate their high school curricula. In the interim, though, there was a dearth of eligible students. Enrollments also fell after Sledd demanded a higher level of discipline and morality as well as academics from his students. Sledd adopted as a motto for the university, "Sound morals, the basis of good citizenship," and clamped down on disruptive students. The student body tested his resolve early in his administration with a mass hazing of the freshmen class. At a morning assembly, the freshmen appeared with shorn heads and the letter *R* for rats, the pejorative term for freshmen, dyed on their scalps. Sledd responded to numerous letters from outraged parents and negotiated a collective guarantee from his students that no future abuses would occur. Not all his actions received the same positive response from the student body. When Sledd canceled the 1905 football season because the players had fallen behind in their studies, several players left school in disgust.[29] Sledd also took decisive action to end high school work at the university. The college had originally maintained three grades of high school referred to as Classes A, B, and C. The lowest grade, Class C, was dropped in 1899. At Sledd's suggestion, the board approved the dissolution of Class B for 1905–6 and Class A for 1906–7. However, it proved impossible to eliminate preparatory classes altogether, and the university still maintained a single year of prep work when Sledd left in 1909.[30]

Sledd's first year as president was transformative and constituted a revolution in itself. He brought stability and decisive leadership at a critical moment. He was able to recruit properly trained faculty, raise admissions standards, and shrink the preparatory department. Things were again looking up when the university was once more rocked by revolution. This one, though, came from outside the university and Lake City, and it disrupted the entire system of higher education.

II

BUCKMAN

5

The Buckman Revolution

The Buckman Act of 1905 is one of the longest and most complex laws enacted by the State of Florida during the Progressive Era. Yet, for a number of reasons, its origins and evolution are mysterious. For one, a copy of the original bill sent to committee does not exist. Consequently, it is impossible to do a before-and-after comparison. The reluctance of the act's authors to publicly explain themselves after the bill's passage further intensified the mystery. Debate on the House and Senate floors was very brief and poorly documented. Even the act's most basic tenets were disputed. For example, were all seven of the white state schools in existence before 1905 truly abolished by the act? The phrase used in the act is "revoked, vacated and abolished." That would seem definitive to most readers and legally unassailable. Yet, in 1909, three of the five members of the Florida State Supreme Court disagreed. They ruled, in the case of the Florida State College, that the act simply renamed the school and changed its character from a coeducational school to a women's college. Was the new University of Florida in Gainesville fundamentally different from the old University of Florida in Lake City? On the surface, they appear to be one and the same. They had the same president, almost identical faculties, and similar course catalogues. The women were already gone, having been removed in 1903.[1]

Dissatisfaction with the existing state of affairs in education was widespread before Florida entered the twentieth century, and it was not confined to any one segment of the polity. Emigrants to Florida continued to clamor for improvements, particularly at the local level, and there was growing sentiment among native Floridians that the status quo was inadequate. Among the state's politicians, progressives lamented the absence of anything that could truly be considered a state university; populists fought to make education more accessible and vocationally relevant; conservatives complained of the high costs of maintaining so many state schools; and all realized that the state schools were holding back the development of both secondary and higher education. Most of this discussion was irrelevant to Florida's Black population. Removed from the political and economic mainstreams, African Americans used the few resources available to them to create and nurture their own educational opportunities.

There had been speculation about possible education reform in the months leading up to the 1905 legislative session. Sledd had heard rumors as early as August 1904.[2] When the legislature convened in the spring of 1905, Governor Broward made it clear in his official message of April 4 that education was a priority for his administration. On the issue of the state schools, Broward's message was simple; the state schools should no longer be "put into the attitude of beggars before the Legislature for the means of existence." To prevent that in the future, the state needed a new system of management whereby the schools would be placed under a single governing entity, and there had to be a steady source of income in the form of a state levy.[3] In response to the governor's message, two proposals for the creation of a board of regents were forwarded to a Special Committee on State Institutions, a joint committee created specifically to review any bills related to the state schools.

The governor did not call for the consolidation, elimination, or relocation of any of the state schools in his message. It was obvious, though, that something along those lines was in the wind. As the proposals for a board of regents came forward, representatives from the counties in which state schools resided were careful to ensure that any new governing board was not empowered to abolish or relocate any existing school. Two such bills were suggested before Henry Holland Buckman, a representative from Duval County, introduced a motion on May 3 to defer further consideration in the House. Buckman stated then that a bill was to be introduced on May 9 that would provide for a state university, a women's college, and a normal school and that the remaining state schools would be run as high schools. On the stated date, Buckman delivered a forty-page bill that was introduced as House Bill No. 361. Buckman's bill was referred to the Special Committee on State Institutions.[4]

Exactly when the process of putting together the bill began is uncertain. In a speech printed in the *Florida Times-Union* on May 15, Buckman stated that he had been working on the bill for three weeks and had been "imbued with the idea" since arriving at the legislature. Suffice it to say, Buckman, and whoever else may have had a hand in the crafting of the law, had to work quickly and deliberately. However, some groundwork had undoubtedly been laid before the legislative session. Sledd and Jere Pound, principal of the East Florida Seminary, were consulted in the months leading up to the 1905 legislative session. Nathan Bryan contacted Sledd for his opinions on higher education in November 1904 to help him with Broward's inauguration speech. Pound communicated directly with Governor Broward in March 1905 to suggest the Georgia Normal and Industrial School as a model for the education of women. This would indicate that gender segregation was being considered at an early date.[5]

On May 15 the two bills on the creation of a board of regents were reported unfavorably by the Special Committee on State Institutions, but a committee substitute for House Bill No. 361 went forward. There were forty-one sections to the revised bill. Sections 1–5 and 7–10 were specific to the dissolution of the seven state schools for white students. Section 6 eliminated the existing boards of trustees for the schools, including that of the Institute for the Deaf, Dumb, and Blind. Section 11 referred to the State Normal and Industrial School and revised an existing statute on this school to indicate that it was now under the joint control of the Board of Education and the newly created Board of Control. Otherwise, the forerunner of FAMU was left untouched. Section 12 created two new schools, the University of the State of Florida and the Florida Female College. The odd names reflected the need to differentiate the new schools from any of the abolished schools. The legislature renamed them the University of Florida and the Florida State College for Women in 1909. That same year, the legislature renamed the Florida State Normal and Industrial School the Florida Agricultural and Mechanical College and dropped the word "Dumb" from the Florida State School for the Deaf, Dumb, and Blind.[6]

Sections 13–15 and 19 created the Florida Board of Control, defined its membership, powers, and responsibilities, and placed the new board under the control and supervision of the Board of Education. The act further indicated that the two boards would act as one joint board on specific matters. For example, sections 16–18 dealt with the way the locations of the new state schools would be determined and gave that responsibility to the joint board. Sections 21 and 22 described the purposes and missions of the University of the State of Florida and the Florida Female College and restricted enrollment to white men and white women, respectively. Sections 23 and 24 dealt with admissions, tuition, and scholarships. Most of the remaining sections concerned mundane matters. However, section 26 made it clear that the state university was also the land grant college, and section 38 stipulated that the Board of Control provide a system of examinations for admission and matriculation. The latter was never implemented.

Oddly, the bill did not create, or re-create, a normal school for white teachers as Buckman had indicated it would on May 1 before he sent the bill to committee. The day before the bill passed the House on May 22, Buckman reassured the state legislators that the white normal institute at DeFuniak Springs would "be transferred to the university[,] . . . strengthening the university and maintaining a normal department there, so that nothing is lost."⁷ Although that may have been his intent, no such transfer occurred, nor was it stipulated in the bill. Instead, sections 21 and 23 allowed for the *possibility* of a coeducational normal school at the otherwise all-male state university, and section 22 provided an option for a female-only normal department at the women's college. However, neither could happen without the approval of the joint board. The act also made no provision for converting abolished state schools into high schools, another of Buckman's assurances.

Once the bill made it to the House floor for debate, it quickly became clear that the votes for passage were there. Numerous amendments were proposed, and all were soundly defeated. The bill passed the House on May 22 with a vote of 34 yeas and 22 nays. The vote in the Senate on May 26 was 16 for and 5 against. The seven counties representing the abolished state schools accounted for many of the negative votes. Governor Broward signed the bill on June 5.

Decades later, Lucius Moody Bristol, a retired sociology professor at the University of Florida, tracked down the surviving members of the 1905 state legislature and sent them questionnaires regarding the passage of the Buckman Act. Representative Eugene Matthews of Bradford County, who chaired the special committee on education, was one of the respondents. According to Matthews, the pro-Buckman forces fell into two groups. The first group consisted of fiscal conservatives who had become increasingly concerned about the rising costs of supporting seven schools and the constant calls for additional schools. In fact, a bill had been introduced in 1905 to make the entirety of the St. Petersburg Industrial and Normal School a state school, and there was a call to make Lakeland High School a state school as well. The second group consisted of educational reformers concerned less with finances and more with the quality of instruction and the proliferation of inferior schools. Matthews further stated that the merits of coeducation had not been given marked consideration and gender separation was taken "more or less for granted—that it was the right thing to do."⁸

Bristol also tapped into the memory of John Gabriel Kellum, chief clerk of the House in 1905 and later the Board of Control's first secretary as well as the business manager for the State College for Women. (He held all three positions concurrently from 1905 to 1917.) Kellum argued that the bill "was primarily an economy measure" but also acknowledged the group of reformers and their impact on the bill. He then added a third group of legislators to the mix who would only vote for the bill if it provided for separate gender-based colleges. Together, the three groups formed a majority in the legislature. Kellum also conceded there was an economic consideration to gender segregation in that it avoided "duplication of accommodations and equipment."[9] In effect, the intent of the act was to create a superior school with a diverse curriculum designed to train white men for their chosen professions, and an inferior school with the more limited course and degree offerings suitable for women's roles as mothers, civic leaders, and teachers. Kellum did not identify the politicians who demanded gender segregation, and we can only surmise their motives. Sexual propriety may have been an issue, but religious beliefs should not have been a factor as all the denominational colleges in Florida, even those inspired by conservative evangelical theology, were coeducational. It is more likely that the votes came from legislators whose vision for higher education leaned toward the prestigious and exclusive Ivy League schools or the one southern antebellum university that retained an aura of distinction in the twentieth century, the University of Virginia. It is also very likely that Henry Buckman shared that sentiment.

The insistence on gender segregation explains why Florida did not consider other choices, including models from other states. One option would have been to create a state university as the primary institution and a combined land grant college and normal school as the second school. A combined land grant and normal school would not have competed equally with the state university in 1905, as land grant colleges and normal schools were considered second-tier institutions. Another option would have been to create a coeducational state university with land grant responsibilities and a separate coeducational normal school. This was a model chosen by several states including Washington and Arizona. Both options, and others, were available *if* coeducation had been a possibility.

Florida's decision to end coeducation put it into the rapidly shrinking group of states that maintained gender-segregated university systems. In fact, Florida is the only state to have been largely coeducational in the nineteenth century to switch course in the twentieth century. In the South, also, prohibitions against female admissions applied only to white students; the historically Black public colleges were coeducational. Southern normal schools and summer schools tended to be coeducational as well.

The male-only universities were sometimes compelled to make exceptions when women insisted on admission to specific professional and graduate programs. North Carolina, for example, allowed some wiggle room for women graduate students, and, under special circumstances, women were admitted to North Carolina State University as early as 1901. The University of Georgia would drop out of the male-only group in 1918, although it restricted female enrollment initially to specific professional programs. Florida followed a similar path in 1925, when it admitted women to academic programs at the University of Florida that were not available at Florida State.

Gender segregation would create numerous problems for Florida's educational leaders, but nowhere more so than with the education of teachers. It is clear from the ambiguous wording and the various options provided in the three sections related to the normal school that the Buckman authors realized they had created a problem and were unable to resolve it. In the final analysis, the Buckman Act kicked the can down the road, so to speak, and the joint board was left to work out the messy details. Ultimately, the joint board decided to reject Buckman's intention for a coeducational normal school at the university and opted, instead, to maintain strict gender segregation in the white normal schools. The joint board's decision undermined the Buckman Act's economic rationale and resulted in a foreseen but undesirable consequence. The net effect of the joint board decision threw the bulk of the normal school students into the State College for Women, making it, not the university, the larger of the two. With greater enrollments came larger operating budgets. Capital outlays for the two colleges would also be more or less equal. Incredibly, the University of Florida's status as the superior academic institution would not equate with superior funding.

Although it was obvious to people at the time, subsequent interpreters of the act often failed to note or appreciate that the law had as much to do with the destruction of a system of secondary education as it did the creation of a new system of tertiary education. The destruction, however, is contained in three pages of the act, while the creation takes up eighteen pages. Henry Buckman referred to the abolished state schools as "nothing more than a separate set of high schools" that had become an "incubus" on the state's educational system. Not everyone agreed with that assessment. Clarence Sowell, in a letter to Governor Broward, decried the elimination of those secondary schools and the benefits they brought to those who did not have access to a local high school. Instead, taxpayers' dollars now supported a state university that the poor could not attend because it required a high school education.[10]

The Florida Board of Control was one of many boards and commissions created by the state legislature to provide oversight and supervision for a wide range of concerns. The number of boards would rise to 150 by 1969, when a government reorganization reduced the number to twenty-five. Among the other 150 boards were the State Racing Commission, the Beverage Commission, the Citrus Commission, and the Livestock Sanitary Board. The members of these boards were appointed by the governor and have been referred to as Florida's "little cabinet." The Board of Control was unique as it was the only board placed under the supervision and authority of one of the twenty-two ex officio executive boards, in this case the Board of Education. It was also the only board to have the heads of four state institutions—the three college presidents and the principal of the School for the Deaf and Blind—reporting directly to it. This odd chain of command—or, as Principal William Hare of the School for the Deaf and Blind deemed it, "our unheard-of dual board control"—was also unique in American higher education. Lastly, the Board of Control was the only state board to do double duty. After 1915, the members of the Board of Control also served on the State Plant Board, created, initially, to take charge of the campaign against citrus canker. In subsequent years, members of the State Plant Board also saw service in the fights against the cotton boll weevil, the Mediterranean fruit fly, and other infestations and diseases. Although the responsibilities of the two boards seem dissimilar, they were associated by the agricultural work of the University of Florida and Florida A&M. The heads of the agricultural programs at the University of Florida, Peter Henry Rolfs and, later, Wilmon Newell, reported directly to the State Plant Board as the state plant commissioner and advised the board on matters related to plant diseases and pests.[11]

As argued by Governor Broward and others, the purposes of a common board of regents or overseers were to restrict competition between the state schools, reduce unnecessary duplication of instruction, and to provide a means of rationalizing and coordinating budget requests among the state schools. Given the clamor for such a board, it was inevitable that it would be a significant part of the Buckman Act. Ironically, though, the act obviated the necessity for a common board when it reduced the number of schools for white students from seven to two and then attempted to make the two noncompetitive. The act also placed two other schools, the School for the Deaf and Blind and the State Normal and the Industrial School, under the Board of Control, and neither would compete with the university or the women's college for either funds or students.

Although the Buckman Act made the Board of Control subordinate to the Board of Education, it provided virtually no guidance as to how or when the boards would interact. In addition to a joint meeting to locate the new schools, the act also refers to joint action regarding the normal schools and the disposition of property from the abolished schools. Section 21 states that the joint board, not the Board of Control, would make decisions regarding the establishment of new academic departments. Joint meetings occurred several times in the years immediately after the Buckman Act, and it may have been, as Bristol speculated, that the act's authors intended for the two boards to work as one body.[12] In later years, joint meetings occurred only sporadically and always to resolve a conflict between the two boards. If unity of action was intended, it was not made clear in the act. A protocol was eventually established whereby the Board of Control made decisions, the decisions were communicated to the Board of Education, and the Board of Education either approved or disapproved.

Whatever its shortcomings—and there were many—the Buckman Act succeeded in its primary purposes. It ended direct state support for secondary education and threw that responsibility back onto the counties. In doing so, it also eliminated five state institutions that seemed unlikely to prosper in a monetarily deprived southern state. The Buckman Act set a path for higher education in Florida that was fundamentally different from the path it had been pursuing. Had the Buckman Act not been passed, Florida's educational history would have likely mirrored that of Georgia, where a host of smaller schools coexisted with and, to some degree, competed with the University of Georgia. With perhaps one or two exceptions, all of Georgia's smaller state schools survived and grew to become state universities and colleges. Georgia Tech even generated two "spin-offs" of its own: Georgia State University and the engineering college at Kennesaw State University. Although it would be impossible to predict what might have occurred in Florida had the Buckman Act not intervened, it is interesting to note that none of the five cities abandoned by the Buckman Act currently host a state university.

If the reasons for the presence or absence of specific features in the Buckman Act elude us today, they were equally mysterious to those who were directly impacted by the act. The act also created a month of institutional uncertainty and placed the faculty of the pre-Buckman schools in an academic limbo. After reading about the law, newly hired engineering professor John Benton concluded: "So far as I can make out[,] the act is an idiotic piece of spite-work, carried through in utter disregard of justice or of responsibility to the wishes of the people." Having accepted a position at a university that no longer existed, Benton threatened to sue.[13] Uncertainty and mystery only intensified the ever-present rumor mills in Tallahassee, Lake City, and Gainesville. Accusations were flying in Gainesville and Tallahassee that the University of Florida was behind the Buckman Act, and university trustee Frank Harris urged President Sledd to take measures to counter those claims. As for himself, Harris stated, "I took no part for nor against the Buckman bill, did not talk to a single member of the legislature concerning it, and I think this was the attitude of the other members of the board, and of the president and members of the faculty as well." He added: "It seems there is little reward for one's performing his duty but it will be seen when the fogs and mists are cleared away. Have hope and faith."[14]

The board of trustees for the old University of Florida held its last meeting on June 14, 1905, the day after spring commencement. Officially, the board no longer existed as the Buckman Act took effect on June 5, the day it was signed by the governor, and the act had abolished the old boards. In closing, the board passed several resolutions, including a warm testimonial to President Sledd. In Sledd the board recognized "a distinguished educator of most excellent Christian character, a Southern gentleman of the highest type, a worthy example for young men, an effective and able organizer, a good disciplinarian, gifted in impartation, an ideal and successful College President." The board further resolved to "heartily recommend" to the Board of Control that Dr. Sledd and his faculty be appointed to their respective positions in the new university.[15]

6

The Immediate Aftermath of Buckman

Of the seven campuses impacted by the Buckman Act, only two would survive after the five men of the Board of Education and the five men of the Board of Control met in July 1905 to determine the fortunate two. The odds-on favorites were Tallahassee and Lake City. Tallahassee was the state capital and the site of Albert Murphree's Florida State College. Lake City's advantage was its possession of a significant and very usable campus, and it seemed unlikely that the state would forsake it. The abandonment of a state university or land grant college campus was unprecedented in modern American history. Florida was soon to become the one and only exception.

The impact would have been less noteworthy had the move occurred only five years earlier. The campus of the Florida Agricultural College then was not significantly larger than those of the other state schools. After 1900, though, the state made significant investments in the land grant college. It erected a science building and, with the help of Henry Flagler, a gymnasium. A modern brick dormitory was being constructed when the decision to relocate came. The state had purchased 200 adjacent acres, tripling the original 100-acre campus. With the additional land and buildings, the University of Florida's campus was, by far, the largest of the state schools. Only Stetson University could boast of a larger one in the state. In addition to the physical plant, tens of thousands of federal dollars had been spent on immovable agricultural improvements, and those would be lost if the university was relocated. There was also the enormous cost of transporting everything that *was* movable, and the Buckman Act made no provision for covering those costs. There were also the psychological costs to consider. How would this decision be perceived by the public, and what of the stress on faculty and students? A draconian decision to move was even more illogical, considering the state's poverty and the fiscal conservatism of its politicians. It seemed unimaginable then, and perhaps more so today, that

Figure 9. Postcard of the former University of Florida campus at Lake City, made shortly after the university moved to Gainesville. The new Science Hall is on the left, and Flagler Gymnasium appears in the background. University Archives Postcard Collection, George A. Smathers Libraries, University of Florida.

the State of Florida would discard one viable campus and create a new one in a pine hammock forty-five miles to the south. In short, Lake City seemed safe.

There was also a perception, particularly in Gainesville, that the Buckman Act was written in such a manner as to favor Lake City and that the newly created Board of Control would be packed with pro–Lake City appointees. Suspicion was heightened when Governor Broward requested a ruling from the Florida Supreme Court as to whether a sitting legislator could serve on a governing board for higher education. The request was prompted by Broward's desire to place Senator Frank Adams, the chair of the Appropriations Committee and his close friend and ally, on the Board of Control. Adams was a key supporter of Lake City. However, the Florida State Supreme Court determined that the Board of Control constituted a civil board, and the state constitution forbade the appointment of legislators to any civil office.[1] It is interesting that this prohibition had not applied to the independent boards of the pre-Buckman schools. Legislators often sat on those boards, and they were not shy about advocating on behalf of their respective colleges. Unable to have Frank Adams, Broward appointed

Adams's brother, Nathaniel—or Nat, as he was called—in his place. That decision could not have pleased Gainesville. In addition to Adams, the original Board of Control included Nathan Philemon Bryan from Jacksonville, Philip Keyes Yonge from Pensacola, Thomas B. King of Arcadia, and A. L. Brown from Eustis. The board first met on June 28, and Bryan was elected chair. To stagger appointments, two of the first five appointees, Brown and Adams, were to serve only two years. Having failed in his purpose, though, Adams would step down within the year.

As Gainesville's indignation and sense of horror at losing the seminary grew, citizens of the town started a letter-writing campaign to the governor. Some of the letters to Broward were from prominent citizens who had backed Broward in the 1904 election despite the presence of a local candidate on the ballot, Congressman Robert Davis. W. S. Broome described a "feeling of unrest and gloom" in Gainesville as it seemed "to be a cut and dried proposition to give the University of Florida to Lake City." John Tench, who had backed Broward over the "drunkard" Davis, noted the widespread support being given to Gainesville at the annual meeting of county commissioners and by a number of county school boards. He also mentioned that there was a defection on the board of trustees of the old University of Florida; Frank Harris was now openly supporting Gainesville.[2] The most emotional letter came from Gainesville mayor William R. Thomas. Thomas keyed on Alachua County's devotion to the East Florida Seminary even though the county supported its own high school and taxed itself to the highest level to do so. Thomas then turned to politics and how the county had "turned its back on an old friend." Finally, he voiced what others had only implied:

> From the day of its establishment, as you are well aware, up to the present moment, the University has been reeking with slander and torn by strife and dissension, until a large majority of the people of Florida have become disgusted and prejudiced against it. Added to the Clute scandal, the DePass muddle, the faculty rebellion last year, the Sledd-Marion fisticuff this last year, the recent report of the legislative committee has sunk deep into the hearts and minds of the people....
>
> Mark my words, Captain Broward [a reference to Broward's days as a steamer captain and gunrunner to Cuban rebels fighting for independence]: if you undertake to establish a University on that heap

of educational ruins, though you may live long, you will not live long enough to be proud of your work; but on the other hand, it will, in my opinion candidly, frankly, but confidentially expressed to you as a friend, be a "thorn in your flesh" as long as you live.³

Thomas's heated letter referenced yet another scandal at Lake City, that of a legislative committee report that was making the rounds in the spring of 1905. As part of its oversight responsibilities, the legislature sent a three-member visitation team at the start of each legislative session to inspect the schools and make recommendations. The visitation teams rarely had anything critical to say about either the schools or their administrators; committee recommendations tended to focus on the obvious needs of each school. The 1905 report, though, painted a disturbing picture of desolation, dereliction, and possible malfeasance at the University of Florida. President Sledd characterized the report "as vicious a collection of falsehoods as could have been put forth under the semblance of the truth." He later confided that the attack "had affected him physically and mentally." Frank Harris published a strong rebuke in the *Ocala Banner* and labeled the report "a piece of political devilment . . . hardly entitled to serious consideration."⁴

As university president for less than a year when the legislators visited the campus, Sledd appeared to have been simply a victim of circumstances. The only criticism aimed directly at Sledd was that he had hired younger professors who lacked the maturity to maintain discipline in the school. That he had managed to recruit a faculty with higher credentials than any university in the Gulf South apparently escaped the attention of the visitation team. Most of the report focused on the "filthy" and "dilapidated" condition of the buildings and grounds, accusations that the agricultural research plots had been mismanaged, and charges that the university trustees had diverted federal funds "contrary to national law."⁵

There was more than a grain of truth regarding the diversion of federal funds. The problems were well documented and had been highlighted as early as 1898, when Alfred Charles True complained to the board of trustees about the use of Hatch funds to pay the college president. Sledd was aware of the issue and would soon undertake measures to correct it. A few months after the report appeared, Sledd relinquished the title of station director and appointed Peter Henry Rolfs, a noted expert in tropical agriculture, to fill the position. At the same time, station personnel were freed of most classroom duties and allowed to focus on their research. The steps taken by Sledd and Rolfs laid the foundation for the station's emergence as one of the nation's largest and most diverse agricultural research and demonstration programs.

Little is known of the three legislators on the visitation team. It was rumored, though, that the team had a bias toward Florida State. Their information on the University of Florida came from disgruntled local sources, and the committee was more than willing to use it. While the investigators' attacks may have been directed at the university, the "clique in town" aimed their guns at President Sledd. In his autobiography, Sledd identified Columbia County's two state representatives, A. J. P. Julian and E. G. Persons, as well as Horace Stockbridge, as the reputed sources for the report. Stockbridge's hostility to the university was long-standing, and it did not abate with the dismissal of Taliaferro. Julian's dislike of Sledd stemmed, in part, from Sledd's refusal to appoint him university physician. The position went instead to chemistry professor Edward R. Flint, who held an MD from Harvard as well as a PhD in chemistry from Göttingen. In retaliation, Julian posted a copy of Sledd's *Atlantic Monthly* article at his pharmacy. But it was Sledd's outspokenness that prompted most of the hostility.[6]

Sledd believed that the university would never be successful as long as it was confined to a "small inland town." He had quietly been advocating Jacksonville as a possible alternative. Warren Candler had also promoted the idea in conjunction with a campaign to establish a Methodist college there. Sledd expressed his views too openly at a meeting of the trustees, and word quickly leaked to the community. This prompted a denunciation of Sledd on the House floor by Representative Persons. Persons linked Sledd's betrayal of Lake City—"an act smacking of Judas Iscariot"—to what he called Sledd's disloyalty to the white race. In his autobiography, Sledd confided, "I stand an innocent man accused of all these things upon the official records of the State of Florida, because [of], as I understand it, all political and personal spite with which I had nothing to do, and of the shadow of the Negro question which writes its dark lines continually upon my career."[7]

The legislative report was probably the final straw that led to the public defection of Frank Harris. Harris had been on the university's board since its reorganization in 1893, and no one was more familiar with the university's problems at Lake City. A month before the joint board meeting in July, Harris and the *Ocala Banner* pointed to local rancor as the source of Lake City's problems: "Lake City has permitted the institution to become mixed up in its local politics and factional fights, and in consequence of which, its hands have not been upheld by its people and its usefulness has been hampered and at times almost paralyzed." Citing the legislative report as but the latest example, the paper noted that all of the college's presidents, "Kost, Kern, DePass, Clute, Yocum, Taliaferro, Sledd, like Shadrach, Meshach and Abednego . . . in turn had to pass through the furnace." In a postscript to the decision to relocate the campus, the *Tampa Herald* put Lake City's loss squarely on the shoulders of Julian and Persons and the legislative report.[8]

Gainesville mayor William Thomas was not the only one with political problems stemming from the Buckman Act. Governor Broward was also in a dilemma. He had just as many friends in Lake City as in Gainesville—both went to Broward in the 1904 election—and they were going to be equally upset if the joint board's decision did not go their way. Broward was open to suggestions, and he received one from former university trustee George Wilson. Wilson argued that the Buckman Act's most glaring defect was its failure to provide for a preparatory school that would serve as a feeder to both colleges. He argued that a coeducational preparatory school was permissible as long as it did not use the name of one of the abolished schools. He suggested Gainesville as the logical site. The day after receiving Wilson's letter, Broward requested a meeting with Jere Pound, presumably to talk about this possibility.[9]

Henry Buckman was receiving letters, too, including one from Mayor Thomas, and he had also heard about the idea of creating a prep school in Gainesville. In an eleven-page letter to Broward, Buckman explained what he believed the act that bore his name was all about. Buckman began by congratulating Broward for his appointments to the Board of Control, and he stressed that his letter was written at his own initiative. "I trust that you will not deem me an officious intermeddler," he said, "if I take the liberty of placing before you some views . . . which the joint Board should take in the establishment and opening of the institutions and particularly that of the University."[10]

Throughout the letter, Buckman stressed his concern that the university "not be a university in name only" and that only those who had passed an examination and taken the necessary preparatory courses be admitted. He realized that this would severely restrict enrollment, but he hoped that Florida's beneficial climate would draw in out-of-state students who "would in time virtually support it." As to Florida students, though, there was no immediate hope: "When we consider that hardly 15% take a university course, that out of forty-six counties, 22 counties have no high school and that the high schools must be the feeders of the institutions, it will not be expected or desired that many students from our own State, for some years to come, will enter this institution." He went on to add that Florida residents should pay tuition as well. "Indiscriminate education" was as harmful as "indiscriminate charity," he argued.

As to the dilemma of Lake City versus Gainesville, Buckman thought it an "unnecessary controversy." He emphasized the importance of maintaining the experiment station without hiatus. If Lake City lost the university, then the station would have to stay in Lake City, at least temporarily. Buckman then switched to the subject of placating Gainesville with a preparatory school. Buckman vehemently opposed the idea for several reasons. First, he could not see why Gainesville would have a greater claim than the towns in South and West Florida that had lost schools. More importantly, the joint board had only to consider the ultimate good of the people and institutions in its decision, and he counseled them to ignore political and sentimental considerations. He further emphasized, "The Act does not authorize the creation of any preparatory departments for the institutions, in fact the whole purpose and intent of the Act was to cut off these preparatory departments and require the counties to levy their own taxes, establish and perfect high schools in each county, and that *the high schools* should be the feeders and preparatory departments for the University and the Female College."

Buckman next turned to the other major decision they would have to make, the election of the college presidents. He noted the acrimony between the University of Florida and Florida State and wanted to put it in the past. To that end, he felt the incumbent presidents, as well as some of their faculty, should be disqualified from serving. Instead, he advised the boards to look outside the state for suitable candidates, particularly for the university: "It should not be a question of dollars and cents as to his salary but the best man in the United States should be sought for and obtained if possible." In closing, he advised the joint board to steel themselves: "Criticism must be expected, possibly from some acrimonious minds, vilification."[11]

Buckman's ambition for a first-class university that would attract tuition-paying students to Florida's superior climate now seems hopelessly naïve. Yet Buckman was not the first person to promote educational tourism in Florida, nor would he be the last. It was prominently on display in the brochures and catalogues of the private colleges in Central and South Florida. Stetson, in particular, painted a paradisiacal picture of what awaited prospective pupils: "The climate of Florida is glorious. It is a land of blue skies, balmy air and sunshine in January, when the frost king holds sway in the

North. . . . The climate is almost a specific for throat and lung troubles, catarrh, rheumatism, nervousness and insomnia. Students who are unable to attend school in the North during the winter find it possible to pursue their studies here regularly and constantly improve in health." The promotion was apparently successful as thirty-eight of its seventy-seven college students came from outside Florida in 1905.[12] Still, it is difficult to defend Buckman's position in light of the tremendous difficulties that Murphree and Sledd faced. The University of Florida, especially, would be hard-pressed to find students, even when admission was free. Buckman was correct on one point, though. The act's primary purpose was to remove preparatory work from the state schools, and there could be no retreat from that central objective. The success of the public colleges depended on the success of the public high schools. This was the core of the Buckman revolution and its one undisputed success. In short, Buckman offered Broward no hope for creating a branch school in either Gainesville or Lake City.

Another elected official receiving a lot of mail from Gainesville in June 1905 was William Holloway, who only recently had left there to become state superintendent. His friends beseeched him to come to his hometown's aid, and to each he replied confidently that Gainesville would be chosen as the site for the university. Holloway had been busy canvassing his fellow members on the Board of Education, and Attorney General William Ellis and Secretary of State Henry Clay Crawford were already in the Gainesville camp. He also felt that Treasurer William Knott could be persuaded to vote for Gainesville. In Holloway's opinion, the advantage lay with Gainesville, not Lake City.[13]

One of the men chosen by Broward for the Board of Control was Thomas "Buck" King, an alumnus of the East Florida Seminary. He was an odd choice if, in fact, Broward intended the university to remain in Lake City, as King retained an affection for his alma mater. King was also getting a lot of telegrams in support of Gainesville, all from people in Bartow, fifty miles north of his home in Arcadia. To King, the telegrams appeared to be coming from different people, but, in fact, the telegrams came from one individual, A. J. Angle, who presumably had the approval of the people who had "signed" the messages. Angle had been recruited by Gainesville business and civic leader Barney Colson, a schoolmate of Angle when both attended the South Florida Military Institute. In all, Angle sent $5.58 worth of telegrams in support of Gainesville, which he billed to Colson.[14] The telegrams were part of a public relations campaign waged by Gainesville that included letters of support from East Florida Seminary alumni spread across the state. The letters often repeated verbatim the contents of a mailer distributed to Seminary alumni and others. The mailers were also sent to Florida newspapers, and Gainesville picked up several endorsements. One of those endorsements came from the *Tampa Tribune*, which had previously stated it would be "folly" to relocate the university to Gainesville.[15] The letters and press statements all stressed the same points about Gainesville's wholesome physical and cultural environments, and all mentioned the positive and friendly relationship between the East Florida Seminary and the town. There was no need to make negative remarks about Lake City; most readers would have understood the implications.

Lake City, on the other hand, seems not to have been as energetic as its rival. There are no comparable letters of support from Lake City in Governor Broward's files. It did pick up a few endorsements from the press including George Wilson's *Florida Times-Union*. However, the attack from Frank Harris and the *Ocala Banner* was a major blow to its position. As part of Lake City's campaign, each of the ten members of the joint board received a glossy pamphlet that hammered home the town's strengths. The pamphlet used visuals to reinforce what Gainesville could not, that there already was a campus in Lake City. The pamphlet also made it clear that, as far as Lake City was concerned, the Buckman Act did not abolish the University of Florida and that it was incumbent upon the boards to justify an unprecedented act if it decided to move the campus.[16]

Lake City reminded the boards of the investments made by the state in terms of physical plant, beautification, and agricultural improvements. Lake City also boasted of its healthy climate, noting that only one student had died at the university in its twenty-year history, "a Cuban of delicate health, who died of pneumonia contracted through exposure." Lake City also pointed out, several times, that it had never experienced an outbreak of malaria or yellow fever, a claim that Gainesville could not make. The health concerns raised by Lake City were very real, although perhaps not appreciated at the time. After the university relocated to Gainesville, malaria would be a persistent health problem there through the 1920s. According to entomology graduate student U. Carr Loftin, 10 percent of the student population at the University of Florida reported to the infirmary in 1912 for malaria treatment, whereas less than 1 percent of the workforce at the Panama Canal Zone did so. Loftin went on to state that eradication of the mosquito breeding areas would have been relatively simple: "If Panama with her tropical rains and with excavations made by buildings, can be

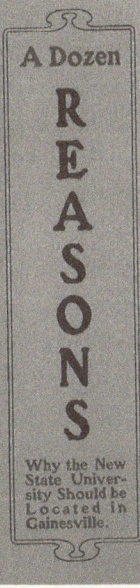

Figure 10. Mailer distributed by the City of Gainesville as part of its successful public relations campaign to relocate the University of Florida there after the passage of the Buckman Act of 1905. State Library and Archives of Florida.

Because It is an ideal location for a University, being near the geographical center of the state and near the center of population, easily accessible from all sections.

Because For fifty years it has been distinctively a college town.

Because Its citizenship is thoroughly imbued with a healthy and enthusiastic educational sentiment.

Because The new University would start off with the accumulated power and prestige of the East Florida Seminary's fifty years of uninterrupted success.

Because The wealth of tradition and sentiment which has grown up about the Seminary would be a rich inheritance to the new University.

Because There would be at once transferred to the new University all the strong affection and powerful influence of the large body of the Seminary Alumni, which is now larger than that of all the other state schools combined.

Because Of the high value placed by her citizens upon educational advantages, as shown by her splendid public and private schools and by the hearty support given the East Florida Seminary during its long and useful career.

Because Of the religious training and large number of scientific lectures given during the National Winter Bible Conference and the Florida Chautauqua held there annually.

Because Of the religious character of the citizens of the community, as evidenced by the large congregations and beautiful church edifices.

Because After thorough investigation as to its healthfulness and desirability, it was selected over all competitors by the Odd Fellows as the location for their National Sanitarium.

Because Of the purity and abundant supply of water. This is shown by analysis to be almost identical with the famous Poland Springs water of Maine.

Because The moral atmosphere of the city, as shown by the purity of home life; the high moral character of its citizens; the strict enforcement of the prohibition laws—the fact that no whiskey is sold, would be of the greatest benefit to the student body.

freed from mosquitoes and malaria, why can't the University of Florida?" He further noted, "Complaints have frequently been made to me by students that the mosquitoes were so thick in the dormitory that they could neither study nor sleep in peace." It was not until 1934 that the university physician could categorically state that no student living in a dormitory had contracted malaria from a campus mosquito, although he also noted that adjacent city property continued to breed mosquitoes that were "carried by wind to the campus."[17]

In an otherwise positive and forward-thinking document, the Lake City pamphlet made one irrelevant taunt at the East Florida Seminary: "We do not wish in this communication to enter into any invidious comparisons or to reflect in the slightest degree upon the faculty, courses or career of any of our sister institutions, but the demands of truth and fairness make it necessary for us to respectfully invite your attention to these elements in the University of Florida in comparing similar elements in our sister institutions in this state." The statement suggests that the university was competing with the seminary, whereas the actual battle was between the two towns. The unnecessary remarks could also have been viewed disapprovingly by the one seminary alumnus on the board, Buck King, whose vote would prove crucial.

Once Jacksonville was no longer an option, President Sledd gave his support to Lake City. It was decidedly lukewarm support; he later confided that the decision to move may have been for the best. The faculty seemed equally indifferent. Farr had no particular preference and noted that both towns had advantages and disadvantages. In a letter to Sledd, E. R. Dickenson, head of the commercial department, wrote of Sledd's "rather chrysalis state" in the public eye in the wake of the legislative report. He urged a change of venue: "In my own private opinion, I believe it would better for us to locate the University in Gainesville. With all of the warring factions out of the way, you could face the future without fear, as you may recall the past without shame."[18]

The members of the joint board began their tours of the prospective sites on June 28, starting in Tallahassee and then traveling to St. Augustine to examine the facilities of the Institute for the Deaf, Dumb, and Blind before arriving in Gainesville on June 30. In Gainesville, the group was entertained at the East Florida Seminary, where Buck King is said to have asked to see his old desk. The group inspected Lake City on July 2 and 3 and returned to Tallahassee on July 4.[19] The two boards convened in Tallahassee on July 5 and established the rules for how the proceedings would be conducted. The

Buckman Act stipulated that the decision regarding the location of the state university had to be made before that of the women's college. Only Lake City and Gainesville had indicated a desire to make formal proposals, but the boards allowed time for other towns to make statements. Gainesville would make the first proposal and would have ninety minutes to make its case. Lake City would follow with two hours, and then Gainesville would have the final word. The hearings were held the next day in the Hall of the House of Representatives.

In its proposal, Gainesville offered $40,000 and 517 acres west of the town, or, optionally, 320 acres west of the town and 15 acres in town. In addition, fourteen local citizens submitted a bid of $30,000 for the properties of the East Florida Seminary. Gainesville would also provide the university with free water. Lake City countered with an equal offer of $40,000, an 11-acre addition to the existing campus, and 800 acres northeast of the town valued at $20,000 that could be sold or used. The bids were remarkably similar in terms of cash and sellable lands: $70,000 from Gainesville and $60,000 from Lake City. However, if Gainesville were selected, the state would also have to reimburse Lake City the $15,000 the city paid to acquire the college in 1883. Still, Lake City appeared to have the proverbial ace in the hole with a physical plant valued at $200,000, roughly equal to the costs of the first four buildings later constructed at Gainesville.

According to Holloway, Attorney General William Ellis and Secretary of State Henry Crawford had already chosen Gainesville before the boards made their inspections. On the Board of Control, Bryan and Adams were firmly in the Lake City camp. Governor Broward would have preferred to abstain but seemed likely to vote for Lake City. This left Knott on the Board of Education and King, Yonge, and Brown on the Board of Control as persuadable votes. Before closing the hearings, the boards heard an argument from several citizens of Tallahassee for having the university situated there. No offers of cash or land were made, though. After dinner, the boards met in closed-door session at the governor's office. The proposals were discussed at length before a vote was taken. The votes were made anonymously on slips of paper, and only the count, 6–4 in favor of Gainesville, was recorded. Tallahassee was then quickly selected as the site for the women's college.[20]

There was considerable speculation then and for many years afterward as to how the individual members voted. However, what appears to be a correct rendering of the votes was leaked to the press within days of the meeting. According to a newspaper account, all of the members of the

Board of Education, save Governor Broward, chose Gainesville, while the Board of Control was split with Bryan, Brown, and Adams voting for Lake City and Yonge and King voting for Gainesville.[21] Partial confirmation came in 1910, when Broward ran for the US Senate. Broward divulged that he had voted for Lake City and that the other three Lake City votes came from the Board of Control. However, it was not until Lucius Bristol questioned William Knott in the 1940s that the initial 1905 press leak was validated. By then, Knott and Attorney General William Ellis were the only surviving members of either board. Ellis had nothing much to say regarding his decision, but Knott gave as his reasons for choosing Gainesville the free water and Gainesville being more central. He also favored Gainesville's "unencumbered" single campus, implying that Lake City would eventually have to expand beyond its existing 300-acre site. He thought Yonge had picked Gainesville because he preferred a new and open campus site "where a studied plan could be followed in arrangement of buildings and campus."[22]

It was left to President Sledd to explain to the northern philanthropists who supported higher education in the South why the State of Florida had made the extraordinary decision to relocate its university. In a report to Rockefeller's General Education Board, Sledd wrote:

> The chief reason for the surrender of the old University and transfer, even at considerable loss, to Gainesville, seems to me to have been the generally prevailing opinion that it would be impossible to make a really great institution in the atmosphere of Lake City; that the town was not, and could not be a suitable place for the proper development and expansion of the institution, owing to certain local conditions which it would be needless to detail: and that to make Lake City the site of this new and larger University would be to invite failure at the onset. . . . This, I say, seems to have been the argument for removal; although other reasons doubtless contributed to the same result.[23]

Sledd's confessions in his autobiography, though, were less guarded and filled with disappointment. Sledd felt that neither town could ever foster the proper environment for a successful university. He also condemned the selection process: "We behold, marvelous to relate, the sale of the state university, and consequently of the educational history and destiny of the state so far as its public activities were concerned, for forty thousand dollars and parcel of land." He added: "If I use strong language . . . it is because I feel strongly. The state university ought to be the greatest thing in the state;

and it is nothing less than a tragedy when its control falls into the hands of the incompetent." The last sentence in Sledd's autobiography reads, "I believed prior to the passage of the Buckman Bill that the state University should be located in Jacksonville, and I believe it no less strongly since the new institution has been located in another small inland town."[24]

Within days after the vote, Nathan Bryan was searching for ways to ease Lake City's loss. Under the terms of the Buckman Act, the joint board had the option of moving the campus of the School for the Deaf, Dumb, and Blind to one of the towns vacated by the act. The offer was made to Lake City, and the town eloquently declined on July 24, stating that its students would be better served by keeping the school in St. Augustine. In fact, Lake City had not yet accepted the loss of the university. It quickly contested the constitutionality of the Buckman Act, and it was not until November that the Florida Supreme Court rejected Lake City's arguments.[25] There were suggestions to create a coeducational normal school in Lake City as a branch of the university, but that idea died in April 1906, when the joint board voted to maintain gender segregation for the normal schools. Nathan Bryan suggested an intriguing idea: he proposed the State Normal and Industrial School move to Lake City. In addition to placating Lake City, the Tallahassee campus could be sold to raise revenue. The proposal gained greater traction in January 1906, when the school's main building burned, destroying its library. However, section 11 of the Buckman Act gave the Board of Education, not the joint board, the power to change the location of the State Normal and Industrial School, and the idea was never given serious consideration.[26] Instead, the 200 acres purchased by the state before the Buckman Act to expand the campus were sold back to Lake City for $23,455. Lake City would eventually find a college for its campus. A schism at Stetson University over President Lincoln Hulley's efforts to lessen Baptist influence there led to the creation of a new Baptist college on the Lake City campus in 1907. Called Columbia College, the *Florida School Exponent* described it as "Baptistic from center to circumference." It operated until 1919. The campus became a veterans' hospital in the 1930s, and the last university building, Science Hall, was demolished in the 1970s.[27]

The vote on July 6 over the location of the University of Florida revealed tensions between the new Board of Control and the members of the Board of Education. Four members of the latter had voted for Gainesville. Lake City's support came from Broward and three members of the Board of Control. Those tensions would be laid bare the following day, when the college presidents were chosen.

The Buckman Act provided a strict protocol for selecting the campuses, but it did not stipulate who would select the presidents or how they would be selected. The power to appoint presidents as well as faculty was clearly assigned to the Board of Control in section 19 of the Buckman Act. However, this and all other powers were "at all times subject to the supervision and control of the State Board of Education." Prior to Buckman, the power to appoint presidents fell to each school's board of trustees, and those appointments were not subject to review by any higher body. This was true in other states as well. It would seem logical, then, for this power to be granted exclusively to the Board of Control. However, as his lengthy letter to Broward indicated, Buckman thought the presidents would be chosen by the joint board. As this would have been an unorthodox method of selection, it is odd that the act did not make this evident.

Rumors that both John Guilliams and Sheats were jockeying for his position had reached Sledd. Guilliams was an associate of Tom McBeath, a former principal of the Jasper Normal Institute, and a member of the faculty of the East Florida Seminary in 1905. By June 27, though, Sledd could report that the "most authoritative information obtainable" indicated he would probably be appointed president; however, he had also "been the object of numerous dirty and vicious attacks." Sledd attempted to get Broward's support, but the governor declined, stating that "it would be a great delicacy in urging any particular candidate."[28]

When the boards met in joint session on the morning of July 7, there was considerable discussion regarding the normal schools. Representative R. W. Storrs of DeFuniak Springs made a plea to keep the normal school there as a branch of the university. No action was taken on Storr's proposal. The joint board's only action was to create a normal department at the women's college as allowed in section 22 of the Buckman Act. The joint board adjourned, and the Board of Control then met separately to consider appointments to the four schools under its purview.[29] The minutes of the Board of Control for the morning of July 7 state that Sledd was selected as president of the university and Murphree as president of the women's college. Murphree, though, declined to accept his appointment and asked for a day to consider it.[30]

The board recessed for lunch and returned in the afternoon. More business was transacted, and then, according to the minutes, the board met with the Board of Education. The minutes of the joint board for that meeting record the following resolution and nothing else: "Be it resolved by the State Board of Education and the Board of Control in joint session that it is the sense of the said Boards in joint session, after a careful reading of the 'Buckman Law,' that the Board of Control has the power to appoint teachers and contract with the same without asking the confirmation of the said State Board of Education." The minutes record only one dissenting vote, from Attorney General Ellis. The Board of Control then resumed its meeting, and President Murphree returned to accept his appointment. Nathan Young was reaffirmed as president of the State Normal and Industrial School, as was William Hare at the Institute for the Deaf, Dumb, and Blind.[31]

Exactly what transpired during the course of that day is uncertain. In a letter to Guilliams the following day, Holloway would only state that "Dr. Sledd won the presidency over tremendous opposition and Prof. Murphree was appointed to the Presidency of the Female College without any opposition whatever."[32] Sledd made an oblique reference to the conflict four years later when the same struggle erupted again with the opposite result. James Marion Farr described a secret session by the Board of Education to annul the Board of Control's decision.[33] It is more likely that Broward sensed the Board of Education would reject Sledd's appointment and reconvened the joint board in the afternoon to settle the matter. It is also apparent that Murphree had been alerted to the Board of Education's machinations, hence his request for a day to consider his appointment. At the day's end, the Board of Education conceded the power of appointments to the Board of Control, but only for the time being.

All in all, the joint sessions of July 5–7 were not an auspicious start for Florida's new system of higher education governance. They were also a harbinger of things to come.

7

The Agony of Andrew Sledd

Like most revolutions, the one precipitated by the Buckman Act spawned chaos and uncertainty. It fell upon President Sledd and the Board of Control to deal with the myriad consequences. The immediate task confronting them was the tremendous and unprecedented burden of moving an entire university forty miles south while simultaneously planning a new campus in a virgin pine hammock. In the midst of all this, Sledd found himself locked in a battle with the state comptroller, A. C. Croom. Andrew Sledd was not the first school administrator to have problems with the man Sledd referred to as "The Czar." William Hare also found Croom worrisome and once asked President Taliaferro for advice on how to handle him. Taliaferro's reply was comical: "As to the form of requisition on the Comptroller for money, you have me, for, apparently, the form has to differ each time." He concluded his letter with, "I am sorry I cannot give you any more information, but if you know the Comptroller, you would not be surprised." John Kellum, as secretary to the Board of Control, and Joseph Guisinger, principal of the St. Petersburg Normal and Industrial School, also complained about Croom. But, whereas others were exasperated and even amused, at times, by Croom's obstinacy, Sledd took offense at the comptroller's failure to perform his duties.[1]

Sledd's problems with Croom began in May 1905, before the Buckman bill became law, and initially concerned unpaid salary vouchers. After Buckman, issues arose over relocation expenditures that had not been budgeted by the legislature as well as federal and state funds allocated to the old University of Florida, which, arguably, no longer existed. It soon became evident, however, that Croom's resistance extended to expenses clearly covered in the budget for the new University of Florida, including mess hall accounts and payrolls for nonsalaried workers. As employees and vendors clamored for payment, a righteously angry Sledd threatened Croom with civil action. It was an empty threat to which Croom replied, "I beg further to say that as 'President of the University' that you are at Liberty at any time to institute legal proceedings to see if you can compel me to pay any account I do not consider a just account against the State of Florida." Sledd sought a legal opinion and was surprised to learn that the Florida Supreme Court had determined in 1850 that the comptroller was the sole arbiter of what constituted a just account.[2] To quell a threatened work stoppage by as yet unpaid African American laborers, Sledd borrowed three hundred dollars on a personal note from a local bank and paid his workers.[3] Sledd's personal loans were only a stopgap measure as pressures mounted. In December, he contemplated resignation. In a heartrending letter, Sledd begged Bryan and the Board of Control to intervene: "It is now the first of December, our men have worked for more than two months and have not received a cent of compensation.... I am actually ashamed to look the men in the face realising the situation. Ashamed for myself who brought them here; ashamed for the Board and the State which permits and perpetuates such gross and inexcusable injustice."[4]

The Board of Control eventually found workarounds to keep the university afloat, but Croom continued to harass Sledd throughout his presidency. In the meantime, though, Sledd had to manage the move from Lake City to Gainesville. Most of the university's equipment was already at Gainesville in June 1906, when a Lake City judge placed a restraining order on further shipments. Nathan Bryan decided to challenge the resolve of the local authorities and asked for a volunteer who would be willing to risk arrest. William Cawthon, then serving as the university's librarian, stepped forward. No arrest came, but Cawthon was unable to find local teamsters to drive the last wagons, and drivers and teams were sent from Gainesville. The last wagons left Lake City on July 23. Cawthon led the wagon train with a shotgun on his lap as Lake City residents lined the street and grimly watched them depart.[5]

At the end of July, Sledd reported that the last of the equipment had arrived in Gainesville and had been unloaded. He requested three weeks leave and retired to his father-in-law's home in Atlanta before returning to Gainesville to prepare for the opening of the new campus. Registration began on September 24, 1906, and an opening ceremony was held the following day. The only buildings available for use were Buckman Hall and Thomas Hall, but the classrooms still lacked blackboards. The buildings were suitably named as both Buckman and Mayor Thomas had some responsibility for the university being in Gainesville. Buckman, though, would have been just as happy had the university remained in Lake City.

Figure 11. When the Gainesville campus opened for registration on September 24, 1906, only Thomas Hall (*foreground*) and Buckman Hall were available. Both were designed as dormitories, but Thomas was used as a multipurpose building until about 1915. University Archives Photograph Collection, George A. Smathers Libraries, University of Florida.

The two buildings were decked out in bunting of the school's colors, not clearly orange and blue. The reporter for the *Florida Times-Union* described them as purple and gold.[6] Although he is the only person to have misidentified the blue as another color, the second color was often disputed. There are references to both gold and orange in early publications, and a school song proclaimed, "we sing to the Blue and Gold, Florida, My Florida." Sledd was also uncertain about the color and referenced both gold and orange in his letters. A consensus on orange was finally reached around 1910.[7]

Nathan Bryan was the keynote speaker for the opening ceremony. He described the years before Buckman as a period in which "the State proceeded to wander and roam in the educational field for sixty years." Bryan then proclaimed the twentieth century as "the age of the specialist" and added: "The so-called learned professions can no longer monopolize the technical instruction of our colleges and universities, but provision must also be made for the expert in other callings, such as teaching, engineering, pharmacy and agriculture. The time is past when 'a soft hand in a kid glove' is the badge of a gentleman. It is no longer undignified to labor. We, as a people, are peculiarly dependent upon skilled labor in almost every calling of life." Bryan also stressed the democratic character of the state university: "This is a public institution for the benefit of the people. It makes no difference how poor you are or how rich you are, just so you are a gentleman and are willing to work. If a boy goes out of Florida to get an education now, it is because he wants to, and not because he has to or ought to do it."[8]

Classes began on September 26. Only 91 students were admitted in the fall semester. Ten additional students enrolled in the spring, which brought a total headcount of 101 for academic year 1906–7, down from 136 the previous year. Students were only required to have passed the eleventh grade to be admitted to either the university or the women's college. Still, 38 students at the university needed remedial work in the subfreshman class. Admission requirements had been set by the Board of Control to be the same as those for the University of Georgia. These were also the minimum requirements for accreditation by the Association of Colleges and Preparatory Schools of the Southern States. The Buckman Act called for a twelfth-grade education at the university and a tenth-grade education at the women's college. This conformed to Buckman's desire to create a university that would attract students from the North. However, it was an unrealistic and unobtainable goal in 1905.[9]

As both Buckman and Sledd envisioned, the higher entrance requirements and the abolition of the state-supported preparatory schools would eventually compel local school districts to elevate their senior high schools. Until then, enrollments would remain low. The following statistics compiled by Sledd from a survey he undertook of white male high school enrollment illustrate the challenges he faced. In Florida's public schools in 1908, there were 160 boys enrolled in the eleventh grade and 91 boys in the twelfth grade. That was the sum total of Florida students available as possible candidates for admission to the university. Three-quarters of the students enrolled in Florida's public schools dropped out before the completion of the sixth grade, and only one-third of 1 percent graduated from high school. And, though the student-age population in Florida had increased 48 percent between 1898 and 1908, the proportion of children enrolled had decreased by 12 percent. Under these circumstances, Sledd wrote, any sudden increases in enrollment would be the "object of suspicion and probable prima facie evidence of educational chicanery and fraud to any intelligent citizen acquainted with all the facts."[10]

Buckman knew this, too, and he accepted the inevitability of low in-state enrollments. As president of the university, Sledd did not have that luxury. It would take some time, but the Buckman Act eventually yielded its desired results. As early as 1914, the first year that the state superintendent reported statistics on grade enrollments in public high schools, there were 1,032 white students in the eleventh grade and 582 twelfth-graders.[11] If we assume similar enrollments of boys and girls (there were generally more girls than boys in the higher grades), then there was an approximate 150 percent increase in enrollment in the six years after Sledd's 1908 survey. Sledd, though, would not be there to take advantage of the increase.

More high schools were not enough; it was also essential for the colleges to work with the high schools to create specific curricula for college-bound students. In March 1906, the Florida Education Association organized the Committee on the Revision of the High School Curriculum with Sledd as its chair. The committee included Murphree and three high school principals. The group met in April and proposed a standard four-year course with math, science, English, and social sciences being taught in each grade. The final report of the committee was sent to the legislature, where Henry Buckman formulated a document entitled "An Act to Prescribe the Course of Study for Public High Schools in the State of Florida." But there is no record that such a bill was introduced, much less voted upon.[12]

Opposition to the Florida Education Association's efforts came from the Florida Teachers Association and the *Florida School Exponent*. In a speech before the Florida Education Association, McBeath condemned efforts to articulate curriculum between secondary and tertiary education or even secondary and primary schools. In words that echoed his opposition to compulsory education, McBeath argued that the three levels of education existed for themselves and that each school turned out "its own particular type of good citizen." In McBeath's scheme, the elementary school provided the rudimentary training needed by the laboring classes; the high school, which he referred to as the "people's college," educated the nation's middle class; and, finally, the college produced the very small class of intellectual laborers. Each level was terminal for its particular type of "good citizen," and the curriculum for each had to be tailored accordingly. He had harsh words for those who thought otherwise: "We hear a great deal said by a class of half-baked thinkers and pseudo pedagogic philosophers about 'articulating' the public school system 'from the kindergarten to the university'; and it seems that the framers of that legal and educational monstrosity the 'Buckman bill,' had something like that impossibility in mind."[13]

McBeath's rebuttal to the Florida Education Association also sought to redeem the antebellum academy. In his vision of the model public high school, McBeath laid out a curriculum that omitted any serious study of the sciences and modern languages because, as he saw it: "These studies belong to the colleges and to the private schools and academies that make it their business to prepare for colleges. The sooner we recognize the fact that these private preparatory schools and academies are an absolute necessity, even to the State colleges, and that the high schools cannot come in and take their places, the better it will be all around. We may just as well accept the fact . . . the public high school is and must of necessity always be a dismal failure as a college preparatory institution."[14]

Although strange to present-day readers, McBeath's views on public and private secondary education and its relationship to higher education were not uncommon in the South. Elsewhere, though, attitudes had shifted dramatically and rapidly in the late nineteenth century. As historian Paula Fass notes, children in the early years of the Republic were expected to enter the workforce well before their teens. Work, not school, gave children an understanding of their place in the world. Schooling beyond grammar grades simply extended childhood and, consequently, economic dependence on the family.[15] This sentiment, however, did not extend to America's privileged classes. In the South, the sons and daughters of the slaveholding gentry were expected to further their education at private academies. Quasi-collegiate military academies thrived in the South, and elite northern colleges drew a disproportionate number of their male students from the upper echelons of southern society.

As Fass further explains, the rise of schooling in the Gilded Age coincided with the revolt against child labor and the resurgence of a family life centered on the upbringing of children. Older values that encouraged independence found their way into new pedagogical theories that promoted education that was both democratic and practical. Schools became vehicles for fostering a child's independence, as rote memorization gave way to a curriculum that stressed problem solving and peer interaction. Children were also encouraged to participate in such extracurricular activities as student government, glee clubs, and athletics. The culmination of this movement was the modern high school, a uniquely American innovation.[16] By the advent of the twentieth century, the high school was a fixture in most of the nation, and the average child's education extended well beyond grammar school. In the South, though, antebellum sentiments persisted well into the twentieth century and retarded the development of public secondary education.

In a letter to Joseph Byrne Lockey, principal of Pensacola High School, Sledd remarked that teachers and principals were better suited to write educational policy for the state than Superintendent Holloway and the Board of Education. Lockey, in turn, suggested that the University of Florida inspect and oversee high school curriculum, but Sledd thought the time was "not yet ripe for the University to assume this natural and proper relation." Yet, he confided, he had submitted a grant proposal to the General Education Board to support a professor of secondary education who would also serve as high school inspector.[17]

The first southern university to appoint a high school inspector was the University of Georgia in 1903. Supported by a grant from the Peabody Education Fund, the Georgia inspector proved a tremendous success. The program was then taken on by the General Education Board, and other states in the region sought funds. Beginning with Virginia in 1905, the General Education Board awarded grants for high school inspectors in all the southern states, with Florida the last to be funded.[18] Under the terms of the grant, the position was to be a faculty appointment at the University of Florida. As such, Sledd would make the nomination to the Board of Control, and its decision, as always, would be subject to final review by the Board of Education.

On February 6, 1908, Sledd informed the General Education Board of his desire to nominate Lockey as the state's high school inspector. Several days later, Sledd was surprised and outraged to read a letter from board general secretary Wallace Buttrick that the board had, upon the recommendation of the Board of Education, already accepted William Sheats for the position.[19] In fact, the Board of Education's recommendation had never been sent to either Sledd or the Board of Control. Sledd did not receive an official notice from Holloway until February 13; it noted Buttrick's acceptance of Sheats. Sledd replied calmly to Holloway that he had yet to receive an application from Sheats and reminded him that the appointment would be made by the president and the Board of Control. Meanwhile, Buttrick telegraphed Holloway that his earlier acceptance of Sheats was "written under misapprehension" and that he was awaiting word from the Board of Control.[20]

Holloway's motivation to appoint his political rival was thought to have been an attempt to keep Sheats out of the 1908 election. Bryan advised Sledd to hire Sheats and warned him that refusing the Board of Education's recommendation could harm his position. Sledd acknowledged Sheats's qualifications for the position but was distressed by Bryan's motivations. "Bryan's attitude troubles me most," he wrote his father-in-law. "He agrees with me that it is purely a political move, said as much; and yet he says 'We want to make all the friends we can.'" He quoted Bryan again in a letter to

Board of Control member Philip K. Yonge, adding that "he never felt it wise to make friends at a sacrifice of principle or a jeopardizing of the cause."[21]

Sledd eventually withdrew Lockey's name from consideration, and Holloway retreated on his desire to appoint Sheats. Discussion between Sledd, Bryan, and Holloway revolved around the possible nomination of George Lynch, a former faculty member of the East Florida Seminary who had taken charge of the Jasper Normal Institute. Once again, Holloway preempted Sledd and the Board of Control and announced to Buttrick that all parties had agreed on Lynch's appointment. Holloway also informed Lynch of the appointment and that he would be working for him, not Sledd, in accordance with the Board of Control's recommendation on January 7, 1908.[22]

When word reached him that, once again, Holloway had bypassed the Board of Control, Sledd lost all semblance of decorum. In two letters to Bryan dated March 30, he described Holloway's actions as "unwarranted, officious and indecent meddling" and threatened to return the money to the General Education Board. He also noted that Holloway—or Mr. H, as he called him—and Lynch were political friends and insisted that Lynch would be "my man and not Holloway's." Sledd also wrote an ill-considered and, apparently, unrestrained letter to Holloway. Farr described Sledd's response to Holloway as "a masterpiece of vituperative denunciation" and urged Sledd not to mail the letter.[23] The letter itself did not survive, but Holloway later referenced Sledd's "contemptuous letter" and Sledd's public apology.[24] The high school inspector appointment proved to be a dress rehearsal for the final showdown with the Board of Education over presidential appointments. The incident had presented Sledd with an opportunity to compromise and build bridges to his political adversaries. But his unwillingness to consider even a competent political appointment underscored the contradiction between his idealism and the harsh political realities he faced and why, ultimately, he was defeated.

During the remainder of his time as president, Sledd had to contend with inadequate budgets as well as political attacks. Croom continued to be a problem, and his recalcitrance only made the dire financial conditions that existed that much worse.[25] Sledd's constant conflicts with state officials eroded his support within the broader university community. Regardless of how they may have about felt about him personally, and there is considerable evidence that he was respected and admired, it was becoming obvious to both town and gown that Sledd was an obstacle to progress. Writing decades later, professor of modern languages Charles Langley Crow commented that Sledd "was not beloved by the members of the Governor's Cabinet," and, consequently, "state warrants went unpaid." He went on to add, "it was also said, perhaps mistakenly, that the professors at the Florida Female College had not been subjected to the same inconveniences."[26]

The departure of Governor Broward eliminated Sledd's only support on the Board of Education. Albert Gilchrist was inaugurated governor on January 5, 1909. On January 30, the Board of Education met and passed a resolution calling for a joint meeting with the Board of Control to discuss the power to appoint college presidents and directing the Board of Control to tender no new contracts until the boards could meet. The board's resolution was backed by an opinion from Attorney General Park Trammel—himself a member of the same board—stating the joint resolution of July 7, 1905, was in error and that the Board of Education had ultimate authority in the appointment of all faculty. Bryan attended the meeting and informed Sledd that "Mr. Holloway is after you and has prejudiced some of the other members I am satisfied. I corrected some of his misstatements, and at one time he became quite angry." He went on to add, "If you have any present row with Holloway, please postpone it until after our March meeting." He also asked Sledd to rush his biennial report to counter arguments raised by Holloway that Sledd's policies were the principal cause of low enrollment at the university.[27]

Sledd's 1909 biennial report to the Board of Control was both a history of his administration and his apologia. The report began with a list of successes: tightened requirements for admission, properly credentialed faculty, the separation of agricultural research and teaching, and the addition of courses in civil and electrical engineering. Repeatedly, he stressed the need for the university not to compete with the high schools. Rather than defend the negative effects of his policies, he enthusiastically embraced the reduction in enrollment: "The results of this choice were in general foreseen but have been more gratifying than might have been anticipated." Noting that there were 225 men enrolled at the old university, as opposed to slightly over 100 in 1908, he remarked, "The policy then adopted ... and since consistently adhered to, threw most of this number back upon the local high schools."[28]

While the boards pondered their next steps, the *Pensacola Evening News* launched an attack on Sledd. The paper's president and manager was William Bloxham Crawford, son of Florida secretary of state and Board of Education member Henry Clay Crawford. In 1889 the Crawford had family moved to Tallahassee, where William Crawford attended the West Florida Seminary. Letters between Crawford and Murphree indicate the two were close. "We must land you this time and now is the time to get busy," Crawford wrote to Murphree. In response, Murphree denied any desire to replace Sledd at Gainesville. He expressed gratitude that the Board of Education supported his appointment, but as a sitting college president who reported to the Board of Control, he could not take any steps to secure the position.[29]

The first of the *Pensacola Evening News* articles appeared on March 6, the same day the joint board met to discuss "the welfare of the University of the State of Florida." The article was addressed specifically to the board members and was not so much an attack on Sledd as it was a paean to Murphree. Crawford even took Murphree's primary weakness, his lack of academic credentials, and made it an asset. Florida, he said, did not need a man with "a string of degrees backing his name" but someone with "executive ability and good common sense."[30] After a lengthy discussion, the Board of Control declined the Board of Education's request to elect presidents by joint ballot. Subsequently, fellow Pensacolan P. K. Yonge gave Crawford a copy of Sledd's report. Crawford asked Murphree for detailed information that would refute Sledd's arguments and pledged total confidentiality: "You know me too well to reiterate my pledge of secrecy as to source of information." Superintendent Holloway requested the same information from Murphree, but, in both instances, there is no evidence to indicate Murphree complied. Regardless, accurate information on enrollment was readily available in the published reports of the state colleges.[31]

A second *Pensacola Evening News* article, this time directly criticizing Sledd, was published on March 23, and there were additional attacks in the *Tallahassee Democrat* and the *Gainesville Sun*. The attacks focused on low enrollment and made unfavorable comparisons with the State College for Women. In a lengthy rebuttal printed in the *Gainesville Sun*, Bryan noted the misleading comparisons with Murphree's college and charged that college enrollment was, in fact, lower there. Female enrollment in noncollege programs at Florida State elevated the overall numbers and obscured the higher college enrollment at the university. Most significant were the large number of female teachers enrolled in subcollegiate normal courses and the small number of male normal school students enrolled at the university.[32] Bryan failed to mention that the disparity in normal school enrollment was the direct result of a decision made at a joint board meeting on

April 2, 1906. Once again, the vote was largely along board lines, with the Board of Education voting against the Board of Control's recommendation that a coeducational normal school be created at the university.

In response to Crawford and the anti-Sledd press, several newspapers came out in support of Sledd. Among them was the *Suwannee Democrat* of Live Oak, which printed a lengthy article by a former faculty member of the university. Another supporter, the *Tampa Tribune,* cynically opined that Sledd's "high character" and "gifts as an educator" were a detriment to success in Florida. Loyal to the last, Frank Harris of the *Ocala Banner* continued to back Sledd and attributed the attacks to "overzealous friends of Prof. Murphree." However, most newspapers stayed out of the fray. When a comparison of the pro- and anti-Sledd newspapers is made, it is difficult to sustain Crawford's assertion that the media campaign was instrumental in Sledd's removal. At best, it provided a cover for the Board of Education's actions.[33]

While Crawford waged his press campaign, Holloway mounted a campaign in Gainesville and enlisted his son Luther to go on his behalf. To Gainesville civic leader Barney Colson, the same man who financed the Bartow telegram campaign in 1905, Holloway wrote: "If the people of Gainesville and the State of Florida ever expect to see a University worthy of the name, it is incumbent upon them, especially the people of Gainesville, to give me all the support possible looking to a change in the head of the institution. . . . You will pardon me for the statement, but if it had not been for my influence and vote in locating the University, Gainesville would not have secured the University, and now when I am asking the people to assist me in protecting the interest of higher education in the State it is their bounden duty to come to my rescue."[34]

Under a threat from Holloway that no further construction would be undertaken at the university as long as Sledd remained, Mayor Thomas wrote a letter urging a change of leadership that was entered into the minutes of the Board of Education. Thomas later retracted the letter, and the retraction letter was also filed with the minutes. Thomas felt that Sledd had been done a "gross injustice" when Holloway used his letter without also divulging his own. It is also possible that Mayor Thomas remembered the potential consequences for towns that meddled in university affairs.[35]

By late March, both Sledd and the Board of Control were resigned to defeat. "It would, in fact, be a relief to me personally to get out but I cannot look without distress upon the probable overthrow of honesty by fraud, of educational policy by political schemes," Sledd confided. He also declined an offer of aid from Wallace Buttrick at the General Education Board. "They would," he argued, "add to the charge never silenced of 'nigger lover,' the further item of 'sold out to the Yankees and the money power.'" Meanwhile, Bryan tried to preempt the Murphree camp by offering the presidency to William Blackman, president of Rollins College. Blackman, though, would only accept a nomination if the Board of Control's jurisdiction over appointments and budgets was reaffirmed. The two boards appeared to be headed for a showdown at a joint meeting scheduled for April 10. Sledd, however, defused the situation by resigning on April 9.[36]

Even so, the meeting on April 10 offered high drama. The Board of Control held its regularly scheduled meeting in the morning, and Sledd's resignation letter was entered into the minutes. His parting comments gave no solace to his opponents; he publicly accused Holloway of orchestrating the attacks and once again defended his position on admissions. "I am only a school man," he said, "[and] I must conduct an educational enterprise along lines of sound educational policy as I understand it. I cannot do more; I will not do less." The board accepted his resignation with "profound regret," and a lengthy commendation of his tenure was entered into the minutes. The board elected Murphree as Sledd's replacement before it adjourned for the morning. Later in the day, the board selected Edward Conradi to succeed Murphree at the Women's College.[37]

The Board of Control met again in the afternoon with the Board of Education present and adopted a lengthy resolution on the Sledd affair. In it, the Board of Control disputed the Board of Education's claim of ultimate authority in matters of appointments and noted that this claim contradicted the joint resolution of July 7, 1905. The resolution further stated that only Sledd's willingness to step down prevented the Board of Control's own resignation and that the board had "submitted to the present situation against our personal inclination to refuse to submit to what appears to us to be a practical dictation by a majority of the Board of Education." Arguing it would be "unreasonable to expect that a man suited to be president of the University would accept employment by the Board of Control, subject to be discharged at any time by the Board of Education," the Board of Control asked the state legislature to give it "supreme" power to select all presidents and faculty.[38]

The resolution dropped an additional bomb when it accused Holloway of bullying the City of Gainesville with the threat of a construction halt at the university unless Sledd left. Both Bryan and Sledd had read Holloway's letter in Mayor Thomas's office. Thomas, however, refused to give them a copy. According to a report in the *Pensacola Journal,* Bryan challenged Holloway at the meeting to produce the letter.[39] The scene was somewhat reminiscent of the 1904 election and Sheats's demand that Holloway produce the Booker T. Washington letter. The Board of Control's resolution was submitted to the legislature, but nothing came of it. Miffed by Bryan's public attack on Holloway, even Henry Buckman refused to intervene. Governor Gilchrist delivered a rebuttal to the Board of Control on April 19. Although he struck a defiant note on the supervisory power of the Board of Education, he mollified his tone when he claimed that only extraordinary circumstances compelled the Board of Education's intervention.[40]

Hattie Carpenter provided what is perhaps the most reasonable explanation for Sledd's ordeal and departure. Carpenter came from Miami County, Ohio, and moved to Miami, Florida, in 1900. She taught school and was a principal there for more than a decade before deciding on a career as a journalist. Carpenter had taken the editorial reins at the *Florida School Exponent* in 1909, two years after McBeath's departure. Her appointment brought a pronounced shift in the *Exponent*'s position on secondary and higher education. "Much of the 'stuff' that you did read about Dr. Sledd was," she reasoned, "as crooked as venom or ignorance could make it. The three gentlemen who are mentioned in this paragraph [Sledd, Murphree, and Conradi] are gentlemen of the highest type. Dr. Sledd is honored by every one who knows him for his fine intellect, for his gentlemanly qualities, and for his fine ideals, which he will never live up to. His contempt for anything which he thinks crooked has given him a reputation, however, for a lack of tact." As to the pretense for which he was dismissed, she blamed low enrollments on the poverty of Florida's high schools and those who headed them. In an obvious dig at McBeath and his supporters, Carpenter added, "If there is any reason for the higher educational institutions of Florida being without the number of students they should have, it is because of the lackadaisical aid of the high school principals, and the gentle 'knocking' of these same mediators."[41]

Sledd's final weeks as university president bear testimony to his character. Sledd rose above the circumstances of his departure and worked closely with Murphree to implement a smooth transition. For his part, Murphree was also conciliatory. His first act upon accepting the presidency was to reappoint Sledd's faculty, allaying the fears of the Board of Control of a mass departure. Publicly, and somewhat hypocritically, he also defended Sledd's position on enrollment. To the *Savannah Morning News* he wrote, "I shall not cater to the people's whim for numbers, but shall maintain the same high standards of scholarship upheld by Dr. Sledd and his able faculty."[42]

The spring of 1909 commencement was Sledd's final public act as university president. Sledd made a brief address to the students, parents, and faculty. Before he could conclude the ceremony, Vice President Farr rose, paid tribute to Sledd, and bestowed upon him the honorary degree of doctor of divinity. The recommendation for the degree, the first honorary degree awarded by the university, came from Bryan and was conferred by the faculty the night before. The faculty had expressed some discomfort with this decision, but they later awarded Sledd with something more useful and appropriate. Upon his departure, the faculty gave him a walking cane "to accompany him thru a long and honorable career in his chosen field of battle—the fight of Truth and Enlightenment against Prejudice and Ignorance."[43]

8

The Fallout from Florida's Sledd Affair

What little standing the budding University of Florida may have had in the academic community received a major blow when the Sledd affair made its way into the influential annual report of the Carnegie Foundation for the Advancement of Teaching. Established in 1905, the Carnegie Foundation would influence and shape American educational policy in the twentieth century while also funneling resources into private and public colleges. The Carnegie Foundation differed from other philanthropic foundations, though, as it encouraged colleges and universities to participate as members. To entice institutions to join the Foundation, Andrew Carnegie established a much-needed pension fund, which became the Teachers Insurance and Annuity Association of America (TIAA) in 1918. The pension was created to support retired faculty but also to encourage older faculty to retire and thus open spaces for younger faculty. Today, TIAA manages over $1 trillion in assets for more than five million active and retired employee accounts at more than fifteen thousand institutions.

Institutions participating in the Foundation agreed to standardize admissions requirements and, in the case of denominational colleges, to shed themselves of any theological influence in their coursework. The Foundation's most enduring contribution to educational standards was in the improvement of articulation between high schools and colleges through the adoption of what became known as the Carnegie unit. Members of the Carnegie Foundation adhered to a minimum standard of fourteen specific units of high school instruction (one semester of coursework equaled ½ unit), with a minimum of 120 contact hours between students and instructor per year in each class as a requirement for freshman admission. It eventually became the standard for high school graduation and college admission throughout the nation.[1]

Carnegie Foundation membership was initially restricted to private colleges and universities. Beginning in 1908, state schools could also apply, and Andrew Carnegie contributed $5 million to the pension fund to accommodate the added retirees. The addition of state universities presented problems and issues for the Foundation that Foundation president Henry S. Pritchett outlined in his 1908 and 1909 annual reports. The 1908 report focused on disparities among the state universities regarding admissions, particularly in the southern states, where the standards were much lower and the sentiments of educators like Tom McBeath all too common. To prepare his 1908 report, Pritchett polled administrators at southern colleges on two questions. First, he asked how long it would take a particular state to adopt the Carnegie standard. Responses ranged from three to eight years. Second, he inquired as to whether the Foundation should temporarily relax its standards to accommodate the southern colleges in the interim. Most respondents argued for relaxation with the assurance that they would soon catch up with the rest of the nation. Sledd, though, wrote an impassioned plea in the negative, and Pritchett quoted extensively from Sledd's response. In the end, the Foundation accepted the southern universities with the understanding that they would raise their standards when they could.[2]

Pritchett's 1909 report looked at other issues that were unique to state universities and included a seven-page section entitled "Politics in State Institutions." Pritchett argued state institutions were more vulnerable to political intrusion: "They are creatures of the state and under the state government." He went on to say: "The state university which educates its legislature to the conception that good educational organization and partisan politics are incompatible has done a notable service to the people of its state. Our stronger state universities have reached this point, and they form to-day the most encouraging exhibits of our program of democratic government." He noted, though, that recent events in several states made him question the independence of public higher education. He cited the situation in Florida as the prime example.

Pritchett was scathing in his assessment of Superintendent Holloway and the Board of Education. He praised Sledd for his determination to improve and defend standards at the university and outlined the difficulties faced by Murphree in accepting a position after the forced resignation of the previous president:

That President Sledd chose to develop a true college with moderate numbers instead of a large college with low standards is immensely to his credit and to the advantage of the state.... It is in fact difficult to understand the attitude of the superintendent of education in this matter, except upon the ground of the universal cry for numbers. It is difficult also to avoid the conclusion that the superintendent of education desired a much more direct interference in the university than is consistent with good administration, and that he had acquired a bias of personal and political hostility. This opinion seemed to be shared by the best men in the state whose opinions I was able to obtain.... The situation is not an easy one for President Murphree. The man who accepts a place from which a scholarly and efficient predecessor has been forced out is on the defensive, at least with scholars who accept the standards which have just been discredited.[3]

President Murphree was undoubtedly displeased with the report as it more than implied that he owed his position to political influence. It also cast doubt on the university's independence and made it even more difficult than it already was to recruit qualified faculty. In a letter to University of Wisconsin president Charles Van Hise, Murphree argued the report did not give a balanced account of what had transpired. Still, he conceded that the relationship between the boards was not conducive to educational progress: "But I do not hesitate to say that in my judgment the supervisory power provided for in our Constitution and granted by our charter to the State Board of Education is an unwise provision. Unless remedied it may in the end give trouble. But the trouble in 1909 was not as serious as the Carnegie Foundation Report imports." He went on to predict that the legislature would eventually grant greater autonomy to the Board of Control.[4]

Murphree enjoyed a brief period of political calm in his first two years as university president that undoubtedly gave him a distorted sense of reality. He had the support of Governor Gilchrist, the Board of Education, the legislature, the Board of Control, and Superintendent Holloway. With Sledd gone, the state comptroller paid the university's bills in a timely fashion. (Croom died in 1912, and presumably all state vouchers were thereafter expedited quickly.) Likewise, the construction logjam broke as the legislature provided funds for several classroom buildings, a gymnasium, and a dining hall. There was also peace between the Board of Control and the Board of Education. Nathan Bryan burned his bridges with the tumultuous April 10, 1909, meeting, and Gilchrist did not reappoint him in May. The less combative P. K. Yonge succeeded Bryan as board chair. The resulting torpor probably convinced Murphree that conflicts had become a thing of the past.

If a common governing board for a state's public universities was the desired goal of progressive educators, it was certainly not evident at the National Association of State Universities. Organized in 1897, the association met annually to discuss the hot issues relevant to public universities. Governance was a key concern, and the association was officially on record in support of independent boards for every school. In response to Murphree's complaints, Van Hise, who was serving as president of the National Association of State Universities, invited Murphree to make a counterargument at the association's 1912 meeting. In his paper, delivered at the evening session of the conference's first day, Murphree framed a strong argument for centralized state boards as a means of reducing political friction. The paper was a springboard for a general discussion that lasted until 10:15. Of the university presidents in attendance that night, eight spoke directly to the issue, and none favored common boards. Several presidents, including Harry Burns Hutchins of the University of Michigan, argued that the very creation of a common board constituted a political attack on higher education. Frank McVey at the University of North Dakota argued that strong charters and clear legislative mandates were more important than the particular system of governance. Sidney Mezes of the University of Texas, which had its own board, acknowledged the possibility that a common board could be preferable under certain circumstances.[5] Van Hise's report on the panel session also rejected central governance but acknowledged its inevitability when state institutions failed to cooperate. Van Hise specifically mentioned Iowa, where a conflict between the state's university, land grant college, and normal school resulted in the creation of a governing board for all three. Van Hise's personal preference was for consolidation of the schools under one institution whenever feasible and independent boards for each school if consolidation was not an option. Variations of Wisconsin's consolidation approach were adopted in other states to create flagship systems with clear legislative mandates. Educational programs were centralized in one institution, and later, when more universities were required, branch campuses were established under the mantel and authority of the founding university.[6]

Murphree's paper did acknowledge several failures in Florida's system of higher education. For one, Murphree thought the state university should break out of its traditional ivory tower and play a larger social role through programs intended to improve the lot of its citizens. He referred specifically to Charles Van Hise's Wisconsin Idea as a model. By invoking the

Wisconsin Idea, Murphree was placing himself in the ranks of the nation's most progressive educators. However, the Wisconsin Idea's success was also attributable to Van Hise's popularity and his ability to openly engage with Wisconsin's political leadership. Although not overtly political, the Wisconsin Idea created bridges between the academic and political worlds that benefited both. In Florida and elsewhere, however, politicians still viewed the state university as one of many institutional dependents that were better seen, rarely heard, but, nonetheless, needed occasional feeding. In regard to funding, Murphree also argued that political tensions were lessened in states that relied on specific tax revenues rather than legislative appropriations. Again, Murphree was criticizing his home state as the battle over the biennial appropriation exhausted the energies of both the Board of Control and the college presidents.[7]

While touting the merits of the Florida Board of Control, Murphree did observe one major flaw in its design. He argued that the major weakness of the Buckman Act was the term of office, four years, for each board member. He felt it should have been much longer. However, the term length was consistent with Florida's other appointive boards and was seemingly designed to constrain the governor's administrative power and protect the boards from executive abuse. Each governor had to contend with administrative boards appointed by his predecessor in the first legislative session of his term. In the case of the Board of Control, the terms of three board members expired shortly after the session ended, and the governor could then appoint his own people. The terms of the other two members ended shortly after the second legislative session ended. A governor could purge the entire board during his tenure, but the term lengths and, more importantly, the times when terms ended prevented him from doing so before the crucial biennial legislative sessions. This setup was true of all boards and commissions in Florida's "little cabinet." The legislature abolished the holdover system in 1945 but made one exception. The one exception was the Board of Control, which retained its original charter.[8]

Whatever the intentions may have been, the Buckman Act failed to provide the Board of Control with the protection from executive abuse that it needed. It is also possible that the authors of the act assumed governors would demonstrate restraint by reappointing sitting board members. Because of the monopoly enjoyed by the Democratic Party, the southern states largely avoided the wholesale purges of gubernatorial appointees that occurred when an opposition party gained power. The first two governors after Broward—Albert Gilchrist and Park Trammel—made only three appointments to the Board of Control and, with the obvious exception of Nathan Bryan's departure, the appointments seem not to have been politically motivated. However, the subsequent three governors—Sidney Catts, Carey Hardee, and John Martin—showed little restraint. Catts would replace four of the board members with his own men. Hardee, in turn, sacked those four, and Martin removed two of Hardee's men. It is interesting to note, though, that one board member, Edgar Lawrence Wartmann of Citra, survived six administrations and provided a small degree of continuity to the board. Wartmann had served on the legislative committee that produced the final draft of the Buckman Act, and his familiarity with the act's complexities would prove helpful. With the exception of the Catts administration, Yonge also stayed on the board through successive administrations and served as the board's chair for more than twenty years. However, unlike Nathan Bryan, Yonge never gave cause for his dismissal. Both Yonge and Wartmann seemed content to complain privately about their lack of power rather than repeat the bloodletting of 1909.

The events that transpired after April 10, 1909, would lay bare the sad reality that the Florida Board of Control had far less power to govern the institutions under its umbrella than the independent boards that managed the pre-Buckman Florida State College, the East Florida Seminary, and the old University of Florida. The boards for those institutions had the power to select and remove presidents and faculty, to prepare and submit budgets to the legislature, and to shape their schools' curricula. The state schools frequently changed their admission requirements without consulting the state superintendent and local school boards. Their 1851 charter even allowed the seminaries to rename themselves, and a subsequent 1859 act empowered the seminaries to award college diplomas. The West Florida Seminary would exercise both powers. There were also discretionary powers unspecified in their charters. As evidenced at the Florida Agricultural College in 1894 and 1903, a state school could go so far as to embrace and then later terminate coeducation without seeking the approval of a legislative or executive agency. Furthermore, there is no record of any legislative or executive body interfering in their internal affairs in the years leading up to the Buckman Act. Conversely, in the twenty-two years after Buckman, the Board of Education would challenge virtually every power ostensibly held by the Board of Control. The January 1905 Florida Supreme Court ruling that the Board of Control would be a civil board further undermined its power. It is known that Governor Broward had wanted to appoint Senators Frank Adams and W. A. Blount to the Board of Control, and there had been speculation that he preferred Henry Buckman over Nathan Bryan.[9] Had the court ruled differently, it would have placed three active legislators on the Board of Control and created an entirely different dynamic between the two boards.

Peace between the boards began to dissipate almost immediately after the spring primary election of 1912. For Murphree, the election pitted two equally unappealing candidates for the position of state superintendent, William Sheats and William Holloway. Murphree had hoped that Fons Hathaway would enter the contest. Hathaway was superintendent of public instruction for Duval County and a graduate of the Florida State College, Class of 1903. When Hathaway declined, Murphree reluctantly supported Sledd's archenemy Holloway. "With reference to myself," Murphree once said, "it is not that Holloway likes me more but Sledd less."[10] Sheats handily defeated Holloway in the 1912 grudge match, and Holloway wasted no time to cast about for another position. In a scene more than reminiscent of 1908, Holloway secured the support of what was essentially a lame duck Board of Education (three of its five members were leaving) to nominate him as the state's high school inspector. The board sent its endorsement directly to Wallace Buttrick at the General Education Board, once again bypassing the Board of Control and the president of the University of Florida, and this time it was Sheats writing angry letters protesting Holloway's action. Murphree was appalled by the entire episode. Among the words used by Murphree to describe the affair were "embarrassing," "disgusting," "nauseating," and "disgrace." He further admitted, "I can now appreciate more fully than ever Sledd's position of a few years ago."[11]

Holloway, though, failed to get his appointment. The Board of Control never responded to Holloway's self-nomination but instead waited for Sheats to take office in January 1913. Of course, Sheats had no desire to appoint his nemesis to any position. Nor did he wish to waste an opportunity to make his own political appointment. A dispute erupted at the 1913 meeting of county superintendents and high school principals when Sheats attempted to "bulldoze" a resolution in favor of having the high school inspector placed under him. When that failed, Sheats decided not to reappoint George Lynch and instead made him supervisor of rural schools. Sheats then pressured Murphree and the Board of Control to replace Lynch with Shelton Phillips, a political supporter.[12]

Sheats also sought the support of the private colleges, which viewed the high school inspector as essentially a taxpayer-funded recruitment officer for the public colleges. President Blackman at Rollins raised this argument with Murphree, who ensured Blackman that Lynch had received "positive instructions... not to canvass students for any college." He went on to add: "The Inspector, as an officer and member of the faculty of the State University, is removed farther from political influences than if he were the shuttlecock of every change in the State Superintendent's office, as he would be under your plan.... A politician will use 'the job' to reward those who helped him get into office. We are facing such a probability at the present time."[13]

The matter was temporarily resolved when the dean of the Teachers College at the University of Florida, Jonathan Thackston, agreed to take on the additional duties of high school inspector. Thackston, though, resigned three years later to serve as dean of the College of Education at the University of Tennessee "at a great increase in pay," according to Murphree, who added, "the disagreeable political situation was also a factor." Once again, Murphree fretted that Sheats would try to install one of his "political henchmen" and suggested George Lynch return to the position. When Sheats rejected that idea, Murphree asked for Sheats's recommendation, and Sheats, who was vacationing in Nova Scotia, replied, "Why the hot haste?" Eventually, Sheats sent a list of ten acceptable candidates, and Murphree chose from that list the erstwhile gun-toting librarian William Cawthon, who, coincidentally, had succeeded Joseph Byrne Lockey as principal of Pensacola High School. This ended what Murphree referred to as the "wishy-washy proceedings."[14]

Patronage was integral to the position of state superintendent, or at least it was to Sheats and Holloway, the only elected superintendents Florida had known. Both relied on their own networks of supporters to attain and retain office. Each could count on specific county superintendents, school principals, and even individual teachers for support. Political disputes erupted annually at the state conventions of the two white teacher organizations, the Florida Education Association and the Florida State Teachers Association. As the *Exponent* described it, there was always an "annual 'scrap' without which there would be no fun at the meetings of the FSTA."[15] The annual meeting of county superintendents and high school principals was another venue for political intrigue. Patronage came with the superintendent's power to appoint instructors at the summer schools. The summer schools were held on the campuses of the state colleges, but the superintendent chose the course content and the faculties. The superintendent also selected the deans of the summer schools, but the deans reported to the presidents. This was less than ideal. The 1910 summer school at the State College for Women was so contentious it erupted into open conflict after the dean made "savage" attacks on President Conradi.[16]

Tensions between Superintendent Sheats and the college presidents came to a head after the legislature passed two laws in 1913 that diminished the superintendent's powers in regard to teacher certification and training. The first law overturned the clause in Sheats's 1893 law requiring examination for teacher certification by granting certification upon graduation from the University of Florida and Florida State. The law also raised the possibility of doing the same for the private schools if they submitted to a review and inspection by the joint board. The law further specified that 15 percent of the students' coursework had to be devoted to pedagogical training and left it to the joint board to determine exactly what that meant. The criteria for certifying schools and curricula were resolved in a series of contentious joint board meetings held in April and May 1914. Eventually, the joint board agreed to criteria suggested by Sheats. Even so, certification of individual teachers from approved schools was not automatic and still contingent upon the state superintendent's signature. This involved a review of courses taken by the student and a determination that the student had met the requirements. Murphree and Florida State president Conradi complained that Sheats approved certificates from the private colleges at a higher and faster rate than those from the public colleges.[17] Problems with certificates continued into the 1920s, with Murphree cautioning one unhappy graduate, "He [Sheats] is so disagreeable and so arbitrary that I hardly know what you may expect."[18]

The second and more troublesome law was the Summer School Act of 1913. The act removed the superintendent's exclusive power to pick faculty for the summer schools and assigned the responsibility to a committee consisting of the superintendent and the presidents of the University of Florida and Florida State. Sheats publicly vented his anger with the law in his 1914 biennial report: "This present State Superintendent has taken much and can endure one more implied insult to gratify the selfish ambition of any who wish to sever his connection as much as possible from the teaching force of the State." He was even blunter when he met with president Conradi and Dean Thackston (representing Murphree) to select faculty for the 1915 summer schools. According to Conradi, Sheats threated to form a coalition of the private colleges, the private normal schools, and the public high school principals for "a fight to the finish" if the state colleges tried "to curtail the dignity and the power of the office of the State Superintendent." Thackston added that Sheats would henceforth "be an unrelenting enemy." Sheats took his campaign to the annual meeting of county superintendents and high school principals and threatened to "cripple, if not annihilate" the public colleges. "It is very unfortunate that we should have situations of this kind," Conradi wrote Murphree, "But it seems they are just bound to come every year or so." To Murphree, Sheats's opposition to the law was "unmistakable evidence of his desire to make a political machine of the Summer Schools by appointment of his favorite political friends."[19]

The Summer School Act had a powerful and positive impact on access to higher education. After 1913, students taking coursework during the summer sessions could apply credits earned to a degree from the college they attended. The summer schools were also coeducational, and women students far outnumbered men. In this way, the University of Florida had its first female graduate, Mary Alexander Daiger, in 1920; many more would follow. A few men graduated from the State College for Women as well, but not until 1938, when Clarence Patrick Priest earned a master's in education. The act also opened the summer schools to any qualified student, and students from outside the field of education began to enroll. The summer school as a distinct entity catering to teachers came to an official end shortly after World War II, when the state universities added regular summer semesters to their catalogues.

The 1920 election would be William Sheats's sixth and final campaign. Once again the election pitted two candidates against one another—Sheats and Pinellas County superintendent Dixie Hollins—who were disdainful of the public colleges. "Both of these men have opposed state institutions, and now both profess the utmost loyalty to these higher institutions of learning," Murphree wrote to University of Florida Alumni Association secretary Ralph Stoutamire. He cynically added, "Mr. Sheats comes out frankly and admits that he has made a mistake by opposing them in the past, but that he is now convinced that they are doing good work and should be supported morally, materially and in other ways."[20] Sheats won reelection in 1920 only to die eighteen months into his last term. Governor Carey Hardee appointed Cawthon to finish the term. Cawthon retained the office in the 1924 election and would serve until 1937. The Board of Control and the presidents no longer had to contend with an antagonistic and contentious state superintendent as Cawthon proved to be a reliable ally of the state colleges.

The disputes with the superintendents were relatively minor skirmishes in the larger context of interagency conflict. The Board of Education would continue to undermine the Board of Control's authority on matters large and small and would always refer to the Buckman Act and the 1909 attorney general's opinion in the Sledd matter as its justification for doing so. But there was another issue left unresolved by the Buckman Act, and that was the matter of how and where Florida's white teachers would be trained. When the legislature revisited the issue in 1913, it threatened the foundation of the Buckman Act and came close to returning Florida to the status quo ante 1905.

III

AFTER BUCKMAN

9

The Quandary of the Normal School

Before Buckman, white teachers in Florida had their choice of four public coeducational normal schools: the State Normal School in DeFuniak Springs; the normal school at the Florida State College; the St. Petersburg Normal and Industrial School; and a revived program at the East Florida Seminary. The authors of the Buckman Act had been unable to reach a consensus on what to do with the normal schools and opted, instead, to leave the matter in the hands of the joint board. The act left the joint board with two possible options. One option was to maintain gender-segregated normal schools at both Florida State and the University of Florida. The second option allowed the boards to create a coeducational normal school at the otherwise all-male University of Florida. A corollary to the second option would have been a branch campus of the university in the same town as the main campus or in another location altogether. There was a logistical rationale for a branch campus as it would have provided a separate space for practical training conducted at a model school, which would have included children of both sexes from ages four to seventeen.

House Representative R. W. Storrs argued before the joint board in July 1905 that the school should remain in DeFuniak Springs as a branch of the state university. A similar idea was floated by Andrew Sledd and Henry E. Bennett, the last principal of the State Normal School. Their suggestion was to kill two birds with one stone and place the normal school in Lake City as a means of reconciliation with that town and to save money on building construction. However, as Buckman pointed out to Broward in his long letter of June 30, 1905, opening a third campus in North Florida would have ignited an uproar in South Florida.[1]

The post-Buckman University of Florida approached the first academic year with the expectation that it would be managing a coeducational normal school. Henry Bennett and William Cawthon were brought from DeFuniak Springs, and Wilbur Floyd and George Lynch were recruited from the East Florida Seminary to teach in the normal school. The education courses were given prominence in the university's catalogue and included coursework aimed at both primary and secondary school teachers. Fifty-one male students were enrolled. Before the academic year ended, though, the joint board notified Sledd that it had decided to maintain strict gender segregation at both colleges. Rather than sustain a rudimentary normal program for a small group of male teachers, Sledd opted to terminate the program altogether and focus on college coursework. A School of Pedagogy was created in 1906, and a bachelor's in pedagogy was offered as an alternative to the subcollegiate normal diploma. However, as the university was mandated to take them, normal students continued to enroll and were unceremoniously placed in the university's preparatory department.[2]

But for the ambiguities in the Buckman Act regarding normal work, the Florida State College for Women seemed destined to be a small liberal arts college. Instead, prospective teachers poured into Tallahassee. In his first biannual report from what was still named the Florida Female College, Murphree confided that he had initially been uncertain about a gender-segregated normal program. "However, after a year and a half of careful observation," he stated, "I have become convinced of the feasibility and value of the present plan of operation." He went on to add that "no disadvantage followed the segregation of the sexes." His enrollment report indicated the need for more teachers. Of the college's four schools, the School for Teachers was, by far, the largest with 133 students. The School for Fine Arts and the School for Industrial Arts had 96 and 71 students, respectively. The School of Liberal Arts, the only school awarding a bachelor's degree, had only 71 students. During this period, approximately two-thirds of all graduates from the Florida State College went on to teach. Many, though, came out of the college's liberal arts, fine arts, and domestic science programs.[3]

Murphree was also a keen observer of educational trends and argued that the normal school of old was no longer de rigueur in pedagogical circles. To support his argument, Murphree conducted a survey of educators in other states and found little support for the continuation of the traditional normal school as an institution separate from the state colleges. Throughout the 1800s, the belief that the educational needs of teachers were better served in specialized schools went largely unchallenged. Support for this argument waned in the twentieth century as colleges of education were introduced in both public and private universities. Gradually, the public normal schools abandoned their original identities and evolved to become colleges and universities. Most were subsumed into state university systems; a few became junior colleges. The private normal schools, for the most part, closed their doors and passed into history.

There would be several legislative attempts to revive an independent state normal school in the early twentieth century. Supporters of a third school were hampered, though, by the lack of support in the executive branch. The election of 1912, however, brought the possibility of change. Park Trammel was elected governor, and Trammel had been a supporter of normal schools as a legislator. He had also voted against the Buckman Act. The election also saw the return of William Sheats, one of the chief advocates for Florida's normal schools.

The Madison School Bill of 1913

By the time Murphree arrived at the University of Florida, the normal program there had already died from "general apathy and general indifference." In a letter to Hattie Carpenter, Murphree expressed doubts as to whether he should revive it.[4] Several years later, Murphree would find himself with not only a viable normal program but a four-year teachers college as well. Both became possible after the Peabody Education Fund decided to dissolve its endowment and divide its remaining assets equally among the southern states to create new teacher training programs. Under the terms of the grants, each state would receive $40,000 from the Foundation to erect a college classroom building. In return, the state would fund a new teachers college. As a teachers college already existed at the State College for Women, the University of Florida was chosen to receive the grant. This raised a concern as to whether Peabody would agree to support a male-only teachers college. The normally articulate P. K. Yonge awkwardly stated their awkward position thusly: "In regard to the co-educational feature, while I believe it would be better not to have any of our institutions of Higher Learning co-educational I don't think it will be possible to get this building with this feature eliminated, so I believe it would be better not to raise this question at all, that is, if we want the building at the University, and I think we ought to have it even with the co-educational feature."[5] If Peabody raised any concerns about the money going to a gender-exclusive institution, they are not mentioned.

Sheats's victory in 1912 intensified the need to get the college operating as soon as possible. In August, Yonge wrote to Murphree to express his frustration with delays in the negotiations: "This Peabody appropriation is, in my judgment, our only hope for securing a teacher's college building for many years to come, if, indeed, we even get it. You know Mr. Sheats' ideas of separate and independent normal colleges for the State, and, of course, you realize that unless the University does its part in training teachers one of the best reasons for the existence of the University falls to the ground."[6] As the Board of Control lobbied hard for legislative support in the winter of 1913, more trouble came from the annual convention of county school superintendents and high school principals held in Ft. Myers. A report from the convention's committee on colleges declared a clear preference for having the new teachers college at the University of Florida be coeducational. President Conradi had hoped the report would not become public, but it was quickly published in the *Gainesville Sun*. The biggest menace to the status quo, however, came from the state legislature, which introduced a bill to take control of the private Florida Normal Institute in Madison and make it a coeducational state normal school.[7]

The Florida Normal Institute was founded in 1907 and was affiliated with the local high school for Madison County. Murphree described it as nothing more than "a cramming school" with a suspiciously low failure rate. The Madison Normal School Bill focused on the needs of rural counties and stressed elementary school training. On paper, it was a modest bill to create a distinctly inferior school that would serve a population the state colleges were unable to serve. To supporters of the Buckman Act, the Madison bill was an existential threat, as the history of state schools prior to Buckman demonstrated that inferior schools inevitably sought to become superior ones. As Buckman himself stated, "The establishment of one normal institution, or state school, never mind what pretext, would be like the hole in the dike." Had the school been created, it likely would have followed the route of state normal schools in other states, and there would now be another public university in a small inland town in North Florida. The bill had one other objectionable feature: the school would be placed under the jurisdiction of the Board of Education, not the Board of Control.[8]

The bill took the Board of Control completely by surprise. On May 6, John Kellum sent Murphree a feverish letter written at 5:00 a.m. urging him to mobilize his students and the people of Gainesville to write letters to their representatives to oppose the bill. The Madison people had already flooded the legislature with support letters, and Kellum pleaded: "Do all you can and get Gainesville people to do all they can. Do it quietly but do it quick." Kellum warned what would happen if the Madison school was funded; South Florida would demand its own school, and West Florida would follow, and then the state would be back to where it was before Buckman.[9]

Murphree followed through and had his students, including some who had attended the Madison school, write letters. Sheats, to the surprise of everyone, stayed on the sidelines. In later correspondence concerning a similar bill, Sheats explained that his efforts were focused on resurrecting the old state normal school, not an inferior normal school that catered to elementary school teachers. The bill passed the House on June 2, cleared the Senate on June 4, and was sent to Governor Trammel for his signature on June 6. On June 11, Murphree wrote to Fons Hathaway to urge him to contact the governor and pressure him to veto the bill. Hathaway complied and sent Murphree a copy of his letter. In it, Hathaway wrote: "The measure is vicious whether so designed or not because it will destroy the policy of higher education in this state which is admired by the whole country.... Veto the bill. It is true you will make some political enemies in doing it, but you will have consciousness of knowing that you have done a patriotic service to the people." Murphree replied, "Your letter to the Governor was a 'peach,' a 'corker,' a 'Jim Swisher.'" After long consideration, Trammel vetoed the bill on June 18. Buckman was "agreeably surprised" at the governor's decision, given Trammel's record as a legislator. As governor, though, Trammel apparently thought it unwise to unravel a complex law that had been in existence for eight years.[10]

The Madison Normal School bill panicked the Board of Control and President Murphree. It was the narrowest of victories, and Murphree was certain that, unless there was a serious change in policy, there would be additional attacks and more attempts to bypass the Buckman Act. Specifically, Murphree became convinced that the University of Florida's teachers college must be made coeducational. His arguments for doing so, however, placed him in the very hypocritical position of supporting coeducation as the president of the University of Florida when he had vehemently opposed it as president of the State College for Women. The situation also placed him in a very peculiar position vis-à-vis the two boards. Gender segregation was a cornerstone of the Buckman Act. The act permitted some latitude by allowing a coeducational normal school at the University of Florida, but the joint board chose not to exercise that option in April 1906. The reasons for doing so were never stated, but, once again, the vote had been largely along board lines, with the Board of Education rejecting coeducation. The decision may have been just spiteful politics; in other words, the Board of Education opposed it because Andrew Sledd and the Board of Control supported it. It is also interesting that there had been a dissenting vote on the Board of Control in 1906; A. L. Brown, who detested Sledd, had sided with the Board of Education. The situation in 1913 was fundamentally different, or so it seemed to Murphree. Holloway had been replaced by Sheats, and Sheats supported a coeducational normal school; A. L. Brown was gone; and Albert Murphree, not Andrew Sledd, was president of the University of Florida.

Murphree submitted his idea to the Board of Control shortly after Trammel's veto. At the time, proponents of the Madison bill were busy trying to find votes to override the veto. Murphree approached several key figures to gain their support, but before he did so he had to explain to his colleague and friend Edward Conradi why he was changing course on the matter of coeducation. Murphree admitted to Conradi that he had strongly opposed coeducation when President Sledd had proposed it in 1906. However, the passage of the Madison bill and the clamor for coeducation at the Ft. Myers convention had changed the situation. He then tried to allay Conradi's fears that many women would transfer from the State College by promising not to offer classes in domestic science, music, and the arts, "which were attractive to girls." Conradi replied that he had expressed his views at Ft. Myers and would do so again at the next Board of Control meeting.[11]

Murphree then sought out two key potential allies, Henry Buckman and William Sheats. This must have been galling to Murphree as he disliked both men intensely.[12] In his letter to Buckman, Murphree noted that the Buckman Act permitted a coeducational normal school and that such a measure would protect the act from future attacks. His letter to Sheats prompted a gleeful, but circumspect, reply: "I hardly know what to say to you in regard to making your normal school co-educational, in fact, I was approached by the other side and expressed some dissent, which somewhat embarrasses me. Since reading your letter I really feel no opposition to your making the school co-educational, but I believe it would be best for me to keep neutral on the question and in the end sustain whatever position you and the Board of Control may take in the matter." Murphree quickly and disingenuously answered that he was not seeking an endorsement but simply an opinion on the matter in order to shape policy for the new department.[13] The Board of Control met on July 5 and heard arguments for either making the university's teachers college coeducational or maintaining the status quo. Afterward, the Board of Control deferred action and requested written statements from both Conradi and Murphree on how the colleges could better serve the needs of Florida teachers.[14]

Conradi's statement began by acknowledging the concerns of those who supported the bill: "The passage of the Madison Normal School Bill by the last Legislature seems to have brought to the minds of some people a keener sense of the need of training elementary and country school teachers. They seem to feel that the state should do more for the training of these teachers than it is doing now." He went on to say that the State College for Women had always offered elementary school instruction and that those who enrolled "enjoyed far better opportunities than they could have enjoyed in any private normal." However, as Conradi noted, an eighth-grade education was a requirement for admission to the normal department, and this was a wise policy: "The State should rather demand that every child be given the opportunity in its home school to complete at least the eighth grade by the time it is fifteen years of age."[15]

Conradi then turned to the proposal that the teachers college at the university be coeducational: "As to the making of the College of Education coeducational, that does not even touch the matter.... There is not a State University in the country that I know of that has an elementary normal school as part of its organization." Conradi also addressed what he believed was Murphree's unspoken reason for advocating coeducation. Namely, that a male-only teachers college would be unable to attract enough students to justify the $10,000 the state was compelled to provide annually in order to receive the Peabody grant. In response to the unstated concern, Conradi noted that the state legislature had just passed the certificate law that allowed the state colleges to award teaching certificates upon graduation and without examination. This law, Conradi believed, would drive both male and female students to the state colleges. Conradi further reminded the board that a coeducational teachers college would effectively end gender segregation at the University of Florida, as the women would be required to take many of their classes in the College of Arts and Sciences with the men.

Conradi then addressed what he felt was the rationale for gender segregation in the Buckman Act:

> If the University is made co-educational, and makes an active campaign for women students, it will make the two institutions for higher learning in the state competitors for students in the same field. Such an arrangement has proved disastrous in several states.... The rivalry

that will ensue will not limit itself to the people immediately interested, but will irradiate in various directions and will soon find its way into the legislature with results that will probably be disadvantageous to both institutions.

Conradi concluded by stating that, if a new normal school should become necessary, it should be under the governance of the Board of Control and located in South Florida.[16]

Conradi's statement was a well-reasoned and finely structured argument on the issue of elementary school training and coeducation. Murphree had little to offer in reply except the fear of what would come if coeducation was not implemented and the perception that there was widespread support for coeducation among the county superintendents and high school principals. Murphree may also have felt that the Board of Control favored coeducation. They had, in fact, supported it in 1906, and the situation in 1913 seemed even more favorable. If so, he was mistaken. In a letter dated the day before Murphree mailed his argument to the Board of Control, Yonge wrote to say that "your conclusion about the attitude of the Board of Control is perhaps wrong." Yonge, himself, was ambivalent. He conceded that circumstances may have forced an exception, but the board needed more information. He considered it perhaps the most the serious question the board had considered.[17] In the end, the Board of Control took Conradi's advice and, like Governor Trammel, decided not to change course.[18]

Despite Murphree's apprehensions, the Teachers College at the University of Florida found success as a male-only program. The college-level coursework emphasized preparation for teaching in secondary education and the fundamentals of school administration. Two of the early graduates quickly landed positions as high school principals, and another was appointed a county superintendent. A traditional four-year subcollegiate normal diploma was offered at both the university and Florida State, but enrollments were never significant and dwindled throughout the 1920s. Eventually, the normal programs were reduced to two years of college, and the LI was replaced with an associate of arts degree.

Madison Again

A final attempt at a normal school law was made in 1919, when a bill was introduced by the House Committee on Education to create not one, but two normal schools. The locations were never publicly stated, but it was assumed that one was the Madison school and the second would be reserved for South Florida. John Guilliams urged Murphree to get behind the bill: "Reconsider your narrow and short-sighted views and come out boldly for better things for the submerged half of Florida's childhood." Murphree denied any active involvement in opposing the bill but thought it senseless to create more schools when the state refused to fund the ones it had.[19] There was one other significant difference between this bill and the 1913 one; the 1919 normal school bill was endorsed by Governor Sidney Catts, who would be sure to sign it if it appeared on his desk.

Sidney Johnston Catts was a political outsider when he came to power in 1917. His 1916 campaign in the Democratic primary played on nativist and anti-Catholic sentiment while also championing Florida's workingman—if that man was white and Protestant. In a peculiar and complicated election that allowed voters to cast votes for their first and second choices, Catts outpolled his opponents in the spring Democratic primary contest. However, inconsistencies in how second-choice ballots were cast placed the decision in the hands of the Florida Supreme Court. The court decided in favor of the runner-up, State Comptroller and former state treasurer William V. Knott. Having been denied the Democratic nomination, Catts ran in the general election as the candidate for the Prohibition Party and the Independent Party and easily defeated Knott. Like other southern populists who came to power, Catts's administration was marked by ugly attacks on immigrants, Catholics, and African Americans. But it also saw significant improvements in public institutions. Reforms were made in the treatment of prisoners and the mentally handicapped, and the state's first compulsory education law was passed. Compared to other gubernatorial administrations of the Progressive Era, Florida's public colleges, or at least its white ones, did well under Sidney Catts.[20]

Catts entered office in 1917 with a determination to upend the status quo. He seized the opportunity to appoint his own men whenever the occasion arose and vowed to purge the Board of Control once in office. Two of his protégés, Joseph Earman, publisher and editor of the *West Palm Post*, and James B. Hodges, a prominent railroad lawyer from Lake City, were placed on the board. Earman and Hodges maintained a multidecade correspondence, and both would fall out with their mentor Catts in the 1920s. Earman served as chair of the Board of Control from April 1917 to 1919, when he was succeeded by Hodges. A third Catts appointee was J. T. Diamond of Milton, who replaced P. K. Yonge on the board and would later serve as the board's secretary. Equally disturbing to the old guard was the dismissal of John Kellum as secretary of the Board of Control. Kellum had been a devoted servant to the board and a confidant of both Murphree and Conradi. Like many establishment Democrats, Murphree had been disturbed by Catts's election and threatened to leave after Catts's purge of the Board of Control.

Although he was initially distrustful of his new bosses, Murphree quickly surmised that he could work with them. Earman, in turn, was amiable and direct, and he publicly referred to Murphree in his newspaper editorials as Kid Murph. Earman also had a peculiar letter-writing style that reflected his career as a journalist. His letters consisted of a series of one-sentence paragraphs that flowed in a telegraphic stream of consciousness. Like his newspaper editorials, his letters often lacked subtlety and ambiguity. Earman was open to advice from the college presidents, and he seemed earnest in his desire to advocate for higher education. He also assured Murphree and Conradi that there would be no political interference while he was chair.[21]

On the matter of the normal school proposal, Murphree warned Earman of the harm that might ensue if the bill passed and was signed into law by the governor. The annual meeting of county superintendents and high school principals once again entered the picture. "We are distressed to learn that a little coterie of County Superintendents are seeking to re-establish the educational situation that was abolished by act of the Legislature in 1905," Murphree cautioned. He cited seven reasons why this "insidious effort" should be defeated. Reason number four read: "It is common knowledge that every Normal School in the United States is not content to remain on a lower scholastic standard than the colleges and Universities of the State in which it may be located. It chafes under the comparison between its standard and that of the State and denominational colleges; and from the outset it begins to strive to duplicate the work of the colleges and offer a college degree, while at the same time it takes its pupils from the tenth grade of the high schools. . . . God save the State of Florida from such a condition!"[22]

He went on to argue that the lack of teachers in Florida stemmed from the low salaries being paid and not the lack of graduates from the teacher programs at the University of Florida and the Florida State College for Women. The counties, he said, "are not paying the wages of a common convict or an ordinary barber." He also commented that the county superintendents supporting the bill, in particular Dixie Hollins of Pinellas County, all aspired to be state superintendent.[23] Earman replied a few days later in a letter marked "Personal and Private" that the bill did not appeal to him. To divert the normal school proponents, Earman published an editorial in his paper that, he argued, would create "a fuss" over the location of these schools: "Anything that will start friction has a tendency to impede. We will see what we will see!" Earman also noted the sensitivity of his letter: "I cannot consistently, as Chairman of the Board of Control, hold office under appointment of the Governor and oppose his desires in the matter." Throughout the legislative debate, Earman publicly voiced support for the bill while working behind the scenes and the back of the governor to undermine it.[24]

After his editorial, Earman forwarded Murphree a telegram from Dixie Hollins. In it, Hollins asked whether the Board of Control would support a bill to make the teachers college at the university coeducational as an alternative to the normal school bill. Earman requested Murphree's opinion on Hollins's proposal. Murphree noted that such a bill was unnecessary as the Buckman Act already allowed for a coeducational normal school at the university. If the legislature wanted to open the Teachers College to women it had only to pass a joint resolution urging the joint board to do so, a measure less complicated than an actual legislative bill. He added, "I beg to say that I strongly favor co-education in the Teachers' College in the University," and concluded with, "Hope you will answer Dixie affirmatively for co-education in Teachers' College." He failed to mention President Conradi's views on the matter.[25]

Shortly after that exchange, Murphree received a letter from Representative Eli Futch of Gainesville. "We are doing our best to put to sleep the bill for the creation of normal schools," Futch wrote. Futch, though, had grown tired of the persistent debates that arose over teacher education and offered a more radical response, "I honestly believe that if I had nothing else of importance on my shoulders at this session, it is possible to do away with one of the fundamental ideas of the Buckman Bill; that is, the idea of separate institutions for men and women." Futch argued that there should be only one coeducational teachers college and it should be located at the State College, not the University of Florida. The University of Florida could then divert funds to other colleges. Although Florida State would become coeducational first in Futch's plan, the university would soon follow. He also reported that Dixie Hollins would support his coeducation effort if the normal school bill failed. Murphree gave Futch his standard opinion on coeducation and warned him that Hollins was a "snake in the grass" who could not be trusted. He did not tell Futch about Hollins's telegram to Earman.[26]

Amid all this discussion, James Hodges informed Earman that the Florida Normal Institute was one of the two schools being offered, and he identified Rollins College as the other. "We don't need them," Hodges stated. He went on to say that if they needed campuses, they should go back to his hometown of Lake City and reclaim the campus that had recently been abandoned by the Baptists.[27] The bill was removed from the House calendar on June 3, 1919, and was given no further consideration. For the next twenty-eight years, the two public colleges for white teachers would continue to administer their separate programs aimed largely at secondary education, while a third coeducational school for African American teachers operated in its own sphere. The matter would not be fully resolved until after World War II. The end of gender segregation in 1947 eliminated the quandary created by Buckman, and the end of racial segregation in 1958 provided more opportunities for Black teachers. Even so, it was not until the expansion of the state university system and the creation of a parallel junior college system in the 1960s that the educational needs of Florida's teachers were fully addressed.

The battles with the legislature over teacher education stemmed more from the vagaries and omissions of the Buckman Act than they did from the unresolved issues of governance. In one of the grander ironies of this history, the Board of Education would gradually concede the domain of teacher education to the Board of Control while it exercised greater control over other aspects of higher education. Those other aspects could be as mundane as a salary increase for a specific instructor or as critical as the biennial budget. The Catts administration also provided a pause in the struggle for power. The struggle would continue where it left off when the Democratic establishment returned to power in 1920.

10

Budget Battles

The Board of Education had defended Sledd's forced resignation in 1909 as an extraordinary action taken to prevent the erosion of public support for the university. No such justification—or any, for that matter—would be made after 1909, even in the case of the something as commonplace as salary increases for two instructors at the State College for Women. The incident occurred in the summer of 1916 after the Board of Control had submitted its salary proposals for fiscal year 1916–17. When the Board of Education returned the proposal, the Board of Control was surprised to see that it now included unsolicited pay increases for Maude Schwalmeyer and Caroline Brevard, instructors in Florida State's School of Education. The Board of Education's amendments further failed to explain how the increases would be funded as the colleges' budgets, once approved by the legislature, provided almost no flexibility. In letters to Yonge and Conradi, Board Secretary John Kellum explained how the situation came to be. He remarked first that he was not surprised to find that it was Schwalmeyer and Brevard who had received the raises as they were the "ones of all the teachers that would try to work politics." He added, "I don't see how the Board can comply with it as it would be perfectly absurd to decrease one teacher's salary to raise another's and especially in this case where I think the teachers to be raised are about the poorest we have."[1]

The Board of Control met on August 14 and rejected the Board of Education's budget amendments. Yonge made his case to the Board of Education on August 16 and requested a joint meeting if his reasons for rejecting the pay raises did not seem satisfactory. Instead, the Board of Control received the following ruling from the Board of Education: "Ordered. That the Secretary notify the State Board of Control that this Board assents to the salary budget of the State Board of Control for the present school year, July 1, 1916, to June 30, 1917. But, in this connection, notifies the State Board of Control that hereafter the State Board of Education desires the privilege of going over the salary budget with the State Board of Control before any contracts for salaries are made for the ensuing year." To drive home the point, the cover letter for the communication specifically referred to the decisions of the Board of Education in the Sledd conflict.[2]

Wartmann, for once, favored resignation over obedience. Kellum recommended that the matter be thrown into the courts to decide once and for all whether the Board of Control had any authority or if it was "a mere figure head." Board of Control member Frank Jennings, who had been appointed by Governor Trammel, struck a more cautious note and hoped "that diplomacy may prevail in the future as it has very largely in the past." Jennings conceded that it might ultimately be decided in the courts, but he was not optimistic that a favorable ruling would be the result. In the end, Professor Schwalmeyer received her raise the following year, and, to accommodate Brevard, a new position was created at the salary she requested. The Board of Education's order to the Board of Control introduced a new and uglier tone to their already tense relationship and set the stage for a series of disputes over budgetary issues that led to more and harsher dictates. Those disputes, though, would have to wait for the end of the Catts administration, four years after Schwalmeyer and Brevard got their raises.[3]

Public universities today derive income from a variety of sources: tuition and fees, federal funds, gifts and endowments, franchise fees, and, finally, state allocations. In the early 1900s, though, public higher education relied largely on tax dollars. Outside the Northeast, few public universities charged in-state tuition. Endowments were meager, the affluent preferring to give to private colleges. In 1916, twenty-two states avoided or mitigated budget battles with their state legislatures by providing higher education its own revenue streams, usually in the form of special millage taxes. These sources had their own downsides in the form of fluctuating property values and the addition of more schools and more departments competing for the same dollars. Still, the revenue streams depoliticized the budget process, and colleges that had them were the envy of those that did not. President Murphree's comments regarding a 1922 millage referendum reflect this sentiment: "The Lord only knows how desperate our institution is and has been on account of the uncertainty, and particularly the wrangling incident every two years at the meeting of our Legislature. I would rather have less appropriation and know that it is definite than to depend upon uncertainty for larger amounts."[4] A millage increase in Florida required a constitutional amendment and voter approval. An increase to support higher education was put to the voters twice, in 1908 and 1922, and was rejected both times.

In the ten years following the departure of Andrew Sledd, appropriations for the white colleges can best be described as barely adequate, while appropriations for Florida A&M can only be described as appalling. Although Conradi and Murphree complained about the lack of support from the legislature, neither president suggested that its school would be unable to function properly without additional funds. Until the legislative session of 1919, the biggest concern was the appropriation for capital projects. Both the University of Florida and the State College for Women were building entirely new campuses, and the appropriation for building construction consumed a significant part of the overall budget. As capital spending is not a recurring expense, the legislature was less reluctant to spend in that area. In general, though, the state legislature found the resources to sustain the white colleges and provide money for physical and curricular growth throughout the 1910s. This changed dramatically after World War I.

The budget issues confronting the state colleges after World War I stemmed from social, political, and economic conditions that were fundamentally different from those of previous and subsequent decades and were often unique to Florida. Furthermore, Florida's economy did relatively well throughout most of the 1920s. While African Americans emigrated northward to escape the oppression of Jim Crow laws, white immigration accelerated, leading to higher property values and increased state revenue. Overall, it was not the type of economy associated with bad budgets. On paper, too, the budget situation seemed to be improving as appropriations for higher education increased noticeably from session to session. However, the budgets fell far short of what the colleges, and specifically the University of Florida, needed.

At the center of the budget crisis was a sudden and unanticipated upsurge in enrollment. As David Levine noted, "World War I proved the preeminence of the expert in modern society." To find them, the nation looked increasingly to its colleges and universities. The impact was felt most in the applied and theoretical sciences, with engineering attracting more students than any other field. On average, land grant colleges across the nation saw larger increases than the liberal arts colleges as students looked for more practical and job applicable training.[5] However, interest in science and engineering was not the only force driving the increase in enrollment. Enrollments had been steadily rising before the war, fueled by the larger numbers of high school graduates. For many students, college became a path to material success and social advancement regardless of the curriculum. For the College Man, as he came to be called, the college experience and its network of friends and associates outweighed any educational value the universities might offer. The postwar decade marked the culmination of a campus culture that emerged in the nineteenth century and persists today. Faddish clothing and behavior, alcohol consumption (even more so after Prohibition), preoccupation with athletics, and a general disdain for anything curricular characterized a certain segment of the student body.[6]

Nationwide, college enrollment rose 57 percent between 1919 and 1928. By comparison, the University of Florida's enrollment increased a staggering 280 percent. Although the total number of women enrolling in colleges continued to increase, increases declined relative to male rates after the war. The Florida State College for Women showed a 100 percent increase, much higher than the national average for both sexes but still far below the University of Florida.[7] Both schools were the beneficiaries of steadily rising numbers of high school students. From 1,215 white students enrolled in the twelfth grade in 1919, the number rose to 2,613 in 1923, and then to 5,784 in 1927.[8] Black twelfth-grade enrollment for the same years was 29, 43, and 171. The development of public high schools also fueled demand for more high school teachers, and the state colleges would help meet that demand.

The University of Florida's exceptional growth was, to some extent, rooted in the university's threefold purpose as state university, land grant college, and teachers college. There were no other choices in Florida for less affluent middle-class parents who wanted to send their sons to a public college other than the University of Florida. Consequently, the University of Florida would find itself riding both postwar enrollment waves, with the serious, technically minded student and the not-so-serious College Man coming to its doors. Alabama had Auburn and Alabama; Mississippi had Mississippi State and Ole Miss; and South Carolina had Clemson and USC. Florida had only UF. The state colleges were also impacted by the Board of Control's open admissions policy. The sole qualification for admission after 1913 was a high school diploma, and the state colleges maintained high school departments for students who lacked access to a local senior high school. Most of the students who entered were unprepared for college work and did not advance to their junior and senior years. Yet the presidents found themselves under constant pressure to encourage new students. The idea that the state colleges should be democratic in their admissions became engrained in the minds of policymakers and would prove unshakable in the postwar period even after it was clearly evident that the policy was no longer sustainable. Despite numerous pleas to either cap enrollment or tighten admissions, the Board of Control was content to maintain the status quo.

The armistice of November 11, 1918, came midway through the fall semester, when the college presidents were preparing their budget requests for the 1919 legislative session. The University of Florida had been placed under military control during the war, and President Murphree based his initial request on the expectation that the university would remain a military camp for the near future. Instead, the university was returned to civilian control in January 1919, and adjustments had to be made on the fly.[9] Academic year 1919–20 was the first full postwar year, and 396 students enrolled at the university in the fall. By the end of 1919–20, the university reported a headcount enrollment of 583, a 57 percent increase over prewar years, making it the first year that the university's enrollment exceeded that of the women's college. It is likely that the sudden increase was seen as a temporary phenomenon fueled by the return of war veterans. If so, Murphree was undoubtedly surprised to find an additional 245 students the following year and 200 more in each of the succeeding years.

Florida's postwar situation was also complicated by a highly charged political climate. The 1916 election had brought Sidney Catts into the governor's mansion, and the Catts administration was noted for its willingness to spend money on public works and state institutions. Perhaps frightened by the Catts revolution of 1916, the legislature granted most of the governor's requests in the 1917 session. Biennial budgets for higher education prior to Catts had been largely stagnant and hovered around $450,000. Under Catts, the appropriation leapfrogged to $645,000 in 1917, still $43,000 less than what Catts's Board of Control requested. The Board of Control submitted another ambitious budget in 1919, but this time the legislature was less inclined to support another dramatic increase.

By late March, Joe Earman and James Hodges realized that opposition was mounting to the Board of Control's 1919 budget request. To Earman, Hodges commented that the legislature was cutting appropriations so severely it would hinder education for the next two years. "They can go to hell," he exclaimed: "I am not going up there to beg them about this thing. It is squarely up to the legislature. They have all the information." Earman decided to act by writing an editorial critical of the legislature in the *Palm Beach Post* entitled "Busy Bees in Tallahassee." Representative Eli Futch wrote to complain that the editorial only antagonized House members. Earman suggested the Board of Control might have to resign if adequate funds were not appropriated. But, he added: "This won't be necessary. They will politic around but when it comes to a showdown THEY ARE GOING TO APPROPRIATE, and they are going to appropriate enough to run them right."[10] Murphree, though, was despondent and "greatly tempted to throw up the sponge." Fons Hathaway suggested to Murphree that the legislature's "niggardly" attitude was a reaction to the current Board of Control. "This is only a surmise," he added.[11] Meanwhile, a student delegation had gone to Tallahassee to protest about conditions on campus. Initially, the legislature had slashed the Board of Control's budget request of $975,000 to $804,000. However, a joint legislative committee restored most of the budget. When the revised budget came out of the committee, Murphree was unhappy to see that, once again, the budget for the University of Florida was lower than that of Florida State.[12]

The election of Cary Hardee as governor in 1920 was a rejection of Catts's populist approach and marked a return to southern economic conservatism. The timing of this shift could not have been worse for higher education in Florida. At the very moment the state needed a populist governor willing to spend money, it was confronted, instead, with a conservative governor appalled at the spendthrift policies of his predecessor. The legislative sessions of 1921 and 1923 would create tensions throughout the system: tensions between the two boards, between the Board of Control and the legislature, and even between the university's faculty and the governor. The situation was further complicated by the creation of a Budget Commission in 1921 consisting of the governor, the comptroller, and the state treasurer. Budget submissions would now be reviewed by the commission, and the commission would send its recommendations to the legislature as well.

The budget prepared by the Board of Control in March 1921 was ambitious and mostly likely unrealistic, but the circumstances that propelled it were extraordinary and dire. The Board of Control requested the budget be doubled, with the bulk of the increase going to the University of Florida. At that time, three of the five men on the board were still Catts appointees, but James Hodges had taken over as chair in 1919 after Joe Earman was appointed to the State Board of Health. In an unprecedented move, the Board of Education prevented the Board of Control from submitting its budget to the state legislature. Instead, the members were summoned to a joint meeting on March 14, 1921, where its budget proposal was rejected. The main point of contention was the allocation for the university. The two boards agreed to the formation of a special committee, with three men from each board, to discuss the situation further.

Also present at the joint meeting was Ernest McLin, a member of the Florida Education Association. McLin was one of several business and civic leaders invited to the meeting to speak on behalf of the colleges. McLin argued that the legislature could raise additional revenue without raising the millage rate, and his views were disseminated in a mass mailer distributed by the University of Florida Alumni Association on March 18. The University of Florida Alumni Association had been organized by the university's Class of 1906, the first graduating class in the post-Buckman era. The association was largely inactive throughout its first decade of existence. After the war, it took on a new character as both a fundraising arm of the university and as a lobby. The association's March 18 flyer, which had a SOS banner at the top, noted that Mississippi provided $1 million more to its universities than Florida, even though Mississippi was far poorer and carried a $5 million bond debt.[13]

The flyer implored people to wire or write the governor and the six men on the special committee to urge them to submit the Board of Control's budget proposal to the state legislature. As a member of the special committee, Superintendent Sheats received numerous letters, and he was not happy with their content. The flyer suggested he opposed the Board of Control's budget proposal when, in fact, he was the only member of the Board of Education who supported the increase. Sheats met with Murphree and F. M. O'Byrne, president of the Alumni Association, to protest this "grave injustice." Ralph Stoutamire, the association's executive secretary, took the blame for the flyer and wrote Sheats a sincere apology. The activity of the association also gained the attention of the legislature. Senator W. J. Singletary of Jackson County accused the university of circulating propaganda and thereby entering into the political process. Murphree responded that the association worked independently and did not consult with any university official.[14]

The special committee met on April 15 and failed to agree on a definite amount. The Board of Education then requested that the Board of Control prepare a budget that did not exceed $500,000 for the University and $600,000 for the State College. Chairman Hodges requested comments from Conradi and Murphree on the revised budget and how they might comply. Rather than reply as an individual, Murphree called upon his

University Council, which consisted of the five deans of the university and Vice President Farr, to deliver a collective response. The University Council submitted its response to the Board of Control on April 18, stating flatly that the Board of Education's budget limit was "inadequate to maintain the institution in a state of efficiency for the next biennium." The Council's response was based on three assumptions: that the course offerings in the catalogue would not be reduced; that the quality of instruction would be maintained; and that enrollment would not be limited. The only reduction the Council was willing to concede was in the area of faculty salaries. But even with the reduction, the university would have to impose a hiring freeze. That was not feasible as professors were already teaching eighteen to twenty-five hours a week. "In reputable schools the maximum number is 15," the Council noted. Classes often had forty-five to sixty-five students when thirty was considered the maximum size acceptable. The Council then returned to the matter of enrollment and presented an enrollment cap as the only alternative.[15]

The response went to great lengths to explain how the previous 1919 budget had been inadequate. That budget did not anticipate an enrollment increase, and much of the budget increase in 1919 went to new courses in sociology, poultry science, and veterinary science. The Council also noted the effects of wartime inflation. By its estimate, the 1919 university budget of $200,000 should have been as high as $500,000. The Council went on to say that a higher budget had not been proposed because the country was still technically at war and "because there existed at that time a peculiar political situation in the state." The overall tone of the response was forceful, but it was also proper and, at times, even deferential. However, it was emphatic in its insistence that the budget suggested by the Board of Education would fall far short of the university's current and future needs and that there would be repercussions. The last sentence struck the following defiant note: "We desire to place ourselves clearly and emphatically on record as protesting against this drastic reduction in the budget of the University and as declaiming all responsibility for the results."[16]

The University Council's response, and particularly the last sentence, provoked a strong rebuke from Governor Hardee. Hardee was puzzled as to how the university had been able to manage affairs with a budget of $200,000 but would be unable to do so with $500,000. He concluded by indicating that President Murphree and the members of the Council were unfit for service and then requested that each member of the Council respond individually unless there was such perfect "unanimity with the membership of the University Council, that a joint communication may fully express your individual views."[17]

Murphree deemed Hardee's letter a "breach of common courtesy." It was certainly a breach of protocol, as the Council's response had been requested by the chairman of the Board of Control, not the governor or the Board of Education. In a letter to James Hodges, Murphree described the letter as "exceedingly insulting and uncalled for," adding: "The Governor has obviously looked for and found something to be offended at upon the part of the University people. If he had had an open mind in replying to our communication addressed to the Board of Control, I feel sure that he would have understood that the University Council meant no threat when it said that it would disclaim all responsibility for the results of the reduced appropriation. We are not Bolsheviks, or labor unionists down here. But we have rights which we think it is our privilege to maintain." As to the governor's implied threat, Murphree stated, "If that is what the Governor meant in the conclusion of his letter, then we are ready to go."[18]

The University Council's report to Chairman Hodges had been an effort in futility, as the Board of Education had already decided to break off negotiations with the Board of Control. On April 28, Hodges awoke to find that the Board of Education had published its own budget proposal in the *Florida Times-Union* without even bothering to inform him. Hodges concluded that the Board of Education's actions could only be explained by the fact that he was a Catts appointee.[19] Murphree explained the situation to House Representative Frank Ellis: "This is the first time in the history of these schools that the State Board of Education has stepped in and prevented the Board of Control from going before the Legislature on the merits of the needs of the institution. Under the circumstances, the Board of Control could do nothing else but step aside and let the State Board of Education handle the matter." Murphree had heard, though, that the governor was willing to make a few concessions and would not object to salary increases for the university as well as small increases for additional staff and new engineering shops. Murphree asked that the amounts requested by the Board of Control "not be urged, lest we get the whole appropriation involved, either by veto or controversy in the House or Senate."[20]

Murphree's information was incorrect, though, and the budget allocation of $500,000 went forward. Meanwhile, an attack on the Board of Control was launched in the Senate. On April 11, Senator Singletary introduced a bill to abolish the Board of Control and place the state schools directly under the Board of Education. Murphree was bewildered and indignant at the attacks and the legislature's stinginess. In a letter to House Representative L. C. Crofton, Murphree asked, "How are we to run the next two years without some additional teachers, and how can we satisfy our men on a salary scale which is $400 less than that allowed the Women's College, how are we to keep up the teaching of engineering without apparatus and machinery, are questions we do not know how to answer?"[21]

With budgetary and legislative issues out of the way, Hardee and the Board of Education used the intersession year to solidify their authority over higher education. Hardee initiated the second purge of the Board of Control by replacing three of Catts's men. He also brought back the conciliatory P. K. Yonge, who was again elected chair. Throughout the 1920s, Yonge would provide a sympathetic ear for the complaints of his presidents and would himself express dissatisfaction with the economic and political reality. But he would be unwilling to risk a confrontation and resigned himself to a role as the bearer of bad news. His approach to arbitration stood in sharp contrast to the combative style of the Catts appointees, and his resolve was quickly tested. In June, the Board of Education presented Chairman Yonge a list of six orders that all but terminated any power or privilege that the Board of Control might have thought it had. Order number six required the Board of Control to give a pay raise in the next legislative session to L. S. Barber, another underachieving instructor at the Florida State College for Women. Order number three stipulated that "all new positions and increases in salaries be reserved for further consideration" and further stipulated that salary requests indicate when a position was new or when a professor was to be given a raise. The orders sent a very clear message to the Board of Control. No longer would the Board of Education be satisfied with exercising its final authority on matters first taken up by the Board of Control. It would now take preemptive action and simply command the Board of Control.[22]

The orders provoked the usual outrage from Board of Control members. John B. Sutton, the sole surviving Catts appointee on the board, labeled the orders "a premedidated [sic] act on the part of the State Board of Education" and urged a showdown: "I would like to see it made an issue and have the matter definitely and finally determined. In other words, if we are subject to the orders and whims of the State Board of Education, then I cannot submit to that construction of the statute by continuing to serve as a member of the Board of Control." He added, "I have always contended, and still contend, that the State Board of Education has no authority to order the Board of Control to do anything."²³ Wartmann, who had already been through several battles with the Board of Education, agreed that action was needed but cynically added that "one of these Chief Moguls will find a comma" that would give new meaning to the Buckman Act. A joint meeting to discuss the matter had been scheduled for July but had to be canceled after the death of Superintendent Sheats. In the interim, the Board of Control submitted its reply on August 10. In it, the Board of Control conceded authority to the Board of Education on the election of presidents, finalized budgets, the creation of new departments, and the question of coeducation. The Board of Control would have authority over the selection of faculty and staff, determining salaries, making rules and regulations, signing contracts, and the preparation of budgets. Without the authority to do so, they argued, the Board of Control had no real reason to exist.²⁴

After the disasters of 1921, Murphree decided on a new course of action for the 1923 legislative session. He bypassed the Board of Control and sent a draft budget directly to Governor Hardee to test the waters along with an apologetic and saccharine cover letter explaining why the budget was so high. The Board of Control also took a different approach in 1923. For the first time, its biennial report included explanations from the college deans and unit heads for how monies would be spent and why they were desperately needed. The result was a litany of academic horrors. The following entry from the University of Florida's lone beleaguered and overworked librarian, Cora Miltamore, adequately conveys the plight faced by the university:

> In the budget, under the caption, LIBRARY, it is recommended that the librarian's salary be at least that of an assistant professor. The duties of the librarian are very confining, beginning, as they do, at eight in the morning and continuing until ten o'clock at night, with, of course, slight intervals in which student helpers are on duty. Most universities pay their chief librarian a full professor's salary. On account of the enormous increase in attendance and about 400 percent increase in the use of the library, it has become an utter impossibility for one librarian to serve the students and faculty and keep the cataloging and care of books up to the demands of the University.²⁵

The new approach was even less successful as Hardee proved to be even more parsimonious in 1923. Twice, Governor Hardee agreed to a budget for the Board of Control only to reduce it each time after meeting with the other two members of the Budget Commission. To the Board of Control,

Murphree stated, "I believe that we face a greater crisis now than we did two years ago." In a letter to John Sutton, Murphree spoke more candidly: "The thing that 'gets my goat' is that Hardee agreed to the amount and said he would approve the sum upon which our last Budget was based, and we know that if Hardee had approved this Budget before the Budget Commission, the Budget would have been recommended as agreed. . . . It looks to me like a very faithless performance."[26] Less than two months later Sutton was off the board. In his last letter to Murphree as a board member, Sutton complained that the Hardee appointees would not support the presidents and would be quick to acquiesce to the governor's demands.[27]

By November 1923, enrollment levels in the College of Engineering at the university had reached the breaking point. Engineering dean John Benton reported that the freshmen class topped 100 and classroom sizes exceeded 40 students for many courses. Murphree urged an enrollment cap of 85 students for the college, but Yonge was unwilling to change course, and then asked Murphree to explain how other universities were handling the situation.[28] A year later, Yonge inquired whether there was a good turnout for the 1924 fall semester. Murphree responded, with more than a tinge of sarcasm: "Yes, we have had a fine opening in point of numbers. In fact, the numbers are so large that we are overwhelmed, embarrassed and distressed. The situation is intolerable! It is dreadful!" He added, "I have never felt so helpless in my life in trying to put in words conditions as they exist here, so that even the Board of Control can fully appreciate the situation, much less making a dent on the minds of the Budget Commission and of the Legislature." Murphree requested permission yet again to limit enrollment only to be rebuffed once more.[29]

Benton was not permitted to cap enrollment, but he was allowed to raise admission standards for engineering students. This provoked an outcry from high school principals and county superintendents and a lengthy protest from State High School Inspector R. M. Sealey: "Has not the College of Engineering already the most severe entrance requirements of any division of the University? The requirement of four units of mathematics, among others, is already unreasonable. Where will it end?" He added that the new math requirement would compel the high schools to hire additional instructors, and they simply did not exist, nor could the counties afford them if they did. Murphree defended the math requirements as essential to the integrity of the university.[30]

Enrollments in the College of Engineering continued to rise despite the new requirements, and Benton again requested a cap in 1925. When Yonge rejected this request as well, Benton suggested a new series of measures that would have made it more difficult to gain admission. These included an application deadline of August 1, which underscores the ease with which students could enroll. Although most freshmen gave notice of their impending arrival before August, some waited until almost the beginning of the fall semester. In theory, students could arrive on registration day with the proper certification and expect to be admitted. In fact, hundreds of students were turned back, not because they were refused admission, but because there was simply nowhere for them to live.[31]

Murphree responded to the budget crisis by first cutting back on maintenance and student services. The results of these cuts were evident when a group of legislators toured the campus at the beginning of the 1923 school year. Senator W. A. MacWilliams criticized the conditions of the dining hall and kitchen and noted that the appearance of the grounds "presented an appearance to me of neglect and lack of care, and are a striking contrast to those of the Woman's [sic] College." Normally, Murphree would have been mortified by such a comparison with the State College, but Murphree told the senator he was glad that he "saw it as it is." Under the circumstances he could ill afford an adequate janitorial staff because every cent was being spent on classroom instruction.[32]

The second area impacted by the budget shortfalls was faculty salaries. In this case, salaries were not cut, as they were already the lowest of any state university in the nation. Rather, salaries were frozen at the level allowed in the 1921 budget. Temporary faculty, some with only a bachelor's degree, were hired at even lower salaries to handle the classroom loads. To encourage faculty retention, Murphree asked to revisit a plan to allow faculty to build residences on the campus "as provided for in the original plans of the University." The Board of Control had approved such a plan in 1913 only to have it rejected by the Board of Education. However, no action was taken on the request.[33]

The Hardee years mercifully came to an end in 1925. Murphree did not know what to expect from the new governor, John Martin, but he may have assumed the worst. In a letter to House Representative Ellis, Murphree warned that another bad budget would threaten the school's accreditation and he would be compelled to curb enrollment. He did not tell Ellis that he had already made several requests to change the admissions requirements and had been rejected each time.[34] The worst, however, did not happen, and the budget for 1925 under Governor Martin was a major improvement over the previous three. But if the budget was higher, so was the student enrollment. The entering class for 1926 topped 900, roughly twice the enrollment for all classes in 1919.

The Hardee years were four of the most difficult for the Board of Control and the state colleges. Any hope that the postwar enrollment boom would be met with a commensurate increase in student per-capita spending were dashed by a conservative governor intent upon curbing all government spending. Any pretense that the Board of Control was in charge of higher education was completely erased. It was evident that the Board of Education under Hardee was intent on exerting its power in every aspect of higher education. The one exception seemed to be the curriculum. The Board of Education had been uninterested in curricular matters and was content to let the presidents and the Board of Control determine what was best. Such restraint, however, did not apply to the education of African Americans. In 1921, the Board of Education issued a directive to effectively end college-level work at the Florida Agricultural and Mechanical College. The directive set off a chain of events that culminated in one of the most dramatic student rebellions in American history.

11

The Ordeal of Nathan Young

Whatever complaints the presidents of the University of Florida and Florida State may have had about conditions at their institutions, they paled in comparison with those that confronted President Nathan B. Young at Florida A&M. His campus was a hodgepodge of twenty wooden structures, many of them in dire need of repair, if not outright condemnation. Particularly atrocious were the dormitories. They were overcrowded, and Young was constantly looking for private homes that would take in students. Young described the men's residences as shacks with stoves for heating and lacking "sanitary arrangements." The women's dormitory was a fire hazard with the college's laundry, kitchen, and bakery attached to it. The centerpiece of the campus was its Carnegie Library, a two-story brick-veneer building that replaced the library lost in 1906, when the school's main building, Duval Hall, was destroyed in a fire. Andrew Carnegie funded public libraries across the nation. A&M's was the first erected at an African American college. Today, it is the oldest endowed building still standing at any of the state universities in Florida.[1]

Young's curriculum was also a hodgepodge, although he described it as multifaceted. All coursework before 1909 was below college grade, with much of it taught at grammar school level. In 1909, the school was organized into three departments—Academic, Agricultural, and Mechanic and Domestic Arts. The Academic Department offered a two-year English normal course, a four-year scientific course, and music instruction. The Agricultural Department consisted of an assortment of courses in horticulture, animal care, and husbandry. The Mechanic and Domestic Arts Department listed fourteen trades but nothing that resembled an engineering program. The closest to a professional program was a successful nursing school supported by the John F. Slater Fund.

The students were distributed by grades with three levels of grammar school, three high school grades, and three "Senior" grades. In 1909, 289

Figure 12. The Carnegie Library at Florida A&M College, date unknown. Florida Memory, State Library and Archives of Florida

students were enrolled, 116 men and 173 women. Of these, 163 were listed as grammar school students, well over half of the total enrollment. In 1916, Congress ruled that Morrill funds could no longer be used to fund primary education. Grammar school–age students continued to arrive after 1916 but were restricted to the model school for education students. To support his ambitious and multifaceted curriculum, Young worked with an annual budget of less than $30,000, of which $23,000 came from federal funds. His state appropriation for operating expenses in 1912 was just over $5,000. Additional federal funding came from the Smith-Hughes Act in 1917, but those funds were specifically earmarked for practical training and further solidified the vocational aspect of the curriculum.[2]

The school acquired a new name in 1909, when it became the Florida Agricultural and Mechanical College. That year also marked the introduction of a four-year college curriculum leading to a bachelor of science degree, though just a handful of students would have qualified for admission. The college would not be fully accredited until 1935. Still, its creation anticipated the needs of Florida's African American communities, and, despite intense opposition from white politicians, the decision to create the college proved irreversible. The inevitable reactionary response came quickly in

June 1909, when State Senator Fred P. Cone, later Florida's twenty-seventh governor (1937–41), launched an attack on A&M. Cone assailed State Superintendent Holloway and the Board of Education for requesting a budget that included a summer school for African American teachers, even though that had been the practice since 1894. Cone's initial assault was unsuccessful, so he turned his attention to a $10,000 construction appropriation for much-needed improvements at A&M. The budget request followed the advice of that year's legislative visiting team, who saw marked improvement at the school but noted the inadequate condition of the buildings.[3]

One of the buildings requested was a sanatorium. The need arose after a typhus epidemic spread through the overcrowded dorms the previous year. The Board of Control was unwilling to put up a fight on behalf of President Young, and the building appropriation was cut. Young pleaded with the Board of Control to use general funds to secure a loan to build the ward and even pledged to pay the interest on the loan personally, "so anxious am I to avoid the risk of an epidemic such as scathed us last year, compared with which the personal risk is nothing."[4] The Associated Press carried the reports of Cone's attacks to other regional outlets. The reports were enough to raise the concerns of Booker T. Washington, who asked Young for his assessment of Cone's influence. Young saw Cone as an opportunist "hoping to ride into politics on the back of the Negro." He was also confident that the Board of Control—"five high-tone gentlemen"—would not change the school's curriculum to appease "blatant-mouthed demagogues" such as Cone.[5]

That Young managed to survive as president for more than twenty years is remarkable and an indication of his diplomatic skills. His excellent relationship with State Superintendent Sheats was also a factor. Matters would change rapidly after the election of Cary Hardee as governor in 1920 and the death of William Sheats in 1922. The backdrop to Hardee's election was a wave of racial violence that prevented African Americans from exercising their constitutional right to vote in the 1920 election. The events of 1920, in turn, were precipitated and shaped by decades of economic, political, and demographic transformation.

As Florida entered the twentieth century, the state began to shed its image as a typical southern state with an economy based in the traditional agricultural commodities of the region. The transportation sector became a major employer and spurred the development of Tampa and Jacksonville. Tariffs on foreign cigars drove cigar makers out of Cuba and into Florida, most notably Tampa. Phosphate mining appeared in the late 1800s and became a major industry in the early 1900s. Tourism took on a new dimension as middle-class vacationers—the so-called "tin can tourists"—flocked to what had been havens for the rich on Florida's beaches. By 1925, tourism surpassed manufacturing and agriculture, combined, as a revenue source for the state. Although Florida's economy was no longer driven by agriculture, agriculture maintained an influence that exceeded its revenue. Tobacco and cotton were cultivated in the Panhandle and northern counties. Truck farming in Central Florida benefited from the growth of the transportation sector, which allowed producers to find regional markets for tomatoes, celery, and other seasonal crops. But the agricultural commodity that would define Florida for the world was citrus.

Florida's new industries changed the state's economic landscape but not the racial status quo. Thousands of Black laborers worked the groves and packinghouses during the winter harvest months, as miners in the phosphate pits, as stevedores on the docks, and as gandy dancers and porters on the rail lines. Although this new and largely wage-earning workforce avoided the debt dependency of tenant farming, it still found itself on the bottom rung of the employment ladder with few opportunities to ascend. As with education, economic progress in African American communities occurred within the narrow confines allowed by the laws and customs of Jim Crow. African Americans in Florida created their own economic opportunities whenever and wherever they could, and with the knowledge that success could be suddenly and violently erased.

Florida's economic transformation coincided with a profound shift in southern demography. In the face of violence and discrimination, hundreds of thousands of African Americans opted to leave their birthplace rather than suffer further poverty, indignity, and harm. The Great Migration, as it came to be known, began in the first decade of the twentieth century and was initially lauded by white politicians who encouraged both Black *emigration* and white *immigration*. Elite satisfaction with the loss of Black citizens, though, gradually turned to despair over the loss of cheap and unprotected labor. The migration intensified with America's entry into World War I as demand for factory labor outside the South increased. Coercive measures were taken to prevent African Americans from leaving, but they could not stop the hemorrhage of human traffic and may have had the opposite effect. Nor did peace and demobilization bring an end to the movement. It was not until the height of the Great Depression that the flood of people abated, only to resume when the next war released a new torrent.

While multitudes fled north, the South's plantation regions were further depleted by southern urbanization and industrialization. In Florida, African Americans often moved south, away from the plantations of West and North Florida and toward economic opportunities that Nathan Young described as "well nigh as attractive" as those outside the South.[6] Urbanization also concentrated African Americans in segregated areas, which undoubtedly gave them a sense of their potential political strength. By the end of the 1910s, African Americans in Florida were determined to reverse more than forty years of social, political, and economic decline and began to organize. Social organizations such as the Colored Knights of Pythias played a pivotal role in creating a statewide network of activists. President Young himself served as a secret correspondent in the NAACP. He took a more visible role in the creation of the Negro Uplift Association in 1919. The goal of the movement was to rejuvenate African American suffrage and break the Democratic Party's monopoly in Florida. Tens of thousands defied election authorities and registered to vote, only to be turned away violently at the polls in November. The election of 1920 was marked by some of the nation's worst political violence, including a massacre in Ocoee that left forty to sixty people dead and destroyed a prosperous African American community.[7]

Cary Hardee campaigned for governor in 1920 with a promise to stop the flight of Florida's Black population. Illogically, Hardee and others were convinced that the only way to prevent African Americans from fleeing oppression was to oppress them even more. Educational policy played a key part in Hardee's campaign. In Hardee's mind, educated Black youth were more likely to leave, and he immediately embarked on a campaign to restrict college-level courses at Florida A&M. Shelton Phillips, state director for the Smith-Hughes–funded Florida State Board for Vocational Education, and J. H. Brinson, state supervisor of Negro Schools, backed Hardee's measures, as did a majority on the Board of Education.[8] The attacks on Young and higher education at A&M coincided with Hardee's assault on the Board of Control and the transfer of near total authority over higher education to the Board of Education. In the case of A&M, the Board of Education would exercise that authority without restraints, and the Board of Control would have few, if any, objections to the Board of Education's actions.[9]

Hardee wasted little time implementing his plans. The Board of Control met on April 11, 1921, and voted to confirm the nominations of the sitting presidents, including President Young. It then conveyed the nominations to the Board of Education. With Sheats and Secretary of State Henry Crawford dissenting, the Board of Education rejected Young's nomination, stating that Young was not "in thorough sympathy with the ideas and purposes for which [the college] was created." The Board of Education scheduled a hearing on the matter for July 29. As secretary of the Board of Education, Sheats informed Chairman Yonge of the meeting, adding the following note: "It is my personal opinion that it would be well for you to be present."[10] At the July 29 meeting, President Young came before the board and defended his policies and actions. Chairman Yonge voiced his support for President Young and assured the Board of Education that "any necessary changes in the curriculum of the school to meet the industrial demands of the State Board of Education" would be made. With those assurances, a majority of the board voted to confirm Young's appointment. Shortly thereafter, Sheats left the meeting.[11]

In Sheats's absence, the Board of Education adopted six resolutions that would redefine Florida A&M's educational mission. The resolutions approved by the board made it clear that the "general academic and classical branches" of knowledge taught at the college were not in conformity with the purpose of the school and that the needs of "the negro youth of the State [were] largely in the fields of agricultural industry and home making." Accordingly, each student, regardless of major, would be required to select a practical vocation and devote four hours each day to the "productive instruction in the vocation of his choice."[12]

The resolutions left absolutely no wiggle room for Young. The board's resolutions made it exceedingly difficult for a student to pursue a college or normal degree while also committing half of each school day to vocational training that the student neither sought nor needed. In a letter to Chairman Yonge, President Young desperately tried to interpret the resolutions in such a way that they did not radically alter his curriculum. But Yonge clearly saw them as dictates, not guidelines, and responded: "I note that you do not understand that the resolution of the State Board of Education contemplates any change in the curriculum. I do not agree with you in this conclusion. In my opinion, the intention of the resolution is to eliminate the classical courses and to offer only agricultural, mechanical, industrial and normal courses." Young replied by denying the existence of any classical course at A&M. The courses in question were those of a more general nature that a student in the sciences or the normal school might take to earn a degree. Languages, in particular, became a point of contention.[13]

Young went on to add that his curriculum paralleled that of other southern Black land grant colleges and that languages were always electives. He also attempted to strike a nerve with the following comment: "I am sure that Florida would not pursue a less liberal educational policy to her Negro citizens than the other Southern States are pursuing toward their Negro citizens, that she certainly would not pursue a reactionary educational policy toward them." Yonge took the bait and made it very clear that the Board of Control was not making the decisions: "Irrespective of what courses of study the Board of Control might recommend, or what you might recommend, or what other colleges may offer, I think when you return from your vacation you had better make up courses of study as required by the resolution of the State Board of Education."[14] Young replied, "The situation is a delicate one . . . and it should not be handled in a drastic way, lest the remedy be worse than the *alleged* disease." He went on to remind Yonge that Sheats had not voted for the resolutions. He closed his letter with the following declaration: "I am leaving Tuesday afternoon for a short vacation before I break down under the uncalled for stress and strain to which I have been subjected because my convictions, born of thirty-three years of teaching, about the work of this College are not wholly in line with educational opinion of those who know practically nothing about the education needs and ambitions of the Negro people. I am free to make the statement to you because you can appreciate somewhat my point of view in the matter."[15]

At the same time Young was fending off attacks to his curriculum, he was also defending his administrative decisions. Specifically, the Board of Control was alarmed by Young's handling of the school's boarding fees and the debts being accrued by his students. According to Young, many students could not afford the boarding fees and had to work off the debt. The ledger for the boarding fee usually showed a deficit but was always reconciled at the end of the biennium.[16] Young also admitted to charging some of his personal expenses to the boarding fund, but he saw that as a perquisite of the position. On January 9, 1922, the Board of Control instructed Young that students could not carry a debt and that sixty-nine students currently in arrears would have to pay or be dismissed.[17]

Throughout his long tenure on the Board of Control, Edgar Wartmann often served as a sounding board for Yonge's questions and concerns. On January 24, Yonge wrote him to get his opinion on the A&M situation. Wartmann replied that he had given up on Young and felt that it was time to let him go. He noted that the Board of Education had already requested his removal once and seemed likely to do so again. Yonge was operating under the same assumption.[18] When it came time for the Board of Control to renew the presidents' contracts for academic year 1922–23, Young was not reappointed. When Sheats was informed of the decision, he replied, much to Yonge's surprise, that he had polled the members of the Board of Education and found a majority "unqualifiedly in favor of Young."[19]

After receiving notification that his contract would not be renewed, Young sent a letter to Sheats imploring as to why, after so many years, he had become "Persona Non Grata." A month later, Sheats informed Yonge that "Young is very loathe to give up his position . . . and it strikes me that he is rather looking to me to save him if I can." He added, "I must say I am really afraid that we will find ourselves worse off if we swap him for some other negro."[20] For two months, Yonge tried to find "some other negro" to take the position but to no avail. The problem was apparent when they compared salaries of presidents at other Black land grant colleges. Young's was the lowest, even though the length of his tenure exceeded all others except James Dudley at North Carolina A&T. By further comparison, Young's salary was lower than that of an assistant professor at either the university or the State College.[21] Inquiries were sent to numerous candidates, and all were asked if they would stress literary over vocational education. Most candidates politely declined the offer, while others were found to be unsuitable. By mid-May, Yonge was ready to terminate the search even though he was still getting suggestions and inquiries as late as June. Yonge informed Sheats that the Board of Control would reappoint Young unless Sheats had another candidate in mind. Sheats answered: "I have not been searching for a person suitable for the presidency of this institution, hence, I am unable to make any nomination. . . . I do not know of any negro outside the State that I believe is his equal." Sheats also sent Young a copy of Yonge's letter with the comment, "I give you this private information for your advantage." Young thanked him.[22]

Young was reappointed by the Board of Control on June 10, but with the stipulation that he no longer draw either funds or provisions from the boarding fund for his personal use.[23] The Board of Education did not act on the appointment at its June meeting. In the interim, Sheats informed Young that he also had the support of Secretary of State Crawford and added, "It is my impression, however, that the confirmation of your nomination is safe." It was the last letter Young was to receive from the superintendent. Sheats died a few days later, and his death dealt the mortal blow to Young's already tenuous position.[24] At a joint board meeting in August, the same meeting in which the Board of Control attempted to delineate the respective powers of the boards, Governor Hardee expressed surprise that the Board of Control's search for a new president at A&M had been suspended. Subsequent to the meeting, Yonge sent him Sheats's letter of March 27 stating that a majority of the Board of Education were "unqualifiedly in favor of Young." A puzzled Hardee replied, "I wish to state that Mr. Sheats did not discuss the matter with me before writing you and I am just a little surprised that he did not do so."[25]

The Board of Control's failure to find a suitable replacement in 1922 only forestalled Young's inevitable demise. It came the following year on June 11. President Young was given less than two weeks to vacate his office after twenty-two years of service. William H. A. Howard, dean of the School of Mechanical Arts, was selected as interim president, effective immediately, and he was ordered to carry out the course of study adopted the previous year. Students would also be required to pay boarding fees in advance. Howard requested a letter from Yonge that would show that he had not solicited the presidency and that his appointment came without prior notice. He also promised to rid the campus of some its "Kicking Horses," a reference to Young's supporters on the faculty.[26] Several days after Young's dismissal, the Board of Control received a letter from the Executive Committee of the Florida A&M Alumni Association requesting information on the reasons for Young's removal. The Board of Control, not wishing to reopen the matter, declined to respond.[27]

What happened next clearly hit the Board of Control by surprise. A student petition was sent to the Board of Control in early October protesting the appointment of Howard. The board declined to respond to the students and instructed Howard to prevent a strike "even if he had to expel the entire student body."[28] On October 11, a Thursday, Howard notified the Board of Control that a student strike had erupted on campus. His report was rather late, as Board Secretary J. T. Diamond stated that the strike had "spread" on Tuesday. In response, Governor Hardee sent two sheriff's deputies to the campus at the college's expense. The students had not responded to "conciliatory" requests by Howard to return to classes, and Howard recommended the dismissal of the strikers. In an admission that the strike was widespread, he confessed it "would paralyze the work of the School but I see nothing else to do." He also attached a list of the strikers' grievances. The grievances centered on unpaid work that they were required to perform as mandated by the Board of Education's resolutions of July 29, 1921. According to the strikers, work that had been paid in the previous year was now being assigned as class work. The strikers also requested amnesty. The last plea read: "That the girls be allowed to wear their colored Sweaters." It is unclear to what this refers, but it may have been an indication that the changes wrought during Howard's tenure had also infringed on student traditions and culture.[29]

By the time Howard made his dilatory report on October 11, students had already been filing back to school, and Howard felt that the tide had turned in his favor. That night, Duval Hall—the replacement building for the original Duval Hall lost in the 1906 fire—went up in flames. Witnesses stated "that it was ablaze in an instant almost from the ground to the top— it evidently having been well oiled." The members of the Board of Control were wired to come to Tallahassee, but only Wartmann and W. L. Weaver of Perry were available. The two arrived on October 15 and constituted themselves a committee of the board. Before going to the campus, they met with the governor and Diamond.[30] Throughout the turmoil at A&M, Diamond would play a critical role as the board's unofficial representative and local adviser. His disdain for the strikers, and African Americans in general, was evident from the start.

At the campus, Wartmann and Weaver met with the faculty; all expressed their continued loyalty to the institution. Weaver and Wartmann concluded, though, that several were in sympathy with the strikers. The men's dormitories were searched for firearms, but none were found, which Diamond attributed to the expulsion, at Yonge's orders, of thirteen strike leaders. The remaining protestors were told to return to classes the next day. Wartmann felt that order had been restored, and Diamond reported that approximately 150 students, out of 339, had returned.[31] Perhaps fearing something akin to the Ocoee massacre, Wartmann also reported on the mood of the white population in Tallahassee: "There is considerable feeling in the city of Tallahassee and any out breaks or recurrence of disorder on the grounds, would, I fear, cause the people to do something that would be very bad." The same day, Homer Thomas, dean of the college, received a threatening letter. Thomas had been sympathetic to the strikers, and, upon receiving the death threat, left town on the next train. Howard fired him the next day for taking leave without permission.[32]

Yonge was in New York when the strike occurred and wrote Wartmann to ask if he had found anything to indicate whether Nathan Young had been involved in the troubles. Young, though, had long since departed and was already serving as president at Lincoln University in Missouri, where he would finish his career, but not before being dismissed in 1927, reappointed in 1929, and then terminally fired in 1931. He died two years later in Tampa.

Yonge also expressed disappointment with Howard's inability to manage the situation but conceded the situation was difficult. Despite the calmer mood, the two white deputies remained on campus as assurance. "Like all negroes who have any responsibility resting upon them," Diamond argued, "Howard, I am certain, prefers for a white man to be near if any trouble should arise." The board had to cover the costs, however, and Diamond was uncertain how they would pay: "If Howard gives up and resigns now or the Board gives up its policy to make the institution function as a Mechanical and Agricultural College as well as Academic, then the 'Classical niggers' will have won." Yonge concurred with Diamond's assessment and blamed the school's troubles on President Young's "ideals."[33]

By October 30 the rebellion appeared to be over. Howard canceled Halloween parties and removed trash from the buildings to reduce the risk of fire. An article appeared in Florida's leading African American newspaper, the *Florida Sentinel*, condemning the removal of Nathan Young and the state's attack on the college. "These articles seem to be splendid proof that we had settled upon the real cause of the 'strike' at the A. and M. College," Diamond remarked and added, "However, the situation there will be in an unsettled condition as long as 'Classical Niggers' continue to use their influence over the state against any Industrial Education."[34] The semester ended without further incident, and all seemed quiet until January 22, 1924, when a women's dormitory, Gibbs Hall, burned. Diamond reported that it was thought to be an accident. Any doubts, though, that peace had settled on the campus went up in the flames of the Mechanic Arts Building the next day. As the locus of vocational educational, it was a prime target. There were also attempts to torch two other buildings. Four guards were hired to watch the buildings at night.[35]

A mood of desperation hung over the Board of Control as it endeavored to bring the situation under control. On March 13, the board met in an adjourned session with E. D. Vestel, a private detective from Orlando. Vestel was hired at ten dollars per day plus expenses, not to exceed one thousand dollars, to investigate and determine who was behind the arson. A few days later, Vestel reported that his plan was to hire undercover agents to infiltrate the student body while also canvassing the Black community. On April 8, he reported he had hired two operatives in Tallahassee's African American neighborhoods, Frenchtown and Smoky Hollow, but they had been unable to discover anything. He advised ending the investigation and joked that "the only thing we have been able to develop is an expense account." He characterized Leon County sheriff Frank Stoutamire's independent investigation as being "absolutely at sea."[36]

In the meantime, Howard acted on his own initiative. On March 19, Diamond reported that Howard had seen him that afternoon to report that several students had agreed to serve as guards without pay. Howard's visit was followed by one from Sheriff Stoutamire, who informed him that Howard had "purchased a lot of pistols and given them to those negro boys to carry while on guard duty." Some had shotguns and Winchester rifles, and, instead of the several guards reported by Howard, there were between eight and fourteen. Stoutamire had been told to cooperate with Howard and would not disarm the students unless ordered to do so by the Board of Control. Yonge replied that Howard had made a grave mistake when he armed the students, and to do so without the authority and direction of the sheriff only compounded the mistake. Even before this incident, Yonge had questioned whether Howard should continue to serve and once again went to Wartmann for counsel. Wartmann noted that Howard did not have a degree sufficient to be a president, a point that had been raised in the student petition before the strike began. Although Wartmann believed Howard was not adequate to the task, he was also concerned that if Howard was let go it would encourage his enemies. He advocated shutting the college until matters were resolved but admitted that others were unwilling to take such a drastic step. Meanwhile, possible successors to Howard were being approached about their willingness to serve. On May 13, Diamond notified Howard that the Board would not reappoint him president. Howard defended his actions and asked why, after his faithful service to the Board, he was "made the goat" for the college's problems.[37]

This time the search for a permanent appointment was short and focused on an individual suggested to State Superintendent Cawthon by Jackson T. Davis. Davis had taken over from Wallace Buttrick as the field secretary to the General Education Board and would later help found the United Negro College Fund. The person he suggested was John Robert Edward Lee, extension secretary of the National Urban League. Like Nathan Young's succession after the firing of Tucker in 1901, Lee was another odd choice as there was nothing in his background to indicate a willingness to weaken African American education. Born a slave in Seguin, Texas, in 1864, Lee already had a long and successful career before getting the offer to come to Florida. Like Young, he had also served as head of the Academic Department at Tuskegee. Lee was also adamant that he be treated fairly.

When asked to come to Florida to meet with the Board of Control, he insisted on travel expenses even if he rejected an offer. Instead, Yonge went to New York City to meet him. Yonge reported back that Lee was "a man of fine appearance, good education, and good common sense." Negotiations continued, and Lee asked the Board of Control to request additional funds from the General Education Board to supplement his salary. Wartmann was afraid the General Education Board would "expect something that we do not desire" in exchange for the money, and the idea was rejected. Instead, Lee was offered a housing stipend and access to the boarding supplies denied to Young. Lee came to Florida on June 14 to meet with the Board of Control and the governor. Hardee "did not much like the appearance of Lee," but an offer was made. On June 19, Yonge wrote that he did not believe Lee would accept the offer. The next day, he received Lee's acceptance via telegram.[38]

By the time Lee arrived in July 1924, Carey Hardee had only six months left in office. His successor, John Martin, was content to leave well enough alone. Lee quietly went to work. The educational path he pursued was fundamentally the same as that of Nathan Young, but no one in a position of power took issue with President Lee's program. Wartmann's objections notwithstanding, Lee would make good use of his connections with the General Education Board. He was forced to seek its assistance early in his administration when the Board of Control informed him that the college would be forced to shut down early in 1925 due to a lack of funds resulting from the expenses accrued during the student upheaval. An emergency bailout from the General Education Board kept the college afloat. Lee subsequently received a grant of $100,000 for building construction that required the state legislature to provide an additional $250,000. The legislature had little choice but to accept it if it wanted to stay in the board's good graces. All told, Lee's first appropriation for the biennium ending in 1927 totaled $450,000, compared to less than $50,000 in President Young's last budget.[39]

Nathan Young had been closely watching the situation in Florida and did not fail to notice the sudden generosity. Upon hearing that Lee had been appointed president, Young sent a rather conciliatory letter to Chairman Yonge expressing his support and the hope that the college's "unfortunate experiences" might bring "clearer vision and more liberal spirit to those who control it." He added, "Institutions, like individuals, oft times are compelled to pass through periods of 'storm and stress' before making the harbor of their hopes." Upon further hearing that the state had increased the college's budget ninefold since his departure, Young was understandably gobsmacked. In a letter to Lee, a copy of which he sent to Yonge, Young remarked: "During the run of the entire 22 years of my service there the total appropriation of the funds made to your school . . . was less than the amount made by this Legislature, which shows progress all of a sudden by leaps and bounds."[40]

Lee's twenty-year tenure as president of Florida Agricultural and Mechanical College—he would die in office in 1944—was marked by increased enrollments, improvements to the physical plant, and enhancements to the school's academic coursework. After Hardee's departure, the Board of Education's resolutions of July 29, 1921, were either forgotten or ignored. Modern languages were reinstated in Lee's second year; the Board of Control did not object. Under Young, students pursuing a college diploma were limited to a bachelor of sciences degree. By 1930, the catalogue offered a bachelor of arts degree, and a student could major in languages as well as other areas of the humanities, social sciences, and fine arts. Provisional accreditation was awarded in 1931 by the Southern Association of Colleges and Secondary Schools and full accreditation in 1935. The college was unable to completely shed its image as a vocational school and continued to offer a plethora of courses in basic trades. However, the emphasis clearly shifted to the arts and sciences and to the school's original purpose, teacher training.

One by one, the remaining shacks and wooden buildings were demolished and replaced with modern structures. Salaries for administrators and faculty were increased. When it was proposed that Lee's salary be raised to $4,000, Governor Fred Cone angrily and publicly stated that "No Negro is worth $4000." Yet, by the end of his term, even Cone could not deny Lee either the praise or the salary he was due. John Temple Graves III, grandson of the man who labeled Sheats the "school crank" and who advocated the removal of African Americans to the Philippines, paid tribute to Lee, calling him "the principal factor in a physical, mental and spiritual growth whose worth to the South is beyond totaling."[41] This adulation coincided with white southern fears of court-mandated school integration and half-hearted attempts to create at least a veneer of equality. This does not diminish, though, what the students fought for and ultimately achieved. The bravery demonstrated by the A&M student body cannot be overstated. Wartmann's fears of a white backlash were all too real, and the students surely understood the potential repercussions of their actions. We must also acknowledge what transpired afterward and that the aims of the revolt were largely achieved. Although the expelled strike leaders would not enjoy the fruits of that victory, there may still have been the solace of knowing that others would. Rather than serve as a permanent barrier to education, Governor Hardee's assault on African American education may have ultimately hastened much-needed improvements and reforms at Florida A&M.

12

President Murphree's Final Battle

The Roaring Twenties in Florida ceased to roar in the winter of 1927. Until then, they roared mightily. The state's population mushroomed 50 percent in the seven years following World War I, with most of the increase occurring in Southeast Florida. Land values skyrocketed in Miami and elsewhere, and state revenues rose accordingly. As land values rose, speculators arrived and fueled what was already an overheated market. An inevitable market correction began in 1925. The market correction became a freefall, though, when a Category 4 hurricane struck just south of Miami on September 18, 1926, causing extensive property damage and killing hundreds. The land speculation had been further fueled by an unregulated and fraud-riddled banking system. Dozens of uninsured banks fell like dominoes in 1926, erasing millions of dollars in depositors' savings in the process. The final blow to the state's economy came in January 1927, when a freeze impacted Florida's citrus harvest. As freezes go, it was climatologically insignificant, but it was enough to spook already nervous investors. In the chaos that ensued, more banks failed, and investors fled the state. Homeowners found themselves paying taxes on property worth far less than its assessed value. To ease their pain, the state lowered millage rates, and the public coffers dwindled.

In 1927, the University of Florida was experiencing its own boom before the bust. With the tight-fisted Hardee gone, the legislature and Governor Martin loosened the purse strings. The 1925 budget was such that the new School of Pharmacy could be elevated to a college. The professional school had first been placed under the College of Arts and Sciences as a cost-saving measure, even though pharmacy required only three years of instruction and the College of Arts and Sciences mandated four. Out-of-state students were, at last, beginning to show up. The Board of Control could not resist the possibility of a new revenue source and increased out-of-state tuition from forty dollars a year to one hundred. As Murphree predicted it would, out-of-state enrollment at UF dropped from 133 in 1925 to 73 in 1927, negating much of the anticipated revenue increase.[1]

Capital improvements were evident at all the state colleges. A&M was getting its much-needed facelift, and the Women's College added several buildings, including a library and a science building. At the University of Florida, the first phase of a massive administrative and classroom complex was finished in 1923, providing the university with an auditorium that could seat the entire student body. To inspire the students during assemblies, Andrew Anderson, an associate of Henry Flagler, donated $50,000 to purchase and install an impressive pipe organ. At the time, it was the biggest cash gift to the university, and the Anderson Memorial Organ is still providing service today. A second phase called for the addition of twenty-eight lecture rooms, administrative offices for the president and other officers, and a massive carillon facing the university's quadrangle. The first phase of a library building was finished in 1925, providing hundreds of study spaces in a grand second-floor reading room. There was little space for books, though. Subsequent phases were to include stack areas and more study spaces. A chemistry building and a second engineering building to accommodate the two disciplines hit hardest by the enrollment crunch were on the approved building list as well. Murphree was also able to fund a campus beautification project and hired the famous landscape firm Olmsted Brothers to prepare a plan. Olmsted had agreed to do it at half its normal rate because they saw college campuses as a potential growth market for landscapers.[2]

With the uptick in enrollment at the University of Florida, there was a critical need for both a student infirmary and a student recreation center. Both functions were being served by wooden barracks buildings constructed when the campus was briefly employed as a military camp during World War I. The barracks became "poster children" in the alumni magazine and inspired a capital campaign led by the YMCA to erect a student union. Murphree enlisted the "Great Commoner," William Jennings Bryan, to act as the front man for the campaign. Bryan had been among the tens of thousands who moved to Florida. His Florida home, Villa Serena, was located next to the estate of his cousin, former governor William Sherman Jennings. Bryan served as a Florida delegate to the 1924 Democratic convention, and without notifying Murphree, much less getting his approval, Bryan nominated Murphree as a candidate for the presidency of the United States. The nomination was ignored and proved to be an embarrassment to both men. Oddly, though, Murphree had been approached about a possible

Figure 13. Architect's depiction of proposed administrative and classroom complex at the University of Florida. Construction started in 1921, but only the auditorium portion was built. University Archives Photograph Collection, George A. Smathers Libraries, University of Florida.

run for the governorship in 1924 but declined owing to the recent death of his wife.[3]

The Board of Control submitted an ambitious budget of $7.5 million for the 1927 legislative session before the cumulative effects of the previous months became apparent. On January 29, Governor Martin, citing the decline in property values, the hurricane, the freeze, and a drop in cotton prices, informed the Board of Control that it could not recommend a budget in excess of $4.5 million. The board was asked to resubmit its request. The board met in special session in Jacksonville on February 5 with the college presidents in attendance. The governor's letter was read into the minutes. Yonge and the Board of Control reduced the budget request to $5.36 million, with the State College for Women taking significantly larger cuts than the university.[4] "I came away from Jacksonville, yesterday, thoroughly depressed and discouraged, as much or more on your account than for any other reason," Murphree told Yonge. Murphree began to look for items that could be cut, including a basketball gymnasium and steel stacks in the library. "If any other cut is required," he informed Yonge, "I see no way out but to reduce the salary scale. That would destroy the morale and disturb the faculty, and I fear would issue in serious embarrassment to the University." In the same letter, Murphree also objected to plans to build a gymnasium at the State College when other needs were more pressing. Board secretary Diamond warned that more cuts might be forthcoming. Murphree wrote back that he was "awfully blue and depressed."[5]

The Board of Control's recommendation was rejected by Governor Martin in a curt letter dated February 16 indicating the $4.5 million target was non-negotiable. This was followed by a letter on February 19 apologizing for the tone of his previous letter: "[I] did not intend, if I have, to in any way write you a letter that might be construed as being rude."[6] Two board members, W. B. Davis and Albert Blanding, took a hard-line stance on further reductions. Davis, who shared a law practice with Claude Pepper in Perry, argued that the board had only to submit its budget request and that it was up to the Budget Commission and the legislature to finalize it. After making its case for why the money was needed, the board needed to be "in the clear" if the budget was reduced. Board member E. W. Lane, president of the Atlantic National Bank and a Martin appointee, disagreed and considered the Budget Commission's numbers to be "very liberal." Lane was also promoting the creation of a plenipotentiary on the Board of Control who would oversee the colleges. Murphree derisively referred to it as the "superman" and "super lord." Lane was also advocating extensive programmatic cuts in higher education, including the elimination of graduate work. "When he gets his superman, a direct agent of the Board at $6000 a year, over all of us, it is barely possible we will have anything left," Murphree lamented.[7]

Florida's failing economy was also having an impact on the fundraising work of the University of Florida Alumni Association. In late January, after the freeze, Executive Secretary Ralph Stoutamire asked Association president Raymer Maguire whether the Association's fundraising and membership drive should be suspended in Central Florida. Raymer Maguire received a law degree from the University of Florida in 1915. He went on to become a successful lawyer in Orlando and a founding partner of Maguire & Voorhis, whose clients included many of the growers in the region. Maguire recommended the campaign be suspended for at least six weeks. By then, the growers would realize that high market prices would compensate for much of their freeze losses. Maguire's letter went on to discuss more mundane Association issues before he turned to the university's budget. Stoutamire had asked whether it would be proper to print President Murphree's budget proposal in the Association's magazine, the *Florida Alumnus*. Maguire reasoned that no one could object to this and stated that, in his opinion, the college presidents needed to be more active and vocal on behalf of their institutions:

> I have thought this matter over a very great deal recently, and I have come to the conclusion that there is very little difference between the operations of a great university and the operation of any other kind of business. The commercial business has to advertise its wares and place them before the public in order that it may procure purchasers and thereby obtain revenue with which to meet expenses and receive a profit. A university must sell its wares to the people of the State who contribute the funds with which to maintain it.... If a State university is unable to present such opportunities to the youth of the State, because of lack of facilities, then it is up to the head of the university to apply to its stockholders, who are the citizens of the State, for more money with which to carry on.[8]

It is doubtful Maguire was familiar with Thorstein Veblen's satirical depiction of university builders as "captains of erudition," similar in drive and ambition to capitalism's "captains of industry." But his perception of a modern university president was not off the mark. University presidents looked to corporations for inspiration and ideas and sought greater efficiency in the delivery of education. Increasingly, universities took on the administrative appearance of a modern corporation, with large numbers of managerial staff. The proliferation of university vice presidents was still a couple of decades in the future, but the numbers of nonteaching staff increased steadily in the 1920s. Andrew Sledd had only a single business manager and one stenographer to support his office. By 1927, that same business manager, Klein Graham, had five people under him, and each college dean, as well as the president, had his own office secretary. Presidents of large public universities, such as Charles Van Hise at the University of Wisconsin, were not at all reluctant to sell their educational wares to both their customers and their financial backers. In Wisconsin and elsewhere, university presidents promoted and advertised the services of their institutions before luncheons of civic and business organizations and in the halls of state legislatures. In Florida, though, it was unclear if presidents enjoyed that freedom.

Maguire sent a copy of his letter to Murphree, and, in a brief reply, Murphree consented to have the budget proposal published. It was, after all, a matter of public record. However, he informed Maguire that the presidents, as subordinates of the Board of Control, could not engage in a public campaign to influence the governor or the legislature. Maguire was puzzled by that and replied: "The phase of the matter which you present had not occurred to me for this reason—I had never thought of you as a subordinate from standpoint of position you occupy with regard to the University of Florida. In other words, I have always looked upon you as the absolute head of the organization. Nevertheless, I realize that technically the Board of Control is a higher authority. But I do not personally regard it as a higher authority in any other particular."[9]

The exchange of letters began early in the winter, before the Budget Commission reduced the Board of Control's budget to $4.5 million. Shortly after the budget meeting in Jacksonville, Murphree wrote Maguire to explain the new budget situation and to caution him about Ralph Stoutamire's confrontational tendencies. He also referenced a proposal being advanced by Senate president William C. Hodges. What Senator Hodges had in mind was an additional fee on automobile licenses that would fund school building projects. Construction requests would then be separated from the Board of Control's requests for continued funding. Murphree went on to talk more about the presidents' relationship with the Board of Control and that board's relationship to the State Budget Commission and the Board of Education: "My opinion is that it is unwise to attempt to put something over the Board of Control and the State Budget Commission. It will only make them mad, and will be an insuperable obstacle to our ultimate goal. Why not lay plans to cooperate in a movement for the building project as above suggested, and suggest to Ralph, who has never been known for his extra amount of tact and good judgment, to refrain from publicity which indicates that the Alumni are making a fight on the Boards?" Maguire concurred in Murphree's assessment of Stoutamire. He also urged Murphree to reconsider his position on campaigning openly on behalf of the university: "Under the circumstances as they now exist, I am strongly inclined to the view, and this is not without basis for the conclusion, that the Board of Control will not object to your taking a more aggressive attitude and will not consider such an attitude one of insubordination."[10]

Murphree's insistence on absolute subordination was somewhat disingenuous given his long history of behind-the-scenes politicking. Yet he had always been careful never to go public with his comments, and he always prefaced letters to politicians and other influential people with a reference to "utmost confidentiality" or "strictest privacy." Murphree had become adept at navigating the backwaters of Florida politics, which made his next reply to Maguire so out of character: "I want to say this finally: The only question in my own mind is, what is the best thing to do in the immediate present for the larger future interest of the University? I am ready to offer myself as a sacrifice, and will do say gladly, if a fight is necessary, and it is thought to be my duty to enter into it. I am for the University, first, last and always. My connection with the institution is of no consequence to me if by sacrificing that relationship I can serve the University in a larger and more effective way."[11]

Maguire closed his next letter by stating, "Your connection with the University of Florida is of tremendous consequence to me and I do not want to see your relationship with it terminated, nor do I want to see your efforts of the past twenty years sacrificed for lack of funds." Murphree, in turn, reiterated his willingness to participate in a public campaign, but he would first seek the Board of Control's approval: "I wish to say again that the politicians at Tallahassee can, in no way, intimidate me. But knowing the temper of some of them, I know that they will use their efforts to kick me out when I begin an active and open campaign against their policies with reference to appropriations. I shall discuss this matter with the Board of Control, which meets here next Sunday night and Monday morning, and ask the Board's approval of an active campaign against the action of the State Budget Commission."[12]

Did President Murphree have Yonge's consent to go public with his comments? It is almost certain he did, and it was Yonge, not Murphree, who had requested the private meeting in Gainesville.[13] The Board of Control could not lobby the governor or the legislature, either as individuals or as a group, nor could it engage in a public relations campaign on behalf of higher education. It could, however, give tacit support to a campaign waged by an alumni association and allow the president to take an active and visible role in that campaign. Regardless, Murphree and Yonge had a long association, and it is unlikely that Murphree would have injured that relationship with a rogue action. Murphree's decision to come out of the shadows in the 1927 budget fight may have stemmed from any number of factors. He was more than thirty years into his career as a college president, and he simply may have felt safe in his position. Or he may have felt that it was pointless to continue as president if his budget was subjected to frequent decimation. He also had options if the worst should happen, and he was asked to step down. He had recently turned down an offer to go to Wake Forest and confided to the president of Furman University that he would have accepted the offer had it been made six months earlier.[14]

As president of the Alumni Association, Maguire would lead the campaign, but he also drew on the support and advice of other association officers. One was Herbert Felkel, editor of the *St. Augustine Record*. Felkel's journalism career got under way in 1907 while he was attending the University of Florida. Felkel founded and served as editor of the *Florida Pennant*, the first genuine student publication at the post-Buckman University of Florida. However, an unsanctioned cartoon and doggerel lampooning the commandant of cadets got him into hot water with the administration, and he was expelled before he could graduate.[15] Another member of Maguire's group was Turner Zeigler "T.Z." Cason (Class of 1908), a prominent Jacksonville physician. Much later in life he would play a pivotal role in the creation of the medical center at the University of Florida. A third member was the association's vice president, Philip "Phil" Stockton May (Class of 1911), a Jacksonville lawyer. May and Cason shared a client and patient in the person of novelist Marjorie Kinnan Rawlings. In 1947, Zelma Cason, T.Z.'s sister, would sue the novelist for invasion of privacy over an unpleasant character that appeared in Rawlings's novel *Cross Creek*. Locals instantly recognized the character as Zelma. Phil May assisted in Rawlings's unsuccessful defense.[16]

Maguire, Cason, Felkel, and May had excellent connections to Florida's economic and political elites. They understood the political process and were accustomed to working with politicians. Their campaign would be far more professional than earlier Alumni Association efforts and would rely as much on persuasion as pressure. Both were applied effectively. Roger Babson oversaw the press campaign, and Murphree kept him informed of the latest "dope" on the budget situation.[17] Babson also put together a fact sheet that became the basis for press contacts as well as speaking engagements. The facts spoke for themselves. The University of Florida was grossly underfunded and in critical need of additional teaching staff and adequate salaries to retain those it had.

Maguire and the Alumni Association team spoke before dozens of civic and professional groups, and at each venue they were usually able to convince the group to send a resolution to the governor and the legislature urging them to approve the Board of Control's original budget request. In late March, Murphree delivered a major address before the State Chamber of Commerce that resulted in the Chamber, at the behest of Peter O. Knight, passing a resolution to restore the millage rate to the pre-1927 level in order to fund education. Among the organizations Governor Martin heard from was the Florida Bar Association. The resolution passed by the Florida Bar was weaker than what Maguire had hoped, largely due to the opposition of two former members of the Board of Control, Francis P. Fleming Jr. and John C. Cooper Jr. Privately, though, Fleming, son of Governor Francis P. Fleming, offered to personally intercede with Governor Martin on behalf of the Board of Control.[18]

By the end of March, Martin was feeling the pressure, as attested by a gloomy letter he wrote to Stanton Walker at the Atlantic National Bank decrying the many friends who were now criticizing him. Martin was unaware that Walker was one of those friends, and Walker shared the letter with Maguire, who, in turn, passed it on to Murphree.[19] On April 13, a bill was introduced in the House to earmark a half mill for building construction at all levels of public education. That same day, John Kellum was busy courting legislators on behalf of the state colleges. After being sacked as secretary to the Board of Control by Governor Catts in 1917, Kellum maintained his position as business manager at Florida State and continued to utilize his Tallahassee connections to gather information. Kellum also met with Governor Martin, who expressed a willingness to use automobile license fees for building construction as well as an increase in the millage rate.[20]

Kellum's information was confirmed in another conversation that Martin had with Herbert Felkel. According to Felkel, Martin would publicly continue to preach economy and voice support for the Budget Commission's proposal. But he made it clear to Felkel that he would not veto the legislature's appropriation if it was higher than the recommendation of the commission. "The fight will be won or lost on the floors of the House and Senate," Felkel proclaimed. Martin also disclosed that midway through the legislative session he would make a special address calling for an automobile license tax that would support higher education. The governor closed his conversation with Felkel by requesting that the Alumni Association cease its campaign.[21]

Maguire thought it too soon to stop. The prevailing opinion in the Alumni Association was that more could be attained from the legislature than from the State Budget Commission, which had expanded to include all cabinet-level officials in 1925. The Budget Commission was also sending mixed messages. At the same time Martin was sounding conciliatory in his conversations with Kellum and Felkel, the Budget Commission was putting additional pressure on the Board of Control and the presidents. The Budget Commission had recommended that $350,000 be taken out of salaries and positions and moved into building construction, and further proposed that salary negotiations be removed from the powers of the Board of Control. Who, exactly, would exercise that power was not stated, but the commission's recommendation on salaries clearly echoed the orders given by the Board of Education in 1922. "What is the use of buildings, unless we have enough teachers to teach the boys who attend the University?" Murphree lamented. He added: "What knowledge the State Budget Commission had of the needs of the University to enable it to make up a budget of the institutions is quite beyond our comprehension. With the exception of the State Superintendent of Public Instruction, I do not believe any other member of the State Budget Commission has spent two hours altogether on this campus in seventeen years."[22]

By May, Murphree had a clearer picture of the budget situation and had been summoned to Tallahassee to appear before the Joint Committee on Appropriations. The rumors concerning an additional source of income for building construction were circulating again, and Murphree urged the Alumni Association to focus on operating expenses, salaries, and equipment. Maguire responded: "We are bending every effort to bring forth the necessary pressure. . . . Copies of resolutions have been coming in from civic groups from points as far south in the State as Key West, and strong ones at that."[23] When Murphree arrived in Tallahassee to speak with legislators, he found that a quorum of committee members was not available. Instead, he met with the governor and the House and Senate leaders, Fred Vals and William C. Hodges. At that meeting, a tentative and somewhat complicated deal was reached whereby education construction would be removed from appropriations. A $4 million building fund was to be established using revenue from several sources including the $1.50 auto license tax as well as a one-cent-per-gallon-of-gas increase at filling station pumps. The new gas tax shifted the tax burden from property owners to automobile owners. John Watson, who initiated the gas tax bill in the legislature, defended the bill by noting that "⅓ of our gas tax is paid by tourists, Negroes and others who pay no ad valorem taxes." Sixty percent of the fund would go to local schools; the remaining 40 percent would be split between the university and the state college. The university's $800,000 share was $300,000 less than the requested amount but $100,000 more than what Murphree confided was absolutely necessary.[24]

With specific revenue streams earmarked for building construction, the legislative appropriation could focus on operating expenses. Martin, Vals, and Hodges suggested a budget that would restore the university's salary and positions requests, and Murphree urged the Alumni Association to accept the deal. Although it was far short of the original budget proposal, there was mutual agreement that it was the best offer they were going to get from the governor and the Budget Commission. If the plan was not accepted, the entire budget would be thrown on the legislature with unpredictable results. Raymer Maguire was less than satisfied with the results of their hard work but grudgingly accepted the outcome: "I can say to you absolutely and unquestionably that I have worked harder on the plan of raising money and on the proposition of obtaining appropriations than I have ever worked on any single proposition, or a number of them, in all my life, and while I won't admit that I am licked I must say that the results are not what I should like."[25]

The final act approved by the legislature and signed by Martin on May 30 differed significantly from the agreement worked out in Tallahassee, but the net effect for the colleges was largely the same. The auto license fee was replaced by a one-quarter mill levy on personal and real property plus two-thirds of the interest accrued on state funds deposited in state banks. The portion allocated to local schools did not go to building construction but, rather, to a Public Free School Equalization Fund to alleviate disparities in tax revenues among the individual counties. Also, 14 percent of the Permanent Building Fund for the State Institutions of Higher Learning was appropriated for the Florida School for the Deaf and Blind and FAMU, with UF and Florida State splitting the remaining 86 percent. In its first six months, the fund took in $437,000. Assuming similar incomes in the remaining eighteen months, UF and Florida State would have earned approximately $752,000 each, or about $50,000 less than the anticipated income. The gas tax proposed in 1927 was implemented in the 1929 session.[26]

It would be an overstatement to characterize the Alumni Association's 1927 campaign as a model for advocacy on behalf of higher education. Yet it clearly marked a new phase in Florida whereby university presidents and their proxies directly engaged not only the public but also those who wielded power. It would have been interesting to see Murphree navigate the new political landscape in subsequent years, but he would die less than eight months after his meeting with Governor Martin. Murphree, though, surely understood the significance of what happened in 1927. Once the 1927 budget was approved, Murphree had to make the difficult decisions regarding which buildings would be constructed and which would have to be put off indefinitely. His primary needs were classroom space and additional dormitories. To meet those needs, Murphree chose not to complete

Figure 14. The University of Florida Auditorium, circa 1925. The north wall remained unfinished until an addition was made in 1977. University Archives Photograph Collection, George A. Smathers Libraries, University of Florida.

the subsequent phases of the library and the administration building. This left exposed on both buildings, massive, unadorned, and unfinished walls that were intended as interior walls. A truncated south wing to the library was built in 1931, but a larger north wing and a stack area were not added until 1949. The blank north wall of the University Auditorium remained until 1977, bearing silent testimony to Florida's economic collapse in 1927 and years of institutional conflict.

Postscript

More Revolutions and Then the Counterrevolution

Unlike the first two presidential appointments, the selection of the University of Florida's third president was not the least bit controversial. After reviewing a list of candidates that included the former high school inspector candidate Joseph Byrne Lockey, who had gone on to a distinguished academic career as a Latin American historian at the University of California, the Board of Control focused on one, US Commissioner of Education John James Tigert. Florida senator Duncan Upshaw Fletcher recommended Tigert for the position and referred to him as "the man for the place." The Board of Control offered Tigert the position in March 1928; he arrived in September while the state was still recuperating from the Bust of 1927. Any hopes for recovery were dashed in October 1929, when the rest of the nation followed Florida into economic depression.[1]

President Tigert saw the University of Florida through the difficult days of depression and world war. He announced his retirement in 1946 just as thousands of veterans arrived to take advantage of the benefits provided by the Servicemen's Readjustment Act of 1944. Enrollment at the University of Florida before the war had never exceeded 3,500. By the end of academic year 1946–47, enrollment had passed the 6,000 mark. The university took all the veterans it could manage, and Florida's private colleges took their share, but there were still thousands of unserved applicants. In response, about 2,000 male veterans were enrolled at the Florida State College for Women in 1946. To sustain the fiction of gender segregation, the men were registered as University of Florida students. Concurrently, a much smaller cohort of women arrived at the University of Florida. These were the wives of male veterans attending the university. The peculiar arrangements at both schools lasted just one year before a sweeping change knocked out one of the central pillars of the Buckman Act.

Millard Caldwell ran for governor in 1944 with a promise to improve Florida's undeniably substandard public school system. A blue-ribbon commission on education issued its report in the winter of 1947, and among its many recommendations was one to end gender restrictions at the white state colleges. Caldwell included the recommendation in his message to the 1947 legislative session, and the legislature complied. With the change, the University of Florida lost whatever claim it might have had to superiority over Florida State. Both institutions would draw from the same pool of high school students and would make similar arguments before the Board of Control and legislature for funding. The two white universities would enjoy a decade of relative calm and growth before the next Buckman pillar collapsed.

The institutional dam created by the Buckman Act was fatally breached in 1956 with the creation of the University of South Florida in Tampa. As Edward Conradi and others predicted in 1913, the flood followed the breach. More state universities emerged in Boca Raton, Pensacola, Orlando, Miami, and Jacksonville, making a total of nine by 1965, one more than the number of state schools that existed prior to Buckman. Arguments from Florida State and the University of Florida that they were different and more deserving than the others fell on the deaf ears of resource allocators and incurred the scorn of South Florida politicians, who had little sympathy for the two institutions located in underpopulated North Florida. From the postwar years until 1970, the University of Florida rose slowly in national rankings of state universities. The 1970s, though, showed significant decline. In a 1978 faculty salary survey of 184 public universities, the University of Florida ranked 157th, below Middle Tennessee State University, Ball State University, and Oklahoma State University. Assistant professors were leaving the university at an alarming rate. As Linton Grinter, dean emeritus of the Graduate School at the University of Florida, noted in 1979, the net result of the legislature's insistence on equality of funding was the maintenance of nine mediocre universities with no center of excellence.[2]

While Florida's universities struggled mightily to maintain even their inferior spots in the national rankings, the state did manage to make a major contribution to the nation's inventory of postsecondary schools. Largely through the brilliance and fortitude of one individual, James L. Wattenbarger, Florida would develop one of the earliest statewide integrated systems of junior colleges. The two-year junior college appeared in the early part of the twentieth century and had become a popular higher education alternative by the 1930s. To some degree, junior colleges replaced the normal school as a teacher conveyor belt for the nation's public schools. The associate of arts in education degree briefly replaced the LI as the requisite teacher degree before it, too, was displaced by the bachelor's in education degree. As with the normal schools before them, America's early junior colleges were stand-alone institutions, each possessing its own curriculum and purpose.

What James Wattenbarger had in mind, though, was something quite different. Wattenbarger himself had graduated from Florida's first public junior college, Palm Beach Junior College, in 1941.[3] Like many junior college graduates, Wattenbarger entered the field of education. He continued his pedagogical training in the College of Education at the University of Florida, where he would earn his next three degrees. The last came in 1950 with the approval of his doctoral dissertation, "The Organization, Administration, and Financing of Public Junior Colleges in the State of Florida." The dissertation was further refined in 1953 with the publication of *A State Plan for Public Junior Colleges*. Perhaps the most influential dissertation ever written at the University of Florida, it became the inspiration for Florida's community college system after Wattenbarger was recruited by Governor LeRoy Collins to transform the dissertation into a plan of action. The plan came to fruition in 1957, when the legislature created the Division of Community Colleges. The plan called for the construction of twenty-eight campuses located in such a way as to provide an easy commute for all but a few potential students. Physical ease of access was further augmented by open admissions. In a departure from university policy, Wattenbarger eschewed the Florida 12th Grade Placement Examination, administered by the State Board of Examiners at the University of Florida, as a requirement for enrollment. Instead, movement from high school to college was carefully articulated by the completion of specific courses enumerated in a common course numbering system. That numbering system was also employed at the junior college level and allowed for the easy transfer of credits to a four-year college. Florida's state universities were compelled to accept junior college graduates, and the associate of arts degree became the academic gateway to the state universities for thousands of students, many from underprivileged backgrounds who otherwise would have been denied admission. Within a few years of the plan's implementation, junior college enrollment in Florida jumped from 600 to more than 6,000. The State Board of Junior [later Community] Colleges was created to govern the new system.[4]

Wattenbarger's initial research began when Florida was still firmly in the grips of Jim Crow segregation. By the time his plan was implemented, Florida was under court order to desegregate its schools, and the painstakingly slow process of desegregation was under way. The first African American admitted to a formerly white university was George Starke, a US Air Force veteran who entered the College of Law at the University of Florida in 1958. Integration was initially limited to professional and graduate schools. Undergraduate programs at all state universities were desegregated in the early 1960s. Ten years after George Starke was accepted, there were still fewer than 100 Black students at the University of Florida. As late as academic year 1978–79, FAMU enrolled more African American high school students than the other four-year state universities combined.[5]

With the end of gender segregation, the slow beginnings of racial integration, and the expansion of the state university system, there remained only one vestige of the Buckman Act of 1905, the Florida Board of Control. It, too, would soon pass into history.

The Florida Board of Control's checkered history came to an end in 1964 with the creation of the Florida Board of Regents. The demise of the Board of Control was hastened by a series of investigations into left-wing activity and homosexuality by the Florida Legislative Investigation Committee, headed by Florida Senate president Charley Johns of Starke. The stated purpose of the Johns Committee was to root out Communist influence in the civil rights movement. When that failed to produce any results, Johns shifted the committee's focus from the Red Menace to the Lavender Menace. In the 1950s and 1960s, gays and lesbians were depicted as subversive elements seeking to indoctrinate naïve youth into a lifestyle deemed perverse and un-American. To do his dirty work, Johns employed investigators familiar with vice squad tactics who had little regard for due process and none for academic proceedings.

Although it was not limited to higher education, or education more generally, the Johns Committee had its most dramatic impact on the University of Florida. At the conclusion of the committee's investigations there, fourteen faculty and staff at the University of Florida were summarily dismissed. No hearings, public or private, were conducted to examine the evidence; they were simply called to the president's office and terminated. Among them were several with decades of teaching experience. Not included among the fourteen who were immediately let go was a law professor named Philip K. Yonge, grandson of former Board of Control chair Philip K. Yonge. His name provided some protection, and he was given a year's leave to find another position. The number of students affected by the investigations will never be known as student records are sealed. Furthermore, expulsion was not always mandated. Gay students under the age of majority were often referred to the infirmary's psychiatric unit for treatment. The head of psychiatry, though, was no fan of the Johns Committee. "Other problems—such as alcohol and heterosexual behavior of students—need investigating more than the homosexuals," contested Dr. Henry C. Schumacher.[6]

By the time the Johns Committee had concluded its attacks, the cumulative effect of decades of political intrusion into the affairs of the Board of Control had taken its toll. A 1963 study on Florida's education needs commissioned by the Board of Control described the ongoing turmoil as "an imposed routine of political flavor, delay, intrusion of wholly extraneous factors, and depreciation of higher education," and concluded, "Continuation of this system would destroy all possibility of achieving greatness for Florida in the space era."[7] The Board of Control's fifty-eight years of contested authority came to an end in 1964 with the creation of the Florida Board of Regents. To reduce outside influence, the new board would have nine members serving nine-year staggered terms. Politics, though, intruded before the new board could even get started. As governor in 1964, Farris Bryant would appoint the first regents, and he attempted to fill all nine seats before his term ended in January 1965. When Governor-elect Haydon Burns challenged Bryant's monopoly on appointments, the Florida Supreme Court ruled in his favor, allowing Burns to name his own appointees. In response, Bryant's entire board resigned in protest. Burn's aggressive move cast a pall over the future of the board.[8]

The Board of Regents was granted the authority to appoint presidents, *without review*, and, after 1967, the Budget Commission no longer approved line-item appropriations for state universities. Authority for campus planning and construction, which had been centralized under the Office of the Architect for the Board of Control, was turned over to each university in 1967. However, some semblance of order was achieved through the Public Education Capital Outlay (PECO) list, a numerical list of buildings approved and ranked by the Board of Regents. Much to the chagrin of University of Florida president J. Wayne Reitz, who vowed never to serve under a chancellor, the legislature delegated executive administrative responsibilities for the state university system to a university chancellor in 1965. By 2000, the chancellor's office had expanded to include two vice chancellors and seven administrative and support staff. Increasingly, the Board of Regents looked to the chancellor for overall direction and budgeting decisions.[9]

E. Travis York, known to all as E. T., was appointed state chancellor in 1974. York was an agriculturalist who had served in various capacities at different land grant universities before accepting the position of provost for agriculture at the University of Florida in 1963. Later, he served as the university's chief academic officer. As someone who had spent a large part of his career in Florida, he was well acquainted with both the strengths and weaknesses of the system he was called upon to lead. He was also aware of the increasing dissatisfaction inside and outside academia with the governance system. York focused on budgeting and was able to convince the legislature and the governor that Florida State and the University of Florida should serve as the state's primary institutions for advanced graduate education and faculty research. York was also sympathetic to the presidents' desires for greater independence. He encouraged more local autonomy regarding capital outlays and advocated, unsuccessfully, for differential tuition rates. Yet, he was committed to centralized governance and opposed any attempts to undermine or circumvent the existing system. York retired as chancellor in 1980 but maintained close ties with his successors as well as administrators at the University for Florida.

Despite the reforms implemented by York and his successors, dissatisfaction with the governance system persisted. In the 1980s and 1990s, there were several legislative attempts to dilute the powers of the Board of Regents. One such attempt came close to fruition in 1980, when the state legislature passed an omnibus bill to create boards of trustees for each state university while also increasing the size of the Board of Regents from nine to thirteen members. The bill also provided a role for the Board of Education in higher education but fell far short of the authority granted in the Buckman Act. Only a veto by Governor Bob Graham prevented the bill from becoming law. There was also displeasure from within the state universities, much of it aimed at the stifling and growing bureaucracy surrounding the regents and the chancellor. A "bunch of micromanaging petty bureaucratic fascists" is how one unhappy department chair described them.[10]

Although there was bipartisan support for reform in the 1980s, it was the ascendency of the Republican Party in Florida in the 1990s that brought radical change. By 1998 the Republican Party controlled both houses of the legislature, the governor's office, and most of the cabinet. The Florida Board of Regents quickly became a target of conservative politicians. The specific catalyst for change was the Board of Regents' reluctance to endorse the creation of a College of Medicine at Florida State and law schools at FAMU and Florida International University. The creation of all three was part of a complicated deal worked out by House Speaker John Thrasher before the 2000 legislative session. The board would eventually relent but only after considerable political pressures were brought to bear. As legend has it, the idea to reorganize the state university system was suggested to Governor Jeb Bush in a dinner meeting with Thrasher during which Thrasher was said to have outlined the plan on a napkin.[11]

Thrasher's plan would not have been possible except for a constitutional revision approved by voters in 1998 that resulted in an overhaul of Florida's cabinet system and a new State Board of Education. Under the new cabinet organization, the positions of state treasurer and state comptroller were combined as the chief financial officer (CFO). The number of elected cabinet positions was reduced to three: the CFO, the attorney general, and the secretary of agriculture and consumer affairs. The remaining cabinet officers would be appointed. The members of the State Board of Education would be appointed by the governor, and the board, in turn, would select the commissioner of education. The revisions eliminated the diffused "collegiate" executive that had existed for more than one hundred years and gave the governor ultimate authority over education.

Higher education was not mentioned in the 1998 constitutional amendment. Yet the revisions became the justification for a bold proposal that would place all public education, from kindergarten through graduate school, under the umbrella of the Department of Education and, by extension, the governor's office. The Blue Ribbon Committee on Education Governance, created in 1999 to explore various possibilities and options, made its final recommendations in February 2000. The most significant structural changes contained in the committee's recommendation included the replacement of the Board of Regents and the State Board of Community Colleges with departmental divisions for both and the creation of local boards of trustees for each of the state universities. The 2000 legislature responded with the passage of the Florida Education Governance Reorganization Act, which embraced most of the recommendations made by the committee. The changes became effective on January 7, 2003, when the Florida Board of Education assumed authority for all aspects of public education. To assure a smooth transition in the interim, the Reorganization Act created the Education Governance Reorganization Transition Task Force. Governor Bush urged the task force to "think big, bold and visionary." Bush, though, had refrained from taking a public position on higher education, providing some hope to supporters of the Board of Regents that he could be persuaded to change course. The two-year delay in implementation also allowed opponents of the Reorganization Act an opportunity to act.[12]

Although support for the Board of Regents came largely from Democratic leaders, several influential Republicans also voiced their support, including Chancellor Adam Herbert and former chancellor E. T. York. York would play a central role in the effort to preserve the Board of Regents and, later, in the campaign to create a Board of Governors. Throughout, York maintained a friendship and correspondence with Jeb Bush and hoped to use his influence to convince the governor to maintain some level of statewide governance. Thinking Bush amenable to alternatives that would be politically less risky, York suggested measures that would soften the blows rendered by the Reorganization Act while maintaining its key features.

York looked to North Carolina as a potential model for Florida. Historically speaking, the two state university systems could not be more different. Florida opted to eliminate its minor schools in 1905, whereas North Carolina chose the path taken by other southern states and allowed its schools to grow and evolve. Academies became normal schools, which became colleges, which became universities. Today, there are sixteen public university campuses in North Carolina, seven of which are campuses of the University of North Carolina. The remaining nine include three formerly white normal schools, the land grant North Carolina State University, and not one, but five, HBCUs, including the designated land grant for African Americans, North Carolina A&T University. Among the UNC campuses, Chapel Hill is the oldest and the flagship campus; UNC Pembroke began as a school for Native Americans; and UNC Greensboro had been the state college for women. UNC also maintains a School of the Arts in Winston-Salem, the first public arts conservatory in the nation.

The University of North Carolina's historical path resembled other flagship systems with the main and branch campuses operating under one Board of Trustees. The campuses outside the UNC network looked to their respective boards for guidance and governance. After World War II, problems arose as each school outside the UNC system became a university and added programs that often duplicated the work undertaken at UNC. By the late 1960s, it was evident that a new governance system was required to restore academic coherence and prevent further conflict and erosion. In a 1971 constitutional revision, the UNC Board of Trustees became the

Board of Governors for all sixteen campuses, and each campus, including those previously under the old UNC Board of Trustees, would maintain its own board of trustees. The thirty-two members of the Board of Governors would determine overall policy for the sixteen universities, mediate disputes over academic programs, and provide guidance to each university. The local boards would select presidents and other key administrators, grant tenure to faculty, oversee distinctly local matters, and submit budget proposals to the Board of Governors. Consequently, North Carolina became the first state with a statewide board of governors and local boards for each university.[13]

On October 2, 2000, York faxed Governor Bush his recommendation for a "modified version of the North Carolina plan" that reduced the powers of the Board of Regents and allowed for the creation of semi-independent local boards. The next day he met with the governor and John Winn, a member of the Board of Education—and, later, commissioner of education—to discuss his plan. He came away from the meeting with the impression Bush was supportive. In a follow-up email he urged Bush to make his views known to the task force. Later that month, University of Florida president Chuck Young and University of Florida provost David Colburn lunched with task force chair Phil Handy, and they both concluded that Handy had already made up his mind and would reject the creation of an intermediate board when the task force made its final recommendations in December. York appealed once more to Governor Bush.[14]

Although York continued to hold out hope that Bush would intercede on behalf of the Board of Regents, others were far less sanguine about the governor's intentions. Opposition to the Reorganization Act suffered a decisive blow in November, when the Council of Academic Vice Presidents stated that an intermediate board was unnecessary and would add "a layer of bureaucracy that may stifle the independence of the local campuses and hamper their advancement." York considered the statement an act of political capitulation and not representative of their actual views. This may have been true to some extent, but York clearly underestimated the degree to which the statement reflected the actual sentiments of the universities. Provost David Colburn, who had signed the statement, explained the situation to York. Although Colburn would have preferred the status quo and the retention of the Board of Regents, that was no longer an option. Given the possible options of independent boards with or without an intermediate board, without seemed the better of the two. In an apologetic email to York, Chuck Young agreed with his provost. Also jumping ship were former UF president Marshall Criser, who agreed to be the first chair of the University of Florida's Board of Trustees, and University of North Florida president Ann Hopkins, who had earlier stated that the loss of the Board of Regents would be a disaster.[15] In despair, York questioned his ongoing commitment to a losing battle. "Perhaps I am too passionate about this," he wrote to Chuck Young. "However, what is being done is obviously wrong and will, I firmly believe, be to the detriment of our university system and especially to the University of Florida. Moreover, it is being done through the exercise of raw political power which is very troubling to me." Two weeks later, the Education Governance Reorganization Transition Task Force issued its final report, and it did not include a recommendation for an intermediate board.[16]

While York and others fought to retain a central board, attention shifted to a proposal made by Senator—and former governor—Bob Graham to put a constitutional amendment on the ballot in 2002 mandating the creation of a board of governors for the state university system. At the time, thirty-five states conferred constitutional status to their governance boards. However, few states provided clear articulation as to the powers and responsibilities of those boards, and only a handful of states allowed the boards to operate even semi-autonomously. Case law more often determined the extent of authority in any particular state. York offered his assistance to Graham, but soon found himself heading the group leading the charge, the Excellence in Education Foundation. (It was York who suggested that the new central board be called the Board of Governors rather than the Board of Regents.) Graham, though, remained the front person for the campaign, and the proposed amendment was frequently referred to as the "Graham amendment." It appeared on the November 2002 ballot as Amendment 11.[17]

The Excellence in Education Foundation argued that a constitutionally protected board would create a firewall between politicians and higher education officials on purely academic matters. The Foundation also noted that, without constitutional protections, even the boards of trustees could be dissolved by legislative act and the trustees removed by any governor at any time. Opponents of Amendment 11 looked to the business sector as an inspiration for governance. "It's a corporate model," stated Phil Handy, "and it works because you define properly what the [Board of Education] does—it sets broad policy, management carries out that policy and the board holds the chief executive responsible." Appropriations were also simplified with the Board of Education assuming more budgetary powers. "For the first time, we'll be funding the entire educational system," Jim Horne noted, "instead of having these food fights over resources." Amendment supporters countered there would be more "food fights" under the new system and pointed to the continuous conflict between Alabama and Auburn as an example of what happened when budget disputes were not properly mediated by a central board.

The Florida Board of Regents ceased to exist on July 1, 2001. It had no impact on the 2001 legislative session and watched impotently from the sidelines as the state legislature diverted critical PECO funds to renovate and enhance The Ringling, Florida's state art museum. This was made possible when The Ringling's administration was transferred from the Department of State's Division of Cultural Affairs to Florida State University in 2000. The 2002 legislative session, the first without a central governing board since the Buckman Act, was an unmitigated disaster for the University of Florida and only slightly less so for higher education overall. Twenty years of steady increases in UF's budget were reversed with the university's agricultural units taking the largest cuts. The University of Florida fared better in 2003 after the university placed more emphasis on government relations. The influence of UF Board of Trustees chair Marshall Criser with Governor Bush may also have been a factor.

In November 2002, Florida voters reelected Governor Jeb Bush but also handed him a political dilemma by approving Amendment 11. In a pattern that has been followed several times since, Bush and the Republicans simply found a way to circumvent a constitutional amendment they had opposed. In this case, Bush would attempt to undermine the Board of Governors by appointing members who were opposed to its very existence. The first chair of the Board of Governors was Tom Petway, who had, in fact, led the campaign against Amendment 11 in the 2002 election. At the board's first meeting on January 7, 2003, Petway announced that the board would simply delegate all authority to the local boards. The *Lakeland Ledger* labeled the Board of Governors "the Pretend Board."[18] When the intent of Governor Bush became obvious, the forces behind Amendment 11 moved to the courts for a remedy, and a new group, Floridians for Constitutional Authority, was formed. Amendment 11's impact had already been felt in the courts before the group could swing into action. In August 2003, the State Board of Education attempted to move funding for a proposed baccalaureate program at the community colleges to the State University System budget. This would have been a direct violation of Amendment 11 had it not been neutralized by a court decision limiting the Board of Education's authority to K-12 and community colleges.[19]

Carolyn Roberts succeeded Tom Petway as head of the Board of Governors in 2004, and the board began to show some signs of life, albeit after the threat of civil suits. The board encouraged enrollment caps at some schools and forwarded a budget request for higher education to the governor and legislature. Former secretary of state Bruce Smathers, a leader in the Amendment 11 fight, was beginning to feel optimistic about the state and status of the board. Florida's business and industry leaders, he argued, did not want the state's university system to be seen as a "banana republic" of squabbling institutions. He also correctly predicted that UF and FSU would eventually close ranks to protect their mutual interests against South and Central Florida. Smathers urged Graham and York to wait until the 2004 legislature passed its budget before pursuing additional civil action. He perceived a "sea change" in Bush's attitude regarding the Board of Governors. "We have almost arrived at the promised land," he declared.[20]

The sea change was likely prompted by Jeb Bush's desire to rein in Republican legislators, whose egregious meddling in the affairs of higher education was beginning to take a toll on the state's reputation. The first major test of the Board of Governors' authority came after the state legislature, with the approval of FSU president T. K. Wetherell, attempted to establish a chiropractic school at Florida State. The legislative effort was spearheaded by Senate president Jim King, who secured an unspecified $9 million appropriation that was widely understood to be seed money for the school. King's efforts to provide academic legitimacy to a branch of alternative medicine were savagely lampooned in the media. He also faced universal opposition by the medical establishment, including seven instructors at FSU's recently opened College of Medicine, who threatened to resign if the school became a reality. King, in turn, threatened retaliation if FSU withdrew its support. A bill to establish the school passed both houses in 2004 but was vetoed by Bush. Bush, though, had promised to sign the bill in 2005, if it came up again. The proposal was then considered by the Board of Governors, which soundly rejected it. The board's disapproval provided more judicious members of the state legislature the leverage needed to kill further consideration of the bill, and Governor Bush avoided a potentially embarrassing situation. The chiropractic school controversy revealed a purpose for the board, but it also initiated a period of acrimony between the board and the state legislature that was not resolved until 2010, when a governance agreement, spearheaded by Chancellor Frank Brogan, sought to define the board's proper authority.

It would be difficult to say anything definitive about the current state of governance in Florida. Clearly, the Board of Governors does not exercise the level of authority that the proponents of Amendment 11 envisioned, but that may simply reflect the Republican Party's monopoly on political power. Under Democratic governors, the Board of Governors might play a different and stronger role. It is also unclear whether the form of governance is crucial. According to Michael Mills, "Changes in state governance structures seem more likely to reflect the unique contexts of the history and the current pressures of each state and may well be the result of the vagaries of the political processes in each state."[21] It may also be, as John Winn argued in 2000, that it does not matter what system is in place: "A review of other models indicates that no one approach is best. Different states have different approaches and differing degrees of central control. No one who has testified or [whom we] talked with has claimed a relationship between governance model and quality of higher education."[22]

Are the state universities better or worse off with a decentralized governance system? Despite the fears of York and others, the universities themselves have not experienced any visible decline since the dissolution of the Florida Board of Regents. The University of Florida entered the cherished top ten of public universities in the 2018 *US News and World Report*'s college rankings and ranked fifth in 2022. Other Florida universities have advanced in the rankings as well. There have been troubling signs, though, of a return to the status quo ante of 1905. Since the dissolution of the Board of Regents, powerful legislators have used their influence to transform two branch campuses of the University of South Florida into small independent colleges. The first new college established after the demise of the Board of Regents was not actually new, although New College is its name. New College was founded in 1960 as a private liberal arts college. It was acquired by the University of South Florida in 1975 and, under special arrangements, served as one of its branch campuses until that relationship was severed by the state legislature in 2001. It has since operated as an independent school with an intentionally small enrollment of fewer than 900 students. In 2012, the state legislature again detached a branch campus of the University of South Florida to create Florida Polytechnic University in Lakeland, another small school with an enrollment of fewer than 1,500 students. The decision was made without input from the Board of Governors and despite the vocal opposition of University of South Florida president Karen Holbrook.[23] Although both New College and Florida Polytechnic serve specific constituencies that might otherwise not be served on a larger campus, it was far less expensive to do so when each was a branch campus. The high administrative costs of maintaining two very small state schools have not gone unnoticed. A bill introduced in 2020 to merge both campuses with the University of Florida was never brought to the floor for a vote.[24]

More troubling, though, are the threats to academic freedom and faculty tenure. The following headline in the *Orlando Sentinel* sounded the tocsin for the 2022 legislative session: "Florida Gov. DeSantis seeks control over universities, targeting tenure and 'politicized' classes." A string of bills intended to undermine or eliminate long-accepted tenets of university governance and faculty and student rights were introduced, including one that would transfer hiring authority from the academic units to the boards of trustees. Bills were introduced to prevent the teaching of critical race theory and other unspecified subject matter deemed subversive. House Bill No. 7, the so-called Stop Woke Act, signed into law by Governor Ron DeSantis, potentially threatened funding for universities delving too deeply into issues of race or gender. Far more ominous were a quote from a high-ranking member of the legislature that the state universities were "socialism factories" and a vow from a member of the Board of Governors to rid the curriculum of "all of the crazy liberal stuff."[25]

It would be naïve to think that any governance system, no matter how strong, could entirely shield state colleges and universities from political interference. It also seems doubtful that any type of governance system can function properly when one political party and one ideological viewpoint exerts undue influence. This has been the case in Florida throughout most of its modern history. The Democratic Party held an almost exclusive monopoly on power from the end of Reconstruction until the 1970s. Conservatives, with occasional disruptions from progressives, populists, and liberals, dominated the Democratic Party when it held power. After a brief interregnum of contested authority in the 1970s and 1980s, the Republican Party has managed the state's affairs since the late 1990s. Every trustee, every member of the Board of Governors, and every member of the Florida Board of Education was appointed during a Republican administration. History provides numerous examples of the potential consequences from this level of absolute political power. Fundamentally, the system of educational governance is far less important than who governs in the state capital.

Notes

Introduction

1. The exception to the three pillars rule is New York. The State University of New York (SUNY) did not originate with a single state university. It emerged, instead, from a statewide network of public teachers colleges. In 1948, the colleges were brought together as one system under a governing Board of Trustees. New York's land grant university, Cornell—a private Ivy League college—is another oddity. Finally, SUNY coexists with CUNY (City University of New York), a university system larger than all but a few of the state systems.

2. John R. Thelin, *The History of American Higher Education* (Baltimore, MD: Johns Hopkins University Press, 2011), provides only three pages on normal schools, whereas the 594-page textbook by John S. Brubacher and Willis Rudy, *Higher Education in Transition: A History of American Colleges and Universities*, 4th ed. (New Brunswick, NJ: Transaction, 1997), somehow manages to avoid the subject entirely. Roger Geiger's monumental *The History of American Higher Education: Learning and Culture from the Founding to World War II* (Princeton, NJ: Princeton University Press, 2015) is the first general history of higher education to place the normal school in its proper context.

3. The pre-Buckman history of the state schools east of the Suwannee River is covered in detail in Samuel L. Proctor, "The University of Florida: Its Early Years, 1853–1906" (PhD diss., University of Florida, 1958); and Francis Arlington Rhodes, "The Legal Development of State Supported Higher Education Florida" (EdD diss., University of Florida, 1948).

4. Gleason to the Trustees of the State Agricultural College, April 10, 1875, in *Report of the Superintendent of Public Instruction for the Year 1876* (Tallahassee), 97–99. Prior to 1894, reports of the state superintendent were issued under an array of constantly changing titles and shifting publication schedules. Reports from the Reconstruction years can also be difficult to find. Beginning with 1894, the reports were issued biannually under the title *Bi-ennial Report of the Superintendent of Public Instruction of the State of Florida for the Two Years ending in [. . .]*; hereafter cited as *Report of the Superintendent*.

5. *Report of the Superintendent*, 1894, 20.

6. *Laws of Florida*, 1903 (Tallahassee), 268–70, chap. 5271, no. 166. The records of the Board of Education indicate the Agricultural Institute's properties sold for $1,000

(Minutes of the Florida Board of Education, April 1, 1907, series 252, State Library and Archives of Florida; hereafter cited as BOE Minutes).

CHAPTER 1. PUBLIC EDUCATION IN REDEMPTION FLORIDA

1. C. Vann Woodward, *Origins of the New South, 1877–1913* (Baton Rouge: Louisiana State University Press, 1951), 438–39; Terry Lee Matthews, "The Emergence of a Prophet: Andrew Sledd and the 'Sledd Affair' of 1902" (PhD diss., Duke University, 1989), 111–13.

2. Oswald Lafayette Parker, "William N. Sheats, Florida Educator" (master's thesis, University of Florida, 1949), 75–79. The word "crank" in nineteenth-century parlance most often referred to a fanatic, not to the annoying person of today who writes intemperate letters to politicians and newspapers.

3. Edward C. Williamson, "The Constitutional Convention of 1885," *Florida Historical Quarterly* 41 (October 1962): 123–24; Eldridge R. Collins, "The Florida Constitution of 1885" (master's thesis, University of Florida, 1939), 69–70; Larry E. Rivers and Canter Brown Jr., "A Monument to the Progress of the Race: The Intellectual and Political Origins of the Florida Agricultural and Mechanical University, 1865–1887," *Florida Historical Quarterly* 85 (Summer 2006): 36–38.

4. *Journal of the Proceedings of the Constitutional Convention of the State of Florida* (Tallahassee: N. M. Bowen, State Printer, 1885), 614–16.

5. Leedell W. Neyland and John W. Riley, *The History of Florida Agricultural and Mechanical University* (Gainesville: University of Florida Press, 1963), 7–9. Rivers and Brown note that the inclusion of section 14 was probably due to the intense lobbying of the African American delegation (Rivers and Brown, "A Monument to the Progress of the Race," 36).

6. David R. Colburn and Richard K. Scher, *Florida's Gubernatorial Politics in the Twentieth Century* (Gainesville: University Presses of Florida, 1980), 101–22.

7. Parker, "William N. Sheats," 79. The charter for the Florida Agricultural College made the state superintendent the president of the college's board of trustees. The legislature amended the charter in 1893 and removed the superintendent from the board.

8. Woodward, *Origins of the New South*, 299; *Biennial Report of the Superintendent of Public Instruction of the State of Florida for the Years 1883 and 1884*, 7; George Gary Bush, *History of Education in Florida* (Washington, DC: GPO, 1889), 11.

9. John R. Thelin, *The History of American Higher Education* (Baltimore, MD: Johns Hopkins University Press, 2011), 59.

10. *Report of the Superintendent, 1894*, 1–60.

11. Ibid.

12. Ibid.

13. Jerrell H. Shofner, *Nor Is It Over Yet: Florida in the Era of Reconstruction, 1863–1877* (Gainesville: University Presses of Florida, 1974), 77–78.

14. Arthur O. White, "Race, Politics and Education: The Sheats-Holloway Election Controversy, 1903–1904," *Florida Historical Quarterly* 53 (1975): 253–72; Joe M. Richardson, "'The Nest of Vile Fanatics': Williams N. Sheats and the Orange Park School," *Florida Historical Quarterly* 64 (1986): 393–406; Antonio F. Holland, *Nathan B. Young and the Struggle over Black Higher Education* (Columbia: University of Missouri Press,

2006), 74. Rivers and Brown note that Sheats's willingness to work with Black educators extended back to his days as superintendent for Alachua County (Rivers and Brown, "A Monument to the Progress of the Race," 30).

15. *Report of the Superintendent, 1894*, 51–52.

16. Data on school attendance in 1905 appears in the Henry Buckman Papers, MSS 00.894, P. K. Yonge Library of Florida History; hereafter cited as Buckman Papers.

17. *Report of the Superintendent, 1904*, 104.

18. *Report of the Superintendent, 1894*, 103.

19. *Florida School Exponent*, January 1898, 5–9.

20. *Report of the Superintendent, 1894*, 109–14.

21. Parker, "William N. Sheats," 122.

22. Glenn Ballard Simmons, *The Consolidation of Higher Public Education in Florida*, 122. The book is a privately printed edition of Simmons's doctoral dissertation submitted to Johns Hopkins University in 1933. Place and date of publication are not provided.

23. *Florida School Exponent*, February 1907, 7.

24. Ibid., February 1897, 11.

25. Simmons, *The Consolidation of Higher Public Education in Florida*, 122. The entire article appears in Simmons's appendix. Original copies are not extant.

26. *Florida School Exponent*, February 1898, 8.

27. Simmons, *The Consolidation of Higher Public Education in Florida*, 122–25.

28. Ibid.

29. *Florida School Exponent*, May 1907, 4.

30. Lucius Moody Bristol, "Development of Higher Education," chap. 5 of "The Buckman Act: Before and After (A Study in Historical Sociology)," 26–28 (unpublished and undated manuscript in the Lucius Moody Bristol Papers, University of Florida); "Message of Governor Francis P. Fleming," *Journal of the Senate*, 1891.

31. *Report of the Superintendent, 1900*, 158; *Report of the Superintendent, 1902*, 161–63.

32. *Florida School Exponent*, January 1898, 11; John Trantham to Albert Murphree, June 2, 1913, box 13; Murphree to Edward Conradi, April 27, 1916, box 15, Administrative Policy Records of President Albert A. Murphree, series P4, University of Florida Archives; hereafter cited as Murphree Records.

33. White, "Race, Politics, and Education," 269–70.

34. *Report of the Superintendent, 1904*, 174.

Chapter 2. A Curse Rather Than a Blessing

1. Leedell W. Neyland and John W. Riley, *The History of Florida Agricultural and Mechanical University* (Gainesville: University of Florida Press, 1963), 22. The campus also included a large oak, known as the "Slave Tree," where enslaved people had been chained and whipped.

2. Reginald K. Ellis, "Florida State Normal and Industrial School for Coloreds: Thomas deSaille Tucker and His Radical Approach to Black Higher Education," in *The Seedtime, the Work, and the Harvest: New Perspectives on the Black Freedom Struggle in America*, ed. Jeffrey L. Littlejohn, Reginald K. Ellis, and Peter B. Levy, 1–27 (Gainesville: University of Florida Press, 2018); Antonio F. Holland, *Nathan B. Young and the Strug-*

gle over Black Higher Education (Columbia: University of Missouri Press, 2006),71–72; Reginald K. Ellis, "Nathan B. Young: Florida A&M College's Second President and His Relationships with White Officials," in *Go Sound the Trumpet! Selections in Florida's African American History,* ed. David H. Jackson Jr. and Canter Brown Jr., 155–56 (Tampa: University of Tampa Press, 2005).

3. Adam Harris, *The State Must Provide: The Definitive History of Racial Inequality in American Higher Education* (New York: HarperCollins, 2021), 53–54.

4. Nathan B. Young, "Florida: Our Contiguous Foreign State," in *These "Colored" United States,* ed. Tom Lutz and Susanna Ashton (New Brunswick, NJ: Rutgers University Press, 1996), 90.

5. *Report of the Superintendent, 1900,* 202–3; Louise Anderson Allen, "Silenced Sisters: Dewey's Disciples in a Conservative New South, 1900–1940," *Journal of the Gilded Age and Progressive Era* 5 (April 2006): 119–37; Ellis, "Florida State Normal and Industrial School for Coloreds," 24–25.

6. Holland, *Nathan B. Young,* 74–75. The most authoritative source on Florida's college finances is a report prepared by the state treasurer at the request of the legislature prior to the Buckman Act. The report is included with other documents found in the Henry Buckman Papers at the P. K. Yonge Library of Florida History at the University of Florida. The report, in ledger sheet form, provides a detailed account of all funds received by the seven state schools from 1881 to 1905; hereafter cited as Treasurer's Report, 1905.

7. Martee Wills and Joan Perry Morris, *Seminole History* (Jacksonville, FL: South Star, 1987), 39.

8. Peter Henry Rolfs, "Founders and Foundations of Florida Agriculture: A Serious and Frivolous Study of Men and Measures," *Proceedings of the Florida State Horticultural Society* (1935), 130; *Report of the Superintendent, 1884; Report of the Superintendent, 1886.* Information on Kost's career can be found in a biographical file in the Samuel Proctor Collection, Manuscript Collection 135, box 49, University of Florida Archives; hereafter cited as Proctor Collection. The Proctor file contradicts the assertion that the library stayed in Tallahassee and became the David Walker Library. Francis Arlington Rhodes, "The Legal Development of State Supported Higher Education Florida" (EdD diss., University of Florida, 1948), 108–9.

9. *Register of the East Florida Seminary, 1887–1888.*

10. *Report of the Superintendent, 1902.*

11. *Florida State College Catalogue 1903–1904* (Tallahassee: J. B. Hilson, State Printer), 14, 156; Treasurer's Report, 1905.

12. The complicated saga of how Florida redeemed its land scrip is recorded in the *Report of the Superintendent, 1873,* 22–31. Florida lost $2,000 when the broker initially contracted by the state was unable to complete the transaction and a second broker was hired.

13. *Report of the Superintendent, 1871,* 6.

14. *Report of the Superintendent, 1878,* 184–85. The resolution was approved on March 7, 1877 (*Laws of Florida,* 9th session, 1877, 149–50). *Report of the Superintendent, 1882,* 17, states that there was $134,900 in the fund as of 1881. Haisley's comments on the purpose

of a land grant college reflect both Redemption sentiments as well as common misconceptions about the Morrill Act. The act did not stipulate the creation of agricultural schools, merely that agriculture and engineering (the practical arts) be taught.

15. *Gainesville Weekly Bee*, January 12 and 26, 1883.

16. Proctor, "The University of Florida: Its Early Years, 1853–1906," 193–221; *The First Annual Catalogue of the State Agricultural College of Florida* (Tallahassee, 1886).

17. Ashley Hurt to his wife, July 27, 1884, Ashley Davis Hurt Papers, University of Florida Archives.

18. *Report of the Superintendent, 1884*, 18.

19. *Report of the Superintendent, 1886*, 14–15. The last mention of Kost and his museum in Florida appears in the college's 1888 catalogue.

20. Ibid., 16. Unlike the state seminaries, the college's charter did not allow it to change its name. Reports from the principals and presidents of the state schools were sometimes included in the superintendents' reports. Enrollment data can be found in the superintendents' reports and in the catalogues issued by the schools.

21. *Report of the Superintendent, 1890*, 9.

22. The Flagler divorce story is told in David Nolan, *Fifty Feet in Paradise: The Booming of Florida* (New York: Harcourt, Brace, Jovanovich, 1984), 135–36.

Chapter 3. Turmoil at Lake City

1. Roger L. Williams, *The Origins of Federal Support for Higher Education: George W. Atherton and the Land-Grant College Movement* (University Park: Pennsylvania State University Press, 1991), 117–22.

2. January 31, 1893, Minutes of the Board of Trustees of the Florida Agricultural College, 1893–1905, series 157, University of Florida Archives; hereafter cited as FAC Minutes.

3. *Gainesville Weekly Sun*, February 9, 1893.

4. *Laws of the State of Florida* (Tallahassee, 1893), 167–68.

5. FAC Minutes, June 22, 1893; *Superintendent's Report, 1894*, 157.

6. FAC Minutes. The letters, dated November 28 and December 5, 1898, are among several inserted into the minute book.

7. FAC Minutes, July 11, 1893.

8. FAC Minutes, July 12, 1893.

9. FAC Minutes, April 17, 1894.

10. Proctor, "The University of Florida: Its Early Years, 1853–1906," 379–406.

11. Ibid.

12. Aurora de Mena, *The Pearl Key, or Midnight and Dawn in Cuba* (Jacksonville, FL: Vance Printing, 1896), 34. The Florida Agricultural College was one of the advertisers in the back of the book. FAC Minutes, April 17 and June 13, 1894.

13. FAC Minutes, June 12 and December 3, 1895; *Superintendent's Report, 1896*.

14. FAC Minutes, February 8 and June 15, 1897.

15. FAC Minutes, July 22 and 23, 1897.

16. Ibid.

17. Peter Henry Rolfs, "Founders and Foundations of Florida Agriculture: A Serious

and Frivolous Study of Men and Measures," *Proceedings of the Florida State Horticultural Society* (1935): 135.

18. FAC Minutes, August 17 and September 7 and 10, 1897. The Summerlin Institute had been a private academy until it was purchased by the City of Bartow in 1894.

19. David B. Danbom, "The North Dakota Agricultural College Controversy of 1893: Scientific Professionalism and Political Patronage," *North Dakota History* 51 (Winter 1986): 12–23.

20. Treasurer's Report, 1905. Florida's situation was not exceptional in the South. Woodward states that Kentucky, Tennessee, and Mississippi reported zero state appropriations to their respective state universities in 1900 (Woodward, *Origins of the New South*, 437).

21. FAC Minutes, June 6, 1901.

22. Taliaferro is the first college president for whom there is a substantial body of correspondence. His records are found in Florida Agricultural College Records, series 162, University of Florida Archives; hereafter cited as FAC Records.

23. Taliaferro to Stockbridge, June 15, 1902; Taliaferro to Carson, August 7, 1902, FAC Records, box 1; FAC Minutes, June 10, 1902.

24. Taliaferro to Carson, May 4, 1903, FAC Records, box 2.

25. Taliaferro to Blount, June 2, 1903, FAC Records, box 2.

26. FAC Minutes, April 9, 1903. The bill's path can be traced in the House and Senate journals.

27. Taliaferro to George Wilson, April 16 and 25, 1903; Taliaferro to Senator W. K. Jackson, April 25, 1903; Taliaferro to Carson, April 11, 23 and 25, 1903, FAC Records, box 2. In his correspondence with Carson, Taliaferro refers to the act as Carson's "victory." Taliaferro's correspondence mentions a public attack on the university bill by Ludwig Bucholz, head of the normal school at Florida State. Bucholz was clearly serving as a proxy for President Murphree, who would have opted to stay above the fray.

28. *Catalog of the Florida State College*, 1903–4, 14.

29. FAC Minutes, June 16 and 26, 1903.

30. John R. Thelin, *The History of American Higher Education* (Baltimore, MD: Johns Hopkins University Press, 2011), 98.

31. Taliaferro to Augusta Barnes, July 2, 1903, FAC Records, box 2.

32. W. K. Jackson to Taliaferro, July 2, 1903; Taliaferro to Jackson, July 3, FAC Records, box 2.

33. Francis Arlington Rhodes, "The Legal Development of State Supported Higher Education Florida" (EdD diss., University of Florida, 1948), 138.

34. Annual report of the president, 1903–1904, FAC Records, box 4.

35. Taliaferro to Davis, May 6, 1903, FAC Records, box 2.

Chapter 4. The Revolutions of 1904

1. Taliaferro to George Wilson, December 19, 1903, FAC Records, box 2.
2. Taliaferro to Carson, April 15, 1904, FAC Records, box 2.
3. Testimony of Professor Gossard, Exhibit D, FAC Records, box 4.

4. Testimony of Professor Cox, Exhibit D, FAC Records, box 4.
5. Taliaferro to Carson, April 15, 1904, FAC Records, box 2.
6. Taliaferro to Wilson, May 9, 1904, FAC Records, box 2.
7. Testimony of Professors Cox, Hume, and Borger, Exhibit D, FAC Records, box 4.
8. Testimony of Professors, Hume, Hadley, Cox, and Blair, Exhibit D, FAC Records, box 4.
9. Testimony of Professor Borger, Exhibit D, FAC Records, box 4.
10. FAC Minutes, June 21, 1904.
11. Bishop Warren Candler to Carson, May 1904; Carson to Andrew Sledd and Sledd's response, May 24 and 27; Sledd to F. W. Simonton, June 27, box 1, series P9, Andrew Sledd Papers, University of Florida Archives, Gainesville; hereafter cited as Sledd Papers.
12. Andrew Sledd, "The Negro: Another View," *Atlantic Monthly*, July 1902, 65–73.
13. For a full discussion of the article and its aftermath, see Terry Lee Matthews, "The Emergence of a Prophet: Andrew Sledd and the 'Sledd Affair' of 1902" (PhD diss., Duke University, 1989); and Bruce Clayton, *The Savage Ideal: Intolerance and Intellectual Leadership in the South, 1890–1914* (Baltimore, MD: Johns Hopkins University Press, 1972), 78–84.
14. Nathan Bryan to Carson, June 28, 1904, box 1, Sledd Papers.
15. Matthews, "The Emergence of a Prophet," 110–18.
16. William Franck to Carson, June 10, 1904, box 1, Sledd Papers; Matthews, "The Emergence of a Prophet," 258; Klein H. Graham Papers, Manuscript Collection 104, University of Florida Archives.
17. L. E. Roberson to Sledd, June 6, 1904, box 1, series P3, Administrative Policy Records of President Andrew Sledd, University of Florida Archives; hereafter cited as Sledd Records.
18. FAC Minutes, July 7, 1904.
19. Taliaferro to Sledd, July 9, 1904, box 1, Sledd Records.
20. Taliaferro to Sledd, July 11, 1904, box 1, Sledd Records.
21. Andrew Sledd, "Autobiography of a Southern Schoolmaster," 123, box 1, Sledd Papers; hereafter cited as Sledd, "Autobiography."
22. Sledd to Karl Schmidt, August 18, 1904, box 1, Sledd Records.
23. A digitized copy of Cox's 1905 survey can be found at http://ufdc.ufl.edu/UF90000063/00001. The original is in the University of Florida Archives.
24. Sledd to the Board of Trustees, April 24, 1905, letterbook 3, Sledd Records; FAC Minutes, May 4, 1905; Sledd, "Autobiography," 145–46. A copy of the article from the *Gainesville Sun* is unavailable.
25. Sledd to Carson, August 9, 1904, box 1, Sledd Records; Sledd, "Autobiography," 124.
26. Sledd, "Autobiography," 128; William J. Bryan to Sledd, July 30, 1904; Sledd's undated reply to Bryan; Sheats to Sledd, undated, 1904, box 1, Sledd Records.
27. Sledd, "Autobiography," 125.
28. "The Educational Situation in Florida," attachment to letter from Sledd to Wallace Buttrick, January 11, 1906, folder 311, reel 27, General Education Board Archives, series

1, Appropriations, subseries 1, The Early Southern Program (Scholarly Resources, Inc. 1993); hereafter cited as GEB. Sledd to Judge Francis B. Carter, undated, 1905, letterbook 4, Sledd Records.

29. Annual Report of the Board of Control, March 6, 1909, box 3; Sledd to S. P. Mays, September 24, 1904; Sledd to W. A. B. Hobbs, September 28, 1904; Sledd to P. H. Cason, October 2, 1904; and other letters to parents in a similar vein, letterbook 1, Sledd Records; Tom McEwen, *The Gators: A Story of Florida Football* (Huntsville, AL: Strode, 1974), 36. The resignations of the football players are documented in the margins of the Record of Scholarship, series 169, University of Florida Archives.

30. Sledd, "The University of the State of Florida," reprint of *Royal Palm Magazine*, March 1906, found in box 1, Sledd Papers. By comparison, Florida State College continued to maintain a three-year high school until the Buckman Act was passed.

Chapter 5. The Buckman Revolution

1. Samuel Proctor, "The University of Florida: Its Early Years, 1853–1906" (PhD diss., University of Florida, 1958), 487, asserts that the original bill exists in the Buckman Papers. There is an edited draft of the final bill in Buckman's papers, but it does not differ substantially from the final bill. A thorough discussion of the Supreme Court ruling can be found in the records of Dean Trusler at the University of Florida. Trusler's analysis of this ruling became a focal point for President John J. Tigert's proposal to change the university's founding date from 1905 to 1853 (Harry R. Trusler to John J. Tigert, April 18, 1935, box 12, Administrative policy records of the Dean of the College of Law, series 41, University of Florida Archives).

2. W. K. Jackson to Sledd, August 10, 1904, box 1, Sledd Records.

3. "Message of the Governor, April 4, 1905," *Journal of the Senate*, 21–22.

4. The public events surrounding the crafting of the Buckman Bill are covered in greater detail in Proctor, "The University of Florida: Its Early Years, 1853–1906," 464–92; and Glenn Ballard Simmons, *The Consolidation of Higher Public Education in Florida* (a self-published and undated version of his 1933 doctoral dissertation at Johns Hopkins University), 133–48.

5. *Florida Times-Union*, May 15, 1905; Pound to Governor Broward, March 17, 1905, Papers of Governor Napoleon Bonaparte Broward, record group 101, series 664, State Library and Archives of Florida, Tallahassee; hereafter cited as Broward Papers.

6. *Laws of Florida, 1909*, chapters 5924–5927 (Tallahassee: Capital Publishing, 1909), 69–70. The edited draft of the Buckman bill found in the Buckman Papers retains the Board of Education's governance of the State Normal and Industrial School.

7. *Florida Times-Union*, May 21, 1905, 24.

8. Lucius Moody Bristol, "The Buckman Act: Before and After (A Study in Historical Sociology)," unpublished manuscript, 1946, 7–8.

9. Ibid.

10. Copy of undated letter by Henry Buckman to the editors of *Outlook* magazine; Clarence Sowell to Broward, November 2, 1905, box 8, Education, Broward Records.

11. W. B. Hare to Sledd, May 25, 1909, box 3, Sledd Records; David R. Colburn and Richard K. Scher, *Florida's Gubernatorial Politics in the Twentieth Century* (Gainesville:

University Presses of Florida, 1980), 132–49. Typically, the members met as the Board of Control in the mornings, adjourned for lunch, and reconvened as the Plant Board in the afternoon.

12. Bristol, "The Buckman Act: Before and After (A Study in Historical Sociology)," 47. The minutes of the joint sessions were kept by the Board of Education. Votes were recorded individually.

13. Thomas Benton to Sledd, June 25, 1905; Sledd to Benton, June 27, 1905, box 2, Sledd Records.

14. Frank Harris to Sledd, June 8, 1905, box 2, Sledd Records.

15. FAC minutes, June 14, 1905.

Chapter 6. The Immediate Aftermath of Buckman

1. Broward to Justices of the Supreme Court of the State of Florida, June 8, 1905, box 3, Napoleon Bonaparte Broward Papers, P. K. Yonge Library of Florida History, University of Florida; Supreme Court Ruling, June 1905, box 9, General Correspondence, Broward Records.

2. W. S. Broome to Broward, May 29, 1905; John Tench to Broward, June 25, 1905, box 8, Education, Broward Records.

3. William Thomas to Broward, May 29, 1905, box 8, "Education," Broward Records.

4. Sledd to Harris, May 28 and June 9, 1905, letterbook 3, Sledd Records; Samuel Proctor, "The University of Florida: Its Early Years, 1853–1906" (PhD diss., University of Florida, 1958), 513–16.

5. *Journal of the Senate*, 1905, "Special Committee to Visit the University of Florida at Lake City," 1078–85. Sledd's point-by-point refutation of the report can be found in Sledd to George Wilson, May 24, 1905, box 8, Broward Records.

6. Sledd, "Autobiography," 146.

7. *Jacksonville Metropolis*, June 1, 1905; Sledd, "Autobiography," 148.

8. *Ocala Banner*, June 10, 1905; *Florida Times-Union*, June 24, 1905. The *Tampa Herald* article was reprinted in the *Florida Times-Union*, July 10, 1905, as a letter to the editor from "A South Floridian." Harris's list of presidents is interesting as neither Kost nor DePass were presidents.

9. George Wilson to Broward, June 24, 1905; Jere Pound to Broward, June 26, 1905, box 8, "Education," Broward Records. Only Pound's response to Broward exists, and the response does not indicate the purpose of the meeting.

10. Buckman to Broward, June 30, 1905, box 8, "Education," Broward Records.

11. Ibid. Some of the points raised in the letter were also stated in documents found in the Buckman Papers. One document appears to be a defense of the act's constitutionality. Buckman's letter to Broward is far more candid and speaks to motivations as well as purpose.

12. *Catalogue of the John B. Stetson University, 1905–1906* (DeLand, FL, 1906), 11. The catalogue contains a register of students and their hometowns. Stetson had a successful exchange program with the University of Chicago, which may also explain its success in attracting out-of-state students.

13. William Holloway to Barney Colson, June 7, 1905; Holloway to Annie Wimberley,

June 7, 1905; among others, letterbook 29, Superintendent of Public Instruction, Letterbooks, 1900-1913, record group 402, series 244, State Library and Archives of Florida; hereafter cited as Superintendent Letterbooks.

14. A. J. Angle to Colson, July 6, 1905, Barney Colson Papers, P. K. Yonge Library of Florida History, University of Florida; hereafter cited as Colson Papers.

15. Proctor, "The University of Florida: Its Early Years, 1853-1906," 501-2; *Tampa Tribune*, May 12, 1905. In most cases, the newspaper endorsements were simply taken verbatim from the Gainesville mailers.

16. *The University at Lake City* (Lake City, FL, 1905). A copy of the pamphlet can be found in the P. K. Yonge Library of Florida History.

17. Ibid. U. Carr Loftin, "Mosquito Conditions at the University of Florida" (master's thesis, University of Florida, 1913), 16; *Biennial Report of the President of the University of Florida to the Board of Control for the Biennium ending June 30, 1934*, 160.

18. James Marion Farr, "The Making of a University: The Personal Memoir of One Intimately Associated with Its Growth," 44, James Marion Farr Manuscripts, Manuscript Collection 28, University of Florida Archives; E. R. Dickenson to Sledd, June 22, 1905, box 2, Sledd Records.

19. Proctor, "The University of Florida: Its Early Years, 1853-1906," 497-99.

20. BOE Minutes, Joint Board, July 6, 1905.

21. Charles Langley Crow, "The Buckman Act" (unpublished manuscript dated April 28, 1937), cites the *White Springs Herald* as the source of the leak. A copy is not available. Crow also mentions a story, later cited by Proctor, that there was an initial vote of 5-5 before Attorney General Ellis switched his vote to Gainesville. But Holloway stated that Ellis was a firm supporter of Gainesville from the beginning. Knott did not mention this story in his reply to Bristol (Proctor, "The University of Florida: Its Early Years, 1853-1906," 512). Tallahassee's last-minute proposal for the university may have stemmed from the very strong possibility of a deadlocked vote.

22. Lucius Bristol, "Lectures on Three Focal Points in the History of Higher Education in Florida" (University of Florida course printout, 1951), appendix 16. Knott's mention of free water seems to be the source for a local legend in Gainesville that free water was the decisive factor in the decision to relocate the university.

23. "The Educational Situation in Florida," submitted to the General Education Board, September 14, 1905, box 2, Sledd Records.

24. Sledd, "Autobiography."

25. BOE Minutes, Joint Board, July 24, 1905.

26. Bryan to Broward, December 21, 1905, box 8, "Education," Broward Records; Kellum to Bryan, January 3, 1906, vol. 1, Secretary John G. Kellum letterbooks, 1905-1907, record group 498, series 1182, State Library and Archives of Florida; hereafter cited as Records of the Secretary.

27. *Florida School Exponent*, June 1907, 7; Kellum to Holloway, June 5, 1907, vol. 2, Records of the Secretary; BOE Minutes, May 3 and June 27, 1907. The minutes of June 27 indicate that Lake City requested the land be sold to the city for a nominal price, but no action is recorded. The figure of $23,455 appears in "History of the Building Develop-

ment of the University of Florida from 1905 to 1945," Edith P. Pitts Papers, Manuscript Collection 50, University of Florida Archives. Pitts cites a report by the Board of Control.

28. Bishop Warren Candler to [his daughter], June 16, 1905, box 2, Sledd Papers; *Bartow Courier*, June 14, 1905 (clipping found in Sledd Papers); Sledd to Thomas Benton, June 27, 1905, letterbook 3; Broward to Sledd, June 24, 1905, box 2, Sledd Records.

29. BOE Minutes, Joint Board, July 7, 1905.

30. BOC Minutes, July 7, 1905, morning session, series 1, State Library and Archives of Florida; hereafter cited as BOC Minutes.

31. BOC Minutes, July 7, 1905, afternoon session; BOE Minutes, Joint Board, July 7, 1905, afternoon session.

32. Holloway to Guilliams, July 8, 1905, letterbook 29, Superintendent Letterbooks.

33. Sledd to Henry Pritchett, April 15, 1909, box 3, Sledd Records; Farr, "The Making of a University," 45.

Chapter 7. The Agony of Andrew Sledd

1. Taliaferro to William B. Hare, June 20, 1903, FAC Records, box 1. After expressing frustration over unpaid warrants, John Kellum joked, "I have nearly lost all my religion on these old accounts." Guisinger was forced to petition the governor in order to get his and his teachers' salaries paid for the month of May 1905. Croom had refused to pay because the pay warrants were dated after passage of the Buckman Act (Kellum to Nathan Bryan, August 5, 1905, Secretary Letterbooks; Guisinger to Broward, August 18, 1905, box 8, Broward Records).

2. Sledd to Broward, May 31, 1905, with letter from Sledd to Croom attached, box 8, Broward Records; Sledd to Croom, August 10, 1905, letterbook 4; Croom to Sledd, August 11, 1905, box 2; Sledd to Bryan, October 16, 1905, letterbook 5, Sledd Records.

3. Sledd to Bryan, August 25, 1905, letterbook 5, Sledd Records.

4. Sledd to Bryan, December 1, 1905, letterbook 5, Sledd Records.

5. Lucius Bristol, "Lectures on Three Focal Points in the History of Higher Education in Florida" (University of Florida course printout, 1951), appendix 17; Samuel Proctor, "The University of Florida: Its Early Years, 1853–1906" (PhD diss., University of Florida, 1958), 525–27. Cawthon did not include the shotgun in his description of events to Bristol. The shotgun was added to the story during an interview with Cawthon held by Samuel Proctor on March 3, 1953.

6. Sledd to Bryan, July 28, 1906, letterbook 7, Sledd Records; *Florida Times-Union*, September 26, 1906.

7. Sledd to Drew Company, May 5, 1906, letterbook 6; Sledd to Mr. Till, December 12, 1906, letterbook 8, Sledd Records.

8. The speech was printed and distributed. A copy can be found in the University of Florida Archives Artifact Collection as registry number 2006.10.

9. Enrollment for the fall 1906 semester can be found in the Agendas and Minutes of the University of Florida General Assembly, November 8, 1906, Series 81, University of Florida Archives. Annual headcount enrollments can be found in the back of the university's catalogue and also appear in the biennial reports to the Florida Board of Control. The Buckman Act gave the Board of Control authority over admission requirements.

10. "Reports to the Board of Control, 1905–1908," box 3, Sledd Records. Oddly, the state superintendent did not keep statistics on students enrolled in specific grades. All but the high school in Tarpon Springs responded to Sledd's survey. The survey, itself, did not survive, only the tallies.

11. *Report of the Superintendent, 1914*, 10. Sledd's predicament was also attributable to the absence of professional programs at the university. The Buckman Act called for the addition of medical programs as well as a law school. A law school was approved in 1909, but Sledd would not be around to take credit for the sudden upturn in enrollment that came when the law students arrived.

12. Sledd to Murphree, J. W. McClung, J. A. Ormond, and W. W. Hall, March 31, 1906; and Sledd to Murphree, April 16 and July 4, 1906, letterbook 8, Sledd Records.

13. *Florida School Exponent*, January 1907, 7–11, and February 1907, 1.

14. Ibid.

15. Paula S. Fass, *The End of American Childhood: A History of Parenting from Life on the Frontier to the Managed Child* (Princeton, NJ: Princeton University Press, 2016), 5.

16. Ibid., 74–85.

17. Lockey to Sledd, April 4, 1907, box 2; and Sledd's reply, April 6, 1907, letterbook 9, Sledd Records. Under the direction of the high school inspector, a standard high school curriculum was finally adopted in 1912. *High School Manual for Florida*, published in the *University Record*, University of Florida, vol. 7, no. 3.

18. J. Patrick McCarthy, "The Articulation of Secondary and Higher Education: Four Historical Models at the University of Georgia," *History of Higher Education Annual* 19 (1999): 42–43.

19. Sledd to Buttrick, February 6, 1908; and Buttrick to Sledd, February 7, 1908; box 3, Sledd Records.

20. Sledd to Buttrick, February 10 and 19, 1908; Buttrick to Holloway, copy of telegram, February 20, 1908; Holloway to Sledd, February 13, 1908; and Sledd to Holloway, February 14, 1908, box 3, Sledd Records. See also Holloway to Sledd, February 18, 1908, letterbook 36, Superintendent Letterbooks.

21. Sledd to Warren Candler, February 12, 1908, box 1, Sledd Papers; Bryan to Sledd, February 4 and 8, 1908; Sledd to Bryan, February 15, March 3 and 20, 1908; Sledd to W. L. Wartmann, February 16, 1908, box 3, Sledd Records; Sledd to Yonge, February 13, 1908, box 1, Phillip K. Yonge Collection, P. K. Yonge Library of Florida History, University of Florida; hereafter cited as Yonge Collection.

22. Holloway to Buttrick, March 10, 1908, box 3, Sledd Records; Holloway to Lynch, March 9, 1908, letterbook 36, Superintendent Letterbooks. The Board of Control minutes simply state that the high school inspector would serve as the superintendent's representative and do not elaborate on lines of authority (BOC Minutes, January 6, 1908).

23. Sledd to Bryan, March 30, 1908, box 3, Sledd Records; James Marion Farr, "The Making of a University: The Personal Memoir of One Intimately Associated with Its Growth," 60, James Marion Farr Manuscripts, Manuscript Collection 28, University of Florida Archives.

24. Holloway to J. P. B. Allan, April 10, 1908, letterbook 42, Superintendent Letterbooks.

25. Report to the Board of Control, March 6, 1907, box 3, Sledd Records; Sledd to E. S. Crill, April 13, 1907, letterbook 10, Sledd Records.

26. Charles Langley Crow, "History of the University of Florida through 1908/09," typescript, 1937, University of Florida Archives.

27. Bryan to Yonge, February 3, 1909, box 1, Yonge Collection; BOE Minutes, January 30, 1909; Bryan to Sledd, February 1, 1909, box 1, Sledd Papers.

28. "Report to the Board of Control for 1909," box 3, Sledd Records. This version of the report did not make it into the official published report.

29. William Crawford to Murphree, March 3, 1909; Murphree to Crawford, March 8, 1909, box 14, Murphree Records. There are four letters from Crawford to Murphree but only one reply from Murphree.

30. *Pensacola Evening News*, March 6, 1909.

31. BOC Minutes, March 6, 1909; BOE Minutes, Meeting of Joint Board, March 6, 1909; Crawford to Murphree, March 12, 1909, box 14, Murphree Records; Holloway to Murphree, March 8 and 10, 1909, Superintendent Letterbooks, vol. 39. Holloway also makes a mysterious reference to a letter that Murphree should read and return to him.

32. *Pensacola Evening News*, March 23, 1909; *Gainesville Sun*, March 14, 1909; *Tallahassee True Democrat*, March 19, 1909; *Gainesville Sun*, March 23, 1909.

33. *Suwannee Democrat*, April 2, 1909; *Tampa Tribune*, March 31, 1909; *Ocala Banner*, April 2, 1909; Crawford to Murphree, April 26, 1909, box 14, Murphree Records. The letter begins with "Your epitaph has been writ."

34. Holloway to Colson, March 9, 1909, Barney Colson Papers.

35. BOE Minutes, April 10, 1909; Sledd to the Board of Control, April 9, 1909, box 3, Murphree Records. That the letter appears in Murphree's files, rather than Sledd's, would indicate that Murphree read the letter.

36. Sledd to Lockey, April 5, 1909, box 3, Sledd Records; Sledd to Buttrick, February 15, 1909, GEB, folder 311, roll 26; William Blackman to Bryan, March 24, 1909; Bryan to Yonge, April 1, 1909, box 1, Yonge Collection. Bryan also considered internal candidates.

37. BOC Minutes, April 10, 1909, morning session. A joint board meeting was held after the morning session, but no action was recorded.

38. BOC Minutes, April 10, 1909, afternoon session.

39. Ibid.; *Pensacola Journal*, April 11, 1909.

40. Buckman to Yonge, April 13, 1909; Bryan to Yonge, April 13, 1909, box 1, Yonge Collection; *Senate Journal*, 1909, "Message from Governor Albert Gilchrist," April 19, 1909, 222–24.

41. *Florida School Exponent*, May 1909.

42. Murphree to Sledd, June 5, 1909; Sledd to Murphree, June 7, 1909, box 3, Sledd Records; BOC Minutes, April 10, 1909, afternoon session; Murphree to *Savannah Morning News*, April 16, 1909, box 14, Murphree Records.

43. Agenda and Minutes of the General Assembly of Faculty, May 24, 1909, series 81, University of Florida Archives; "Resolution of the Faculty," undated, box 1, Sledd Papers; Crow, "History of the University of Florida through 1908/09."

CHAPTER 8. THE FALLOUT FROM FLORIDA'S SLEDD AFFAIR

1. Roger Geiger, *The History of American Higher Education: Learning and Culture from the Founding to World War II* (Princeton, NJ: Princeton University Press, 2015), 384–85; Arthur Levine and Scott Van Pelt, *The Great Upheaval: Higher Education's Past, Present, and Uncertain Future* (Baltimore, MD: Johns Hopkins University Press, 2021), 76–77.

2. *Annual Report—Carnegie Foundation for the Advancement of Teaching* (New York, 1908), 64–73. Among the public colleges, only Kentucky and the University of North Carolina agreed with Sledd.

3. *Annual Report—Carnegie Foundation for the Advancement of Teaching* (New York, 1909), 94–95.

4. Murphree to Charles Van Hise, October 2, 1911, box 15, Murphree Records.

5. *Transactions and Proceedings of the National Association of State Universities of the United States of America*, vol. 10, 1912 (Burlington, VT), 208–42.

6. *Report of the Commissioner of Education for the Years Ended June 30, 1912*, vol. 1 (Washington, DC: GPO, 1913), 92–93.

7. Murphree's commitment to the Wisconsin Idea must be questioned. As late as 1919, Murphree stated, "We are not ready to follow Wisconsin's lead in this direction" (Murphree to the Board of Control, June 6, 1919, box 14, William C. Hodges Papers; hereafter cited as Hodges Papers).

8. David R. Colburn and Richard K. Scher, *Florida's Gubernatorial Politics in the Twentieth Century* (Gainesville: University Presses of Florida, 1980), 134.

9. Samuel L. Proctor, "The University of Florida: Its Early Years, 1853–1906" (PhD diss., University of Florida, 1958), 494.

10. Murphree to Asa Clark, January 31, 1910, box 14, Murphree Records.

11. Murphree to Vice President Farr, June 12, 1912, box 24, Murphree Records.

12. Murphree to A. P. Bourland, January 25, 1913, box 15, Murphree Records.

13. Murphree to Blackman, March 17, 1913, box 15, Murphree Records.

14. Murphree to Yonge, August 8 and 21, 1916, box 3, Yonge Papers; Sheats to Murphree, telegrams, August 15 and 16, 1916; Murphree to Yonge, September 23, 1916, box 13, Murphree to E. C. Sage, June 7, 1917, box 17, Murphree Records.

15. *Florida School Exponent*, January 1898, 4.

16. Conradi to Yonge, June 21, 1910, box 2, Yonge Papers.

17. Chapter 6540, *State Laws of Florida*, 1913; BOE Minutes, Joint Board, May 14, 1915, Agendas and Minutes of the University of Florida General Assembly of Faculty, September 30, 1914, series 81, University of Florida Archives; Murphree to Kellum, February 14, 1916, box 13, Murphree Records.

18. Murphree to Mrs. Glenn McKay, November 21, 1921, box 18, Murphree Records.

19. Chapter 6498, *Laws of Florida*, 1913; *Bi-ennial Report of the Superintendent of Public Instruction of the State of Florida for the Two Years Ending in 1914;* Murphree to J. C. Adkins, May 10, 1913, box 15; Conradi to Murphree, April 7, 1915; Thackston to Murphree, undated, box 16; Murphree to Wartmann, March 3, 1915; Murphree to Yonge, April 3, 1915, box 3, Murphree Records; BOC minutes, April 9, 1915.

20. Murphree to Ralph Stoutamire, February 16, 1920, box 18, Murphree Records.

Chapter 9. The Quandary of the Normal School

1. "Report to the Board of Control on Teacher Education," January 31, 1906, box 1, Yonge Papers; Buckman to Broward, June 30, 1905, box 8, "Education," Broward Records.

2. *Catalogue of the University of the State of Florida, 1905–1906*, 89–122. Student rolls are published in the back of the catalogue. The university had made the decision to restrict enrollment to men until the joint board made its decision.

3. "Report of the President of the Florida Female College," February 15, 1907, box 1, Yonge Papers. The report also noted that there were sixty children enrolled in the model school and kindergarten. "Report of President Edward Conradi," July 25, 1913, box 2, Yonge Papers.

4. Murphree to Conradi, January 31, 1910; Murphree to Carpenter, March 14, 1910, box 14, Murphree Records. By 1908, the normal program at the university existed only on the pages of the catalogue as it had no students. The catalogue for 1906-7 shows seven normal school students and none in the catalogue for 1907-8. Sledd's School of Pedagogy also failed to attract students. It was not revived in 1909, when Murphree created the first colleges at UF: Law, Arts and Sciences, Agriculture, and Engineering.

5. Yonge to Murphree, July 13, 1911, box 14, Murphree Records.

6. Yonge to Murphree, August 19, 1912, Murphree to Yonge, box 3, Murphree Records. Murphree shared similar concerns about Sheats's views with Buck King (Murphree to T. B. King, June 21, 1912, box 15, Murphree Records).

7. Murphree to Yonge, March 17 and June 14, 1913, box 3, Murphree Records.

8. Murphree to Yonge, March 14 and 17, 1913; Murphree to Wartmann, July 26, 1913, box 3, Murphree Records. The quote from Buckman appears in a proposal made to the Board of Control attached to the letter to Wartmann. Murphree to State Representative W. T. Martin, June 4, 1913, box 13, Murphree Records.

9. Kellum to Murphree, May 6, 1913, box 13, Murphree Records.

10. Sheats to Murphree, May 8, 1919, box 13; Murphree to Hathaway, June 11 and 14, 1913; Murphree to Buckman, June 11, 1913; Buckman to Murphree, July 5, 1913, box 15, Murphree Records.

11. Murphree to Conradi, June 23, 1913; Conradi to Murphree, July 1, 1913, box 15, Murphree Records.

12. Murphree's opinions of Buckman and Sheats were expressed in a number of letters. For examples, see Murphree to W. A. Rawls, March 14, 1921, box 19; and Murphree to Conradi, April 27, 1916, box 16, Murphree Records.

13. Murphree to Buckman, July 8, 1913; Sheats to Murphree, July 1 and 25, 1913; Murphree to Sheats, July 24, 1913, box 15, Murphree Records.

14. BOC Minutes, July 5, 1913.

15. "Report of President Conradi," July 25, 1913, box 2, Yonge Papers. The Buckman Act actually required a tenth-grade education at Florida State. Subsequent to the act, the Board of Control lowered admission standards for both UF and FSU.

16. Ibid.

17. "Report of President Murphree," July 26, 1913, box 2, Yonge Papers; Yonge to Murphree, July 25, 1913, box 3, Murphree Records.

18. BOC Minutes, August 4, 1913.

19. Guilliams to Murphree, April 22, 1919; Murphree to Guilliams, May 1, 1919, box 17, Murphree Records. The university's normal school included a two-year elementary professional course that first appeared in the catalogue in academic year 1914-15. The elementary course was one of four courses available in the normal school. The university did not report enrollment data for the specific courses, but there were only 31 students enrolled in the entire normal school in academic year 1919-20 (*University of Florida Course Catalog, 1919-1920*, 194).

20. Wayne Flynt, *Cracker Messiah: Governor Sidney J. Catts of Florida* (Baton Rouge: Louisiana State University Press, 1977). This superb biography is the only detailed study of the Catts administration.

21. Ibid., 126-27.

22. Murphree to Earman, April 16, 1919, box 3, Murphree Records.

23. Ibid.

24. Earman to Murphree, April 22, 1919, box 3, Murphree Records.

25. Earman to Murphree, April 30, 1919, Murphree to Earman, May 1, 1919, box 3, Murphree Records.

26. Futch to Murphree, May 3, 1919, Murphree to Futch, May 5, 1919, box 3, Murphree Records.

27. Hodges to Earman, May 1919, box 8, Hodges Papers.

Chapter 10. Budget Battles

1. Conradi to Yonge, July 31, 1916; Wartmann to Yonge, July 19 and 26, 1916; Kellum to Yonge, August 1, 1916, box 3, Yonge Papers. An elementary school in Tallahassee was named after Brevard. The Caroline Brevard Grammar School is on the US National Register of Historic Places and now houses community services for the Leon County School District.

2. BOC minutes, August 14, 1916; Yonge to Sheats, August 16, 1916; Sheats to Yonge, October 23, 1916, box 3, Yonge Papers.

3. Wartmann to Yonge, July 26, 1916; Jennings to Yonge, February 2, 1917; Conradi to Yonge, March 31, 1917, box 4, Yonge Papers.

4. Murphree to Edward Comegyo, April 4, 1916, box 15; Murphree to Frank Ellis, May 12, 1921, box 19, Murphree Records. Most states, including Florida, operated on a biennial budget. Florida's legislature met on odd-numbered years.

5. David O. Levine, *The American College and the Culture of Aspiration, 1915-1940* (Ithaca, NY: Cornell University Press, 1986), 32-51. Enrollment for land grant colleges rose 65 percent between 1919 and 1928.

6. Roger Geiger, *The History of American Higher Education: Learning and Culture from the Founding to World War II* (Princeton, NJ: Princeton University Press, 2015), 408-22; Helen Lefkowitz Horowitz, *Campus Life: Undergraduate Cultures from the End of Eighteenth Century to the Present* (New York: Knopf, 1987).

7. *Report of the Board of Control for the Biennium Ending 1930*; "Biennial Report of the President of the University of Florida to the Board of Control for the Biennium Ending June 30, 1930," 47. Figures for Florida State were derived from enrollment reports in the

college's catalogue. Florida State experienced a brief drop in enrollment after the war only to rebound very rapidly.

8. *Report of the Superintendent, 1920, 1924, 1928.*
9. Murphree to Eli Futch, May 6, 1919, box 13, Murphree Records.
10. Hodges to Earman, April 2, 1919; Earman to Hodges, April 26, 1919, box 14, Hodges Collection.
11. Murphree to Hathaway, May 6, 1919; Hathaway to Murphree, May 7, 1919, box 17, Murphree Records.
12. Murphree to Bryan Mack and Joe Earman, May 6, 1919; Murphree to Earman, May 17, 1919, box 4; Murphree to Wartmann, May 21, 1919, box 3, Murphree Records.
13. F. M. O'Byrne to J. B. Hodges, April 11, 1921, box 3, Yonge Papers. The bulletin is attached.
14. Stoutamire to Sheats, April 15, 1921, box 2, Records of Superintendent Sheats; Conradi to Murphree, May 19, 1921, and Murphree's reply, May 23, 1921, box 18; Murphree to Frank Ellis, April 23, 1921, box 19, Murphree Records.
15. Murphree to Hodges, April 27, 1921, box 3, Murphree Records.
16. Ibid.
17. Hardee to University Council, May 5, 1921, box 13, Murphree Records.
18. Murphree to Hodges, May 7, 1921, box 3, Murphree Records.
19. Hodges to Murphree, April 28, 1921, box 3, Murphree Records.
20. Murphree to Frank Ellis, May 21, 1921, box 19, Murphree Records.
21. L. C. Crofton to Murphree, April 12, 1921, and Murphree's response, April 14, 1921, box 13, Murphree Records.
22. BOC minutes, June 10 and June 20, 1922; Conradi to Yonge, July 13, 1922, box 7, Yonge Papers.
23. Sutton to Yonge, July 7, 1922, box 7, Yonge Papers.
24. Wartmann to Yonge, July 31, 1922; Kellum to Yonge, July 15, 1922; and Yonge's reply July 24, 1922, box 7, Yonge Papers. In this series of letters, Yonge wrote that Trammell had come to regret his 1909 opinion. BOC minutes, July 20, 1922.
25. Murphree to Hardee, October 10, 1922, box 13, Murphree Records; *Report of the Board of Control for the Biennium Ending 1922*, 70.
26. Murphree to the Board of Control, April 12, 1923; Sutton to Murphree, April 13, 1923; Murphree to Sutton, April 16, 1923, box 3, Murphree Records. Sutton had been captain of the 1914 Florida football team. After leaving the Board of Control, he became an early Florida football booster.
27. Sutton to Hon. G. P. Garrett (UF Alumni Association), June 9, 1923, copy attached to a letter from Sutton to Murphree of the same day, box 3, Murphree Records.
28. Murphree to Board of Control, November 8, 1923, Yonge to Murphree, November 14, 1923, box 9, Yonge Papers.
29. Murphree to Yonge, September 27, 1924, box 3, Murphree Records.
30. Murphree to Sealey, February 6, 1924; Sealey's protest is attached. See also letter from Sam McInnis, principal in Auchula, to Murphree, February 16, 1924, box 21, Murphree Records.

31. Yonge to Murphree, January, 19, 1925, box 14, Murphree to F. M. O'Byrne, secretary of the University of Florida Alumni Association, October 28, 1920, box 1, Murphree Records. Benton finally received permission to limit enrollment in 1926. The announcements for 1926 state: "Pending the provision of enlarged facilities for instruction, the right is reserved to limit the number of freshmen admitted to the College of Engineering, to such number as can be properly accommodated with the present facilities" (*University of Florida Catalog 1925–1926*, 45).

32. MacWilliams to Murphree, November 7, 1923; Murphree to MacWilliams, November 8, 1923, copies sent to the Board of Control, box 9, Yonge Papers.

33. Murphree to Board of Control, October 8, 1921; Murphree to Board of Control, February 12, 1921, box 3, Murphree Records; BOC Minutes, March 3, 1913.

34. Murphree to Ellis, May 13, 1925, box 13, Murphree Records.

Chapter 11. The Ordeal of Nathan Young

1. Young to Earman, April 8, 1919, box 16, Hodges Papers; Nathan Young to P. K. Yonge, March 20, 1908, box 1, Yonge Papers.

2. Antonio F. Holland, *Nathan B. Young and the Struggle over Black Higher Education* (Columbia: University of Missouri Press, 2006), 72–75; *Report of the Board of Control for the Period ending December 31, 1912*, 20, Exhibit "B." A&M reported more than 100 grammar students enrolled in the model school in 1923 (William Howard to Diamond, October 18, 1923, box 9, Yonge Papers).

3. *Journal of the Senate*, "Report of Legislative Visiting Committee," May 21, 1909, Nathan Bryan to P. K. Yonge, June 8, 1909, box 1, Yonge Papers.

4. Nathan Young to Yonge, June 19, 1909, box 1, Yonge Papers. Cone's attack only delayed the construction of the sanatorium. A college pictorial brochure depicts a sanatorium in 1916, which also served as a training facility for the college's nursing program. It later became a hospital serving Tallahassee's Black community.

5. Holland, *Nathan B. Young*, 89–90.

6. Nathan B. Young, "Florida: Our Contiguous Foreign State," in *These "Colored" United States*, ed. Tom Lutz and Susanna Ashton (New Brunswick, NJ: Rutgers University Press, 1996), 90.

7. Paul Ortiz, *Emancipation Betrayed: The Hidden History of Black Organizing and White Violence in Florida from Reconstruction to the Bloody Election of 1920* (Berkeley: University of California Press, 2005), 142–228. Young's participation in the events of 1920 is found at 165–68 and 180. See also Holland, *Nathan B. Young*, 92–94.

8. Holland, *Nathan B. Young*, 91. As Holland points out, the post of state supervisor of Negro schools was funded by the General Education Board with the idea of improving African American education in the South. In Florida, and probably elsewhere in the South, it had the opposite effect as Brinson worked diligently to undermine educational opportunities for Black students.

9. Holland, *Nathan B. Young*, 90–97, and Reginald K. Ellis, "Nathan B. Young: Florida A & M College's Second President and His Relationships with White Officials," in *Go Sound the Trumpet! Selections in Florida's African American History*, ed. David H. Jackson Jr. and Canter Brown Jr. (Tampa, FL: University of Tampa Press, 2005), 165–69, chronicle

Young's ordeal with state officials. Both argue that the Board of Education and the Board of Control worked in concert. A fuller examination of the record, though, indicates that the attacks against Young were initiated by the governor and some members of the Board of Education without Yonge's knowledge or input. Nevertheless, Yonge, too, felt that A&M's curriculum gave too much emphasis to the liberal arts, and he did not oppose the resolutions adopted by the Board of Education.

10. Sheats to Yonge, July 27, 1921, box 2, Records of Superintendent Sheats; Holland, *Nathan B. Young*, 96–97; BOC Minutes, April 11, 1921; BOE Minutes, June 22, 1921.

11. BOE Minutes, July 29, 1921.

12. Ibid.

13. Young to Yonge, August 10, 1921; Yonge to Young, August 12, 1921, box 6, Yonge Papers.

14. Young to Yonge, August 13, 1921; Yonge to Young, August 15 1921, box 6, Yonge Papers.

15. Young to Yonge, August 15, 1921, box 6, Yonge Records.

16. Holland, *Nathan B. Young*, 99–100.

17. Ibid.; BOC Minutes, January 9, 1922. Only three of the sixty-nine were unable to make payment.

18. Yonge to Wartmann, January 24, 1922; Wartmann to Yonge, Janaury 26, 1922, box 6, Yonge Papers.

19. BOC Minutes, March 13, 1922; Sheats to Yonge, March 27, 1922, box 2, Records of Superintendent Sheats.

20. Young to Sheats, April 3, 1922; Sheats to Yonge, April 5, 1922, box 7, Yonge Papers; Sheats to Yonge, May 5, 1922, box 2, Records of Superintendent Sheats.

21. The comparison with other African American presidents appears in a document called appendix A in box 7 of the Yonge Papers, but it is unclear who compiled the information and to what document it appended. Salaries of faculty and administrators were published in several sources including the annual reports of the Board of Control.

22. Yonge to Wartmann, May 15, 1922, box 7, Yonge Papers; Yonge to Sheats, May 23, 1922; Sheats to Young, May 24, 1922; Young to Sheats, May 25, 1922; Sheats to Yonge, May 24, 1922, box 2, Records of Superintendent Sheats.

23. BOC Minutes, June 10, 1922.

24. Sheats to Young, June 14, 1922, box 2, Records of Superintendent Sheats.

25. Yonge to Hardee, August 15, 1922; Hardee to Yonge, August 26, 1922, box 8, Yonge Papers.

26. BOC Minutes, June 11, 1923. Holland, *Nathan B. Young*, 161–62.

27. BOC Minutes, June 11 and July 9, 1923; Holland, *Nathan B. Young*, 161–62; Executive Committee of the Florida A&M Alumni Association to the Board of Control, June 15, 1923; Howard to Yonge, June 16, 1923; J. T. Diamond to Yonge, July 17, 1923, box 8, Yonge Papers.

28. BOC Minutes, October 8, 1923.

29. Diamond to Yonge, October 14, 1923; Howard to Yonge, October 11, 1923, box 9, Yonge Papers. Leedell W. Neyland and John W. Riley, *The History of Florida Agricultural and Mechanical University* (Gainesville: University of Florida Press, 1963), 78–81,

attribute the student strike to the decision that boarding fees be paid in advance. They also questioned whether the fires were deliberate: "Since no one was apprehended and since the losses were not attributed to arsonists, it must be assumed that the fires started accidentally. Nevertheless, the rapidity with which they occurred bespoke the probability of irregularity." Neyland and Riley's book was published in 1963. Over time, the origins of the student protest and the cause of the fires were acknowledged and even celebrated by the FAMU community. See, for example, Evan Miles, "The Fires of FAMC," October 3, 2012, the *FAMUAN* online, http://www.thefamuanonline.com/2012/10/03/the-fires-of-famc.

30. Diamond to Board of Control, October 14, 1923; Wartmann to Yonge, October 15, 1923, box 9, Yonge Papers.

31. Wartmann to Yonge, October 15, 1923; Diamond to Board of Control, October 14 and 16, 1923, box 9, Yonge Papers. Diamond named the thirteen expelled students, ten men and three women.

32. Wartmann to Yonge, October 15, 1923; Howard to Yonge, October 16, 1923; box 9, Yonge Papers. A threatening letter purporting to be from the KKK was also sent to Howard accusing him and similar Black educators of causing the flight of African Americans northward by failing to provide suitable schools in the South. Yonge, Hardee, Diamond, and Howard were convinced the letter came from a Young supporter and not the Klan (Yonge to Wartmann, October 22, 1923; Diamond to Yonge, October 23, 1923, box 9, Yonge Papers).

33. Diamond to Yonge, no date (only second page exists); Yonge to Diamond, October 8, 1923, box 9, Yonge Papers.

34. Diamond to Yonge, November 2, 1923; Diamond to Board of Control, November 6, 1923; Howard to Yonge, October 30, 1923, box 9, Yonge Papers.

35. Diamond to Board of Control, January 22, 1924; BOC Minutes, March 10, 1924. Neyland and Riley relate that three students were brought before Prudential Committee and questioned about the Gibbs fire (Neyland and Riley, *The History of Florida Agricultural and Mechanical University*, 79). No charges were made, but the three were expelled. No mention of this is made in the Yonge Papers or the minutes of the Board of Control.

36. BOC Minutes, March 13, 1924; Vestel to Yonge, March 17 and April 8, 1924, boxes 9–10, Yonge Papers.

37. Diamond to Yonge, March 19, 1924; Yonge to Diamond, March 21, 1924; Wartmann to Yonge, March 20, 1924; Yonge to Wartmann, March 22, 1924; Yonge to Weaver, March 22, 1924; Diamond to Howard, May 13, 1924; Howard to the Board of Control, June 9, 1924, boxes 9–10, Yonge Papers. Howard subsequently disappears in the historical record. He is not listed in the college catalogue for academic year 1924–25.

38. Lee to Yonge, March 25, 1924; Yonge to Diamond, May 25, 1924; Yonge to Wartmann, June 14, 1924; Wartmann to Yonge, June 16, 1924; Weaver to Yonge, June 18, 1924; Yonge to John Cooper, June 14, 1924; Yonge to Albert Blanding, June 19, 1924; Lee to Yonge, telegram, June 20, 1924, box 10, Yonge Papers.

39. Leedell W. Neyland, *Twelve Black Floridians* (Tallahassee: Florida Agricultural and Mechanical University Foundation, 1970), 28–29.

40. Young to Yonge, September 10, 1924; Young to Lee, June 8, 1925, box 10, Yonge Papers.

41. Neyland, *Twelve Black Floridians*, 30–31; Wikipedia on John Temple Graves.

Chapter 12. President Murphree's Final Battle

1. Murphree to the Board of Control, March 6, 1925, box 6, Murphree Records.

2. Murphree to the Board of Control, March 6, 1925, and October 10, 1925, box 6, Murphree Records. Murphree credited H. Harold Hume, who was then employed at the Glen Springs Nursery, with getting Olmsted to do the work.

3. The capital campaign did not go well. A considerable sum was lost in a 1924 bank failure because the campus YMCA director failed to insure the deposit. Bryan died in 1925, and the Bust of 1927 ended any further fundraising efforts. The remaining assets from the campaign went unused until the Works Progress Administration funded the construction of the Florida Union in 1939. The capital campaign is extensively documented in box 14, Murphree Records. Bryan's nomination of Murphree is mentioned in Samuel Proctor and Wright Langley, *Gator History* (Gainesville: South Star, 1986), 34.

4. BOC Minutes, February 5, 1927.

5. Murphree to Yonge, February 15, 1927; Murphree to Diamond, February 18, 1927; Diamond to Murphree, February 18, 1927; Martin to Yonge, February 16, 1927, copy of letter, box 7, Murphree Records.

6. BOC Minutes, February 19, 1927.

7. W. B. Davis to Yonge, March 1, 1927; Lane to Yonge, February 23, 1927, box 13, Yonge Papers; Murphree to Diamond, February 16, 1927, box 7, Murphree Records.

8. Maguire to Stoutamire, January 27, 1927, copy sent to Murphree, box 21, Murphree Records.

9. Murphree to Maguire, January 31, 1927; Maguire to Murphree, February 2, 1927, box 21, Murphree Records.

10. Murphree to Maguire, February 11, 1927; Maguire to Murphree, February 28, 1927, box 21, Murphree Records.

11. Murphree to Maguire, March 1, 1927, box 21, Murphree Records.

12. Maguire to Murphree, March 3, 1927; Murphree to Maguire, March 5, 1927, box 21, Murphree Records.

13. Yonge to Murphree, February 19, 1927, box 13, Yonge Papers.

14. Murphree to J. W. McGlothlin, February 3, 1927, box 21, Murphree Records.

15. The *Independent Florida Alligator* traces its origins to a publication that appeared in 1906 called the *University News*. Sledd's records, though, paint the publication as a moneymaking scheme by someone who enrolled at the university but never attended classes. Only six issues were printed (Sledd to Bryan, January 28, 1907, vol. 8, Sledd Records). The cartoon appears in the *Florida Pennant* 1, no. 4 (February 1908). The cartoon does not appear among the numbered pages of the publication, and there is nothing on its reverse side. It is likely that the page was inserted after the edition was reviewed and approved by the faculty committee on publications. Felkel had been a student at the Florida State College when the Buckman Act was passed (George M. Chapin, *Florida, 1513–1913: Past, Present and Future*, vol. 2: *Biographical* [Chicago: S. J. Clarke, 1913], 78–

79). Agendas and Minutes of the University of Florida General Assembly of Faculty, vol. 2, September 29, 1908, series 81, University of Florida Archives.

16. The story of *Cason vs. Rawlings* is told in Patricia Nassif Acton, *Invasion of Privacy: The Cross Creek Trial of Marjorie Kinnan Rawlings* (Gainesville: University of Florida Press, 1988).

17. Murphree to Maguire, March 5, 1927, box 21, Murphree Records.

18. Maguire to Murphree, April 14, 1927; Murphree to Maguire, April 16, 1927, box 21, Murphree Records.

19. Maguire to Murphree, March 29, 1927 (letters attached), box 21, Murphree Records.

20. Kellum to Yonge, April 13, 1927, box 13, Yonge Papers.

21. Maguire to Murphree, April 19, 1927 (copies of Felkel and Cason letters attached), box 21, Murphree Records.

22. Murphree to J. C. Jenkins, April 4, 1927, box 21, Murphree Records.

23. Murphree to Maguire and Maguire to Murphree, May 3, 1927, box 21, Murphree Records.

24. Murphree to Maguire, May 9, 1927, box 21, Murphree Records; Watson to Yonge, June 12, 1927, box 14, Yonge Papers.

25. Maguire to Murphree, May 11, 1927, box 21, Murphree Records.

26. *Laws of Florida, 1927,* chap. 12012; Diamond to Yonge, February 7, 1928, box 14, Yonge Papers.

Postscript: More Revolutions and Then the Counterrevolution

1. Records related to the presidential search can be found in the January-February 1928 folder, box 14, in the Yonge Papers.

2. "Conversation with Linton Grinter and Mike Gannon," *Conversation* (television program), 1979, WUFT-TV, Gainesville, FL, https://ufdc.ufl.edu/AA00052503/00001/.

3. Palm Beach College and St. Petersburg College both claim to be Florida's oldest public community college. The dispute centers over the origins of St. Petersburg College as a private school.

4. James L. Wattenbarger, *A State Plan for Public Junior Colleges: With a Special Reference to Florida* (Gainesville: University of Florida Press, 1953). James L. Wattenbarger and Harry T. Anderson, "A Succinct History of the Florida Community College System," in the manual prepared for the Board of Trustees of the Florida College System, 2012, https://afc.memberclicks.net/assets/docs/community%20college%20history.pdf

5. *Desegregation Status Report for 1977-78 and 1978-79,* Florida Board of Regents, 1979, 83-84.

6. *St. Petersburg Times,* February 26, 1960. Yonge's story was related to me in 2021 by Roy Hunt, professor emeritus of the University of Florida's College of Law, who met Yonge years after his departure from Florida. The story is supported by circumstantial evidence in the records of the University of Florida. Many articles and monographs, as well as two documentaries, have focused on the Johns Committee. Jennifer Paul Anderson and Thomas V. O'Brien, "Pork Choppers, Presidents, and Perverts," *American Edu-*

cational History Journal 43 (2016): 75–92, provides a solid overview of the committee's impact at the University of Florida and the University of South Florida.

7. *Report of the Space Era Education Study* (Tallahassee: Florida Board of Control, 1963).

8. David J. Nelson, "William Haydon Burns," in *The Governors of Florida*, ed. R. Boyd Murphree and Robert A. Taylor (Gainesville: University Press of Florida, 2020), 535–36.

9. "The Chancellor and the Legislature (A Parable)," box 6, E. T. York Papers, series P25, University of Florida Archives; hereafter cited as York Papers. Within the York Papers is a series entitled "Higher Education Governance" that includes York's extensive email correspondence as well as numerous published reports on governance issues in Florida and elsewhere.

10. Ken Wald to E. Travis York, October 29, 2002, box 7, York Papers.

11. The napkin story and the reorganization efforts are explored in depth in Michael R. Mills, "Stories of Politics and Policy: Florida's Higher Education Governance Reorganization," *Journal of Higher Education* 78 (2007): 162–87.

12. Higher Education Governance, box 6, York Papers.

13. Higher Education Governance, box 8, York Papers.

14. York to Bush, fax, October 2, 2000; York to Bush, October 4, 2000; Chuck Young to York and Adam Herbert, copy to David Colburn, October 31, 2000; York to Bush, November 14, 2000, box 6, York Papers.

15. David Colburn to York, November 29 and 30, 2000; Chuck Young to York, November 30; Bruce Smathers to York, December 1, 2000, box 6, York Papers.

16. York to Young, December 1, 2000, box 6, York Papers.

17. The activities of the Excellence in Education Foundation are documented in boxes 7 and 8 of the York Papers.

18. The activities of Floridians for Constitutional Authority are documented in box 8 of the York Papers. The files include a detailed account of the board's first meeting given to York by Richard Briggs, the faculty representative on the Board of Governors.

19. York to Dexter Douglas, Jon Mills, and Thom Rumberger, November 2, 2003, box 8, York Papers.

20. Smathers to York, August 25, 2003; Smathers to York, October 2, 2003, box 7; Smathers to York, March 16, 2004, box 8, York Papers.

21. Mills, "Stories of Politics and Policy," 162.

22. John Winn to York, December 4, 2000, box 6, York Papers.

23. Although it was given no say in its establishment, the Board of Governors was tasked with overseeing Florida Polytechnic's opening and development.

24. "Bill to Merge Florida Poly, New College into UF Dies in Florida Legislature," *Tampa Bay Times* (online), March 6, 2020.

25. *Orlando Sentinel*, June 6, 2022.

Sources

Those Who Came Before

The merits and characteristics of the Buckman Act have been argued in several doctoral dissertations and in the unpublished works of Lucius Moody Bristol. All were written before 1960. The consensus interpretation viewed the act as the progressive denouement to a complicated and less than inspiring fifty-year prehistory. The act was signed into law by Governor Napoleon Bonaparte Broward, a populist and progressive Democrat, who targeted the plight of the state colleges in his 1905 legislative address. These same historians also focused on the aspects of the act relating to governance and the establishment of the Florida Board of Control. The creation of a single board to govern multiple institutions seemed a remarkably advanced idea for its time, preceding as it did similar bodies in other states. These views are most evident in the works of Glenn Ballard Simmons, Francis Arlington Rhodes, and Samuel Proctor. The sole dissenting voice on the progressive merits of the Buckman Act was that of Lucius Bristol.

Bristol taught sociology at the University of Florida from 1920 to 1940. Ill health forced Bristol into special status in 1940, but the exigencies of war called him back into the classroom, if only briefly. As part of his special-status assignment he was asked to take on several projects. During those years, and then after his official retirement in 1947, Bristol produced several works on higher education that examined key points in Florida's history, including the Buckman Act. Bristol's study of the Buckman Act was completed in 1945 and revised the following year. Copies of the manuscript were distributed but never published. Gender segregation was one of the facets of the Buckman Act that intrigued Bristol as it seemed out of place for an ostensibly progressive law. As he deconstructed the act further, he found other features in the bill that puzzled him, specifically the sections related to governance and teacher education. He also questioned the efficacy of the act, noting several features that were abandoned early on or even completely ignored. His research also led him to evidence that the Buckman Act could not have passed without the strong support of southern conservatives as well as progressive reformers. Bristol was still unraveling the act and its repercussions when he died in 1953 and his last unfinished manuscripts were turned over to Julien Yonge, curator of the P. K. Yonge Library of Florida History at the University of Florida.

Bibliography

MANUSCRIPT COLLECTIONS

State Library and Archives of Florida

Minutes of the Florida Board of Control, Series 1.
Minutes of the Florida Board of Education, Series 252.
Papers of Governor Napoleon Bonaparte Broward, Series 664.
Records of Superintendent William Sheats, Series 249.
Secretary John G. Kellum, Letterbooks, 1905–1907, Series 1182.
Superintendent of Public Instruction, Letterbooks, 1900–1913, Series 244.

University of Florida Archives, Public Records Series

Administrative Policy Records of President Albert A. Murphree, Series P4.
Administrative Policy Records of President Andrew Sledd, Series P3.
Agendas and Minutes of the General Assembly of Faculty, Series 81.
Florida Agricultural College Records, Series 162.
Minutes of the Board of Trustees of the Florida. Agricultural College, Series 157.

University of Florida Archives, Manuscript Collections

Lucius Moody Bristol Papers
Charles Langley Crow Manuscripts
James Marion Farr Manuscripts
Klein H. Graham Papers
Ashley Davis Hurt Papers
Morgan Family Collection
Edith Pitts Papers
Edward Powers Collection
Samuel Proctor Collection
Andrew Sledd Papers
E. Travis York Papers

P. K. Yonge Library of Florida History, Manuscript Collections

Napoleon Bonaparte Broward Papers
Henry Buckman Papers
Barney Colson Papers
James C. Hodges Papers
Philip K. Yonge Collection

FLORIDA GOVERNMENT DOCUMENTS

Bi-ennial Report of the Superintendent of Public Instruction of the State of Florida for the Two Years Ending in [. . .]. (Published biannually under the same title beginning with 1894. Previous reports were printed irregularly under different titles.)
Journal of the Proceedings of the Constitutional Convention of the State of Florida. Tallahassee: N. M. Bowen, 1885.

Journal of the Senate
Laws of Florida
Report of the Board of Control for the Biennium ending [. . .].
Report of the Space Era Education Study. Tallahassee: State Board of Control, 1963.

PERIODICALS AND NEWSPAPERS

Annual Report—Carnegie Foundation for the Advancement of Teaching
Florida School Exponent
Florida Times-Union
Gainesville Weekly Bee
Gainesville Sun
Ocala Banner
Orlando Sentinel
Pensacola Evening News
Pensacola Journal
Tampa Tribune
Transactions and Proceedings of the National Association of State Universities of the United States of America

COLLEGE PUBLICATIONS (TITLES VARY)

Catalog of the Florida Agricultural and Mechanical College
Catalogue of the Florida Agricultural College
Catalogue of the John B. Stetson University
Florida State College Catalogue
Register of the East Florida Seminary
University Record of the University of Florida

MICROFILM SOURCES

General Education Board Archives. Scholarly Resources, 1993.

SECONDARY SOURCES

Allen, Louise Anderson. "Silenced Sisters: Dewey's Disciples in a Conservative New South, 1900–1940." *Journal of the Gilded Age and Progressive Era* 5 (April 2006): 119–37.
Anderson, Jennifer Paul, and Thomas V. O'Brien. "Pork Choppers, Presidents, and Perverts: The Response of Two University Presidents to Attacks on the Privacy and Academic Freedom of Professors by the Florida Legislative Investigation Committee, 1956 to 1965." *American Educational History Journal* 43 (2016): 75–92.
Bristol, Lucius Moody. "The Buckman Act: Before and After (A Study in Historical Sociology)." Unpublished manuscript completed and distributed in 1946. A copy can be found in the Lucius Moody Bristol Collection in the University of Florida Archives.
———. "Lectures on Three Focal Points in the History of Higher Education in Florida." University of Florida course printout, 1951.
Bush, George Gary. *History of Education in Florida.* Washington, DC: GPO, 1889.

Chapin, George M. *Florida, 1513–1913: Past, Present and Future*. Chicago: S. J. Clarke, 1913.

Clayton, Bruce. *The Savage Ideal: Intolerance and Intellectual Leadership in the South, 1890–1914*. Baltimore, MD: Johns Hopkins University Press, 1972.

Colburn, David R., and Richard K. Scher. *Florida's Gubernatorial Politics in the Twentieth Century*. Gainesville: University Presses of Florida, 1980.

Collins, Eldrige R. "The Florida Constitution of 1885." Master's thesis, University of Florida, 1939.

Danbom, David B. "The North Dakota Agricultural College Controversy of 1893: Scientific Professionalism and Political Patronage." *North Dakota History* 51 (Winter 1986): 12–23.

Ellis, Reginald K. "Florida State Normal and Industrial School for Coloreds: Thomas deSaille Tucker and His Radical Approach to Black Higher Education." In *The Seedtime, the Work, and the Harvest: New Perspectives on the Black Freedom Struggle in America*, ed. Jeffrey L. Littlejohn, Reginald K. Ellis, and Peter B. Levy, 1–27. Gainesville: University of Florida Press, 2018.

———. "Nathan B. Young: Florida A & M College's Second President and His Relationships with White Officials." In *Go Sound the Trumpet! Selections in Florida's African American History*, ed. David H. Jackson Jr. and Canter Brown Jr., 153–72. Tampa: University of Tampa Press, 2005.

Fass, Paula S. *The End of American Childhood: A History of Parenting from Life on the Frontier to the Managed Child*. Princeton, NJ: Princeton University Press, 2016.

Flynt, Wayne. *Cracker Messiah: Governor Sidney J. Catts of Florida*. Baton Rouge: Louisiana State University Press, 1977.

Geiger, Roger. *The History of American Higher Education: Learning and Culture from the Founding to World War II*. Princeton, NJ: Princeton University Press, 2015.

Harris, Adam. *The State Must Provide: The Definitive History of Racial Inequality in American Higher Education*. New York: HarperCollins, 2021.

Holland, Antonio F. *Nathan B. Young and the Struggle over Black Higher Education*. Columbia: University of Missouri Press, 2006.

Horowitz, Helen Lefkowitz. *Campus Life: Undergraduate Cultures from the End of Eighteenth Century to the Present*. New York: Knopf, 1987.

Levine, Arthur, and Scott Van Pelt. *The Great Upheaval: Higher Education's Past, Present, and Uncertain Future*. Baltimore, MD: Johns Hopkins University Press, 2021.

Levine, David O. *The American College and the Culture of Aspiration, 1915–1940*. Ithaca, NY: Cornell University Press, 1986.

Loftin, U. Carr. "Mosquito Conditions at the University of Florida." Master's thesis, University of Florida, 1913.

Lutz, Tom, and Susanna Ashton, eds. *These "Colored" United States*. New Brunswick, NJ: Rutgers University Press, 1996.

Matthews, Terry Lee. "The Emergence of a Prophet: Andrew Sledd and the 'Sledd Affair' of 1902." PhD diss., Duke University, 1989.

McCarthy, J. Patrick. "The Articulation of Secondary and Higher Education: Four Historical Models at the University of Georgia." *History of Higher Education Annual* 19 (1999): 25–55.

Mills, Michael R. "Stories of Politics and Policy: Florida's Higher Education Governance Reorganization." *Journal of Higher Education* 78 (2007): 162–87.

Murphree, R. Boyd, and Robert A. Taylor, eds. *The Governors of Florida*. Gainesville: University Press of Florida, 2020.

Neyland, Leedell W. *Twelve Black Floridians*. Tallahassee: Florida Agricultural and Mechanical University Foundation, 1970.

Neyland, Leedell W., and John W. Riley. *The History of Florida Agricultural and Mechanical University*. Gainesville: University of Florida Press, 1963.

Nolan, David. *Fifty Feet in Paradise: The Booming of Florida*. New York: Harcourt, Brace, Jovanovich, 1984.

Ortiz, Paul. *Emancipation Betrayed: The Hidden History of Black Organizing and White Violence in Florida from Reconstruction to the Bloody Election of 1920*. Berkeley: University of California Press, 2005.

Parker, Oswald Lafayette. "William N. Sheats, Florida Educator." Master's thesis, University of Florida, 1949.

Proctor, Samuel L. "The University of Florida: Its Early Years, 1853–1906." PhD diss., University of Florida, 1958.

Report of the [U.S.] Commissioner of Education for the Year Ended June 30, 1912.

Rhodes, Francis Arlington. "The Legal Development of State Supported Higher Education Florida." EdD diss., University of Florida, 1948.

Richardson, Joe M. "'The Nest of Vile Fanatics': Williams N. Sheats and the Orange Park School." *Florida Historical Quarterly* 64 (1986): 393–406.

Rivers, Larry E., and Canter Brown Jr. "A Monument to the Progress of the Race: The Intellectual and Political Origins of the Florida Agricultural and Mechanical University, 1865–1887." *Florida Historical Quarterly* 85 (2006): 1–41.

Rolfs, Peter Henry. "Founders and Foundations of Florida Agriculture: A Serious and Frivolous Study of Men and Measures." *Proceedings of the Florida State Horticultural Society* (1935): 129–36.

Shofner, Jerrell H. *Nor Is It over Yet: Florida in the Era of Reconstruction, 1863–1877*. Gainesville: University Presses of Florida, 1974.

Simmons, Glenn Ballard. *The Consolidation of Higher Public Education in Florida*. A self-published and undated version of his 1933 doctoral dissertation at Johns Hopkins University.

Sledd, Andrew. "The Negro: Another View." *Atlantic Monthly*, July 1902, 65–73.

Thelin, John R. *The History of American Higher Education*. Baltimore, MD: Johns Hopkins University Press, 2011.

The University at Lake City. Lake City, Fla., 1905. (Presentation publication prepared by the City of Lake City for the members of the Florida Board of Control and the Florida Board of Education prior to the selection of the site for the University of Florida. The only known extant copy located at the P. K. Yonge Library of Florida History.)

Van Ness, Carl. "Florida's Sledd Affair: Andrew Sledd and the Fight for Higher Education in Florida." *Florida Historical Quarterly* 87 (Winter 2009): 319–52.

Vickers, Raymond B. *Panic in Paradise: Florida's Banking Crash of 1926*. Tuscaloosa: University of Alabama Press, 1994.

Wattenbarger, James L., and Harry T. Anderson. "A Succinct History of the Florida Community College System." *Florida College System Trustees Manual*, 2012.

White, Arthur O. "Race, Politics and Education: The Sheats-Holloway Election Controversy, 1903–1904." *Florida Historical Quarterly* 53 (1975): 253–72.

White, Arthur O., and Ronald K. Goodenow, eds. *Education and the Rise of the New South*. Boston: G. K. Hall, 1981.

Williams, Roger L. *The Origins of Federal Support for Higher Education: George W. Atherton and the Land-Grant College Movement*. University Park: Pennsylvania State University Press, 1991.

Williamson, Edward C. "The Constitutional Convention of 1885." *Florida Historical Quarterly* 41 (October 1962): 116–26.

Wills, Martee, and Joan Perry Morris. *Seminole History*. Jacksonville: South Star, 1987.

Woodward, C. Vann. *Origins of the New South, 1877–1913*. Baton Rouge: Louisiana State University Press, 1951.

Index

Page numbers in *italics* refer to illustrations

Adams, Frank, 79, 114
Adams, Nathaniel, 80
Anderson Memorial Organ, 162
Angle, A. J., 85
Association of Colleges and Preparatory Schools of the Southern States, 97, 159
Atlantic National Bank, 164, 169

Babson, Roger, 168
Beecher, Charles, 36
Bennett, Henry E., 120
Benton, John R., 65, 77, 143–44
Bethune-Cookman University, origin of, 15–16
Blackman, William, 105, 115
Blanding, Albert, 164
Blount, W. A., 114
Blue Ribbon Committee on Education Governance, 179
Brevard, Caroline, 132–33, 202n1
Brinson, J. H., 150, 204n8
Bristol, Lucius Moody, 72, 76, 90
Brogan, Frank, 184
Broome, W. S., 80
Broward, Napoleon Bonaparte, 49, 61, 64, 70, 79–80, 83, 89, 113–14
Brown, A. L., 80, 89, 125
Bryan, Nathan Philemon, 61, 64, 71; as chair of the Board of Control, 80, 89, 94, 114; conflict with Board of Education, 100–106, 110; speech at opening of the University of Florida, 96–97
Bryan, William Jennings, 162
Bryant, Farris, 177
Buchholz, Ludwig, 192n27

Buckman, Henry Holland, 70–74, 95, 97, 106, 114, 123, 125; his interpretation of the Buckman Act, 83–85
Buckman Act, 3–8, 51, 55, 76, 89, 98; bill history, 69–73; creation and membership of Florida Board of Control, 75–76, 112–13; dismantling of, 173–76; on gender segregation, 72–74, 124–26; impact on secondary education, 83–84, 97; on normal schools, 72, 74, 120; overview of, 71–72; on racial segregation, 71; repercussions of, 78–79, 91–93
Budget Commission, 137, 142, 164, 166–67, 169–70
Burns, Haydon, 177
Bush, John Ellis (Jeb), 179–84
Buttrick, Wallace, 100–101, 105, 114

Caldwell, Millard, 174
Candler, Warren A., 60, 82
Carnegie, Andrew, 108–9, 146
Carnegie Foundation for the Advancement of Teaching, 108–10
Carpenter, Hattie, 106, 122
Carson, Charles A., 44, 50–51, 60–61, 192n27
Cason, Turner Zeigler, 168
Cason, Zelma, 168
Catts, Sidney, 113, 128–31, 136
Cawthon, William S., 20, 95, 115, 117–18, 120, 157, 197n5
Chipley, William Dudley, 43
City University of New York, 187n1
Clute, Oscar, 44–48; allegation that he was gay, 47–48
Colburn, David, 181
Collins, LeRoy, 175
Colson, Barney, 85, 104

Index

Columbia College, 91
Cone, Fred P., 148, 159
Conradi, Edward, 116–17, 174; appointment as president of Florida State, 105; on normal schools, 125–27
Cooper, John C., Jr., 169
County superintendents and high school principals, annual meeting of, 114–15, 117, 122, 127, 129, 143
Cox, Nicholas H., 57–59, 63
Crawford, Henry Clay, 85, 89, 151
Crawford, William Bloxham, 102–4
Criser, Marshall, 182–83
Crofton, L. C., 141
Croom, A. C., 94–95, 110
Crow, Charles Langley, 65, 101–2

Daiger, Mary Alexander, 117
Davis, Jackson T., 157
Davis, Robert W., 55, 80
Davis, W. B., 164
DePass, James, 43–44
DeSantis, Ronald Dion (Ron), 186
Desegregation of Florida higher education, 176
Diamond, J. T., 128, 154–57, 163
Dickenson, E. R., 88
Du Bois, W. E. B., 30; comment on William Sheats, 18
Dudley, James, 153

Earman, Joseph, 128–31, 136–37
East Florida Seminary, 22, 31–32, 80, 92, 120–21; governance of, 14, 23–24; origin of, 3–4; transfer to Gainesville, 4
Edgar, George M., 32
Education Governance Reorganization Task Force, 179, 182
Edward Waters University, 16
Edwin M. Stanton School, 16
Ellis, Frank, 140, 144
Ellis, William, 85, 93
Excellence in Education Foundation, 182

Farmers' Institute, 50–51
Farr, James Marion, 60, 62–63, 65, 93, 101, 107
Fass, Paula, 99

Felkel, Herbert, 168–69, 207n15
Flagler, Henry, 41, 55, 162
Fleming, Francis P., 23, 169
Fleming, Francis P., Jr., 169
Fletcher, Duncan Upshaw, 173
Flint, Edward, 65, 82
Florida: Crash of 1927, 161; economic and demographic changes, 148–50; immigration and education, 14–16; racial violence, 149–50
Florida Agricultural and Mechanical College: accreditation, 159; arson, 155–56, 205–6n29, 206n35; attacks by Fred Cone, 148, 204n4; buildings, 146, 148, 158, 171, 204n4; curriculum, 146–48, 159; curriculum, attacks on, 150–52; enrollment, 147, 204n2; funding, 30, 146–47, 158–59; governance, 14, 71, 194n6; impact of Morrill Act of 1890, 28–30; origin as State Normal School for Colored Students, 6, 13; proposal to move to Lake City, 91; student protest, 154–57
Florida Agricultural and Mechanical University, 3, 6, 176, 179
Florida A&M Alumni Association, 154
Florida Agricultural College, 22–23, 32, 196n27; admission of women, 45–46; board of trustees, 14, 23–24, 188n7; creation of commercial department, 45; enrollments, 40, 46; Flagler Gymnasium, 41, 55; funding, 49, 192n20; origin of, 4–6; renamed University of Florida, 51–52; siting in Lake City, 37; termination of coeducation, 52–55
Florida Agricultural Experiment Station, 40
Florida Agricultural Institute, 7, 51, 187n6
Florida Bar Association, 168–69
Florida Board of Control, 173; admissions policy, 135–36; appointments to, 112–13; budgetary matters, 163–69; composition of first board, 79–80; conflicts with Board of Education, 92–93, 100–106, 116, 132–33, 137–44; creation in Buckman Act, 71, 75–76; demise of, 176–77; normal schools, 120–27; powers of, 111–13
Florida Board of Education: attacks on Florida A&M, 150–52, 204–5n9; constitutional revision of 1998, 179–83; creation of, 13–14;

normal schools, 124–25. *See also* Florida Board of Control
Florida Board of Governors, 182–86
Florida Board of Regents, 176, 178–79; dissolution of, 179–83
Florida Constitutional convention of 1885, 6, 12–14; Article 12, 13–14; creation of Florida Board of Education, 13; creation of normal schools, 13; role of Black delegates at, 13, 188n5
Florida Democratic Party, 12, 18, 24–25, 112, 150, 186
Florida Division of Community Colleges, 175
Florida Education Association, 98, 115, 138
Florida Education Governance Reorganization Act of 2000, 179
Florida International University, 179
Florida Legislative Investigation Committee, 176–77
Florida Memorial University, origin and early history of, 16
Florida Normal Institute, 123, 131
Florida Pennant, 168, 207n15
Florida Polytechnic University, 185
Florida School Exponent, 20–21, 81, 106
Florida Sentinel, 156
Florida Southern College, 15
Florida State College. *See* West Florida Seminary
Florida State College for Women: appropriations, 171; building construction, 162; coeducation, 173–74; enrollments, 121, 135, 202–3n7; faculty, 132, 141; normal school, 126–27, 201n15; summer schools, 116–17
Florida State Plant Board, 75
Florida State School for the Deaf and Blind, 71, 75, 171
Florida State University, 174, 178–79, 183–84; College of Medicine, 179, 184
Florida Supreme Court, rulings on Buckman Act, 69, 79, 114
Florida Teachers Association, 12, 21, 115
Florida Times-Union, 42–43, 86, 96
Florida 12th Grade Placement Examination, 175
Florida University. *See* West Florida Seminary

Floridians for Constitutional Authority, 183
Floyd, Wilbur, 120
Freedmen's Bureau, 17–18
Futch, Eli, 130, 136

Gainesville, 20, 24, 37, 104–5; campaign for university, 63, 79–80, 83–88, 87; malaria, 86, 88; selection as site for university, 3, 89–91, 196nn21–22
Gainesville High School, 21, 24
Gainesville Sun, 24, 42–43, 64, 103, 125
General Education Board, 20, 30, 100–101, 114, 157–58
Gibbs, Jonathan C., 12, 17
Gibbs, Thomas Van Renssalaer, 12–13, 28
Gilchrist, Albert, 102, 106, 110, 113
Gleason, William Henry, 5–6
Graham, Daniel Robert (Bob), 178, 182
Graham, Klein, 61, 165
Graves, John Temple, 12
Graves, John Temple, III, 159
Grinter, Linton, 174
Guilliams, John, 92–93, 128
Guisinger, Joseph, 94, 197n1

Haisley, William P., 36, 190n14
Hampton Institute, 30
Handy, Phil, 181–82
Hardee, Cary, 113, 117, 139–40; attacks on Florida A&M, 148, 150–52, 161
Hare, William, 75, 93–94
Harris, Frank, 44, 77, 80–83, 86, 104
Hatch Act of 1888, 40, 42, 44
Hathaway, Fons, 114, 124, 137
Haygood, Atticus G., 40
Henderson, John A., 34
High school curriculum, 98–100, 198n17
High school enrollments, 97, 135
High school inspectors, 100–101, 143
Historically Black colleges and universities, 2–3, 15–17, 73. *See also* Florida Agricultural and Mechanical College
Hodges, James B., 128, 131, 136–37, 140
Hodges, William C., 166, 170
Holbrook, Karen, 185
Holladay, Alexander Quarles, 40

Hollins, Dixie, 117, 129–30
Holloway, Luther, 104
Holloway, William H., 91; conflict with Andrew Sledd, 100–106, 109–10; election of 1904, 24–25; election of 1912, 114; his support for Gainesville as site for UF, 85
Hopkins, Ann, 182
Howard, William H. A., 154–57, 206n32, 206n37
Hulley, Lincoln, 91
Hume, H. Harold, 59, 207n2
Hurt, Ashley Davis, 38
Hutchins, Harry Burns, 111

Jackson, W. K., 53
Jasper Normal Institute, 18, 20, 92, 101
Jennings, Frank, 133
Jennings, William Sherman, 49, 162
Johns, Charley, 176–77
Julian, A. J. P., 82–83
Junior Colleges, 122, 131, 174–75

Kellum, John Gabriel, 72–73, 94, 123, 129, 132–33, 169, 197n1
Kern, F. L., 40
King, Jim, 184
King, Thomas B., 80, 85, 88–89
Knight, Peter O., 168
Knott, William V., 85, 89, 128
Kost, John, 31–32, 39, 190n8

Lake City, 3, 6, 131; campaign for university, 86, 88; response to losing university, 91, 95; selection of as site for the Florida Agricultural College, 18, 37–38, 40; town-gown relations, 42–48, 58, 62, 82–83; veterans' hospital, 91
Lane, E. W., 164
Law, Evander M., 7
Lee, John Robert Edward, 157–59
Little, Wilbert A., 20
Lockey, Joseph Byrne, 99–100, 115, 173
Lofton, U. Carr, 86, 88
Lynch, George, 101, 114–15, 120

MacWilliams, W. A., 144
Madison Normal School Bill, 123–27
Maguire, Raymer, 164–71

Marion, Melville C., 60, 63–64
Martin, John, 113, 144, 158, 161, 163–64, 168–71
Matthews, Eugene, 72
May, Philip Stockton, 168
McBeath, Tom, 12, 92, 106; on compulsory education, 21; on high school curriculum, 98–99; on state schools, 21–23; on William Sheats, 24
McCreary, H. H., 24
McLin, Ernest, 138
McNair, Warren, 8
McVey, Frank, 111
Mena, Aurora, 46
Mezes, Sidney, 111
Mills, Michael, 185
Miltamore, Cora, 142
Morgan, Ida, 54
Morrill Act of 1862, 4–5, 27–28; sale of Florida bonds and income from, 36
Morrill Act of 1890, 6; impact on Black state colleges, 28–30
Murphree, Albert Alexander, 51, 98; appointment as president of the Florida Female College, 92–93; appointment as president of the University of Florida, 103–7, 110; appointment as president of the West Florida Seminary, 32; on appropriations, 112, 133–34, 163–71; attributes of, 32–34, 59, 61; conflicts with William Sheats, 114–18; death, 171; disputes with Governor Hardee, 137–44; on enrollments, 85, 161–62; on normal schools, 121–30; relationship with governing boards, 110–12, 165–67; statues of, 33, 34; tenure at Florida State College, 32–36
Murphree, Jennie Henderson, 34

National Association of State Universities, 111
National Urban League, 157
New College, 185
Newell, Wilmon, 75
Normal schools (public), 20, 22, 34; after Buckman, 91–92, 104, 120–31; Florida Constitution of 1885, 13–14; development in US, 1–2, 121–22; early development in Florida, 6–7
North Carolina, development of state universities, 180–81

Oberlin College, 28, 30
O'Byrne, F. M., 138
Ocala Banner. See Harris, Frank
Ocoee massacre, 150, 155
Ogden, Robert Curtis, 30
Olmstead Brothers, 162, 207n2

Palm Beach Junior College, 175, 208n3
Peabody, George, 20
Peabody Education Fund, 20, 100, 122
Pensacola Evening News, 102
Pepper, Claude, 164
Persons, E. G., 82–83
Petway, Tom, 183
Phillips, Shelton, 114, 150
Pound, Jere, 70, 83
Powers, Henry C., 47
Priest, Clarence Patrick, 117
Pritchett, Henry S., 109–10
Public Education Capital Outlay, 177, 183

Rawlings, Marjorie Kinnan, 168
Reconstruction, 5–6, 13, 17–18, 36
Reitz, J. Wayne, 177
Republican Party of Florida, 5, 12, 178–86
Robert Hungerford Normal and Industrial School, 15
Roberts, Carolyn, 184
Robertson, L. E., 62
Rogers, Daisy, 45
Rolfs, Peter Henry, 31, 44, 47, 75, 81
Rollins College, 15, 105, 131
Russell, Albert J., 14, 32, 38–40

Schmidt, Karl, 63
Schwalmeyer, Maude, 132–33
Sealey, R. M., 143
Secondary school attendance, 19, 97–98
Seminary Act of 1851, 4
Servicemen's Readjustment Act of 1944, 173
Sheats, William Nicholas, 43, 48, 100; conflicts over high school inspector, 114–15; conflicts over Summer Schools, 116–17; dismissal of Thomas Tucker, 30; election of 1904, 24–25, 62–65; election of 1912, 114, 122; election of 1920, 117; on Florida A&M, 30, 151–53; on Florida Agricultural College, 6, 18; history of public education in Florida, 16–18; on normal schools, 122, 124–25; on race and education, 18, 188–89n14; on Reconstruction, 17–18; role at constitutional convention of 1885, 12; on state schools, 23–25; on teacher certification, 19–20, 116
Singletary, W. J., 138, 140
Sledd, Andrew, 44, 165; appointment as university president, 60–62; *Atlantic Monthly* article on race relations, 60–61; on colleges in the South, 11, 61, 109; conflict with William Holloway, 100–106, 114; fight with Professor Marion, 63–64; influence on Buckman Act, 70–71; on normal schools, 120–21; opinion on sites for university, 82, 88, 90–91; resignation as president of the University of Florida, 105–7, 198n11
Smathers, Bruce, 184
Smith-Hughes Act of 1917, 147, 150
South Florida Military Institute, 7, 22
Starke, George, 176
State appropriations for higher education, 134, 136–44
State Board of Community Colleges, 175, 179
State Normal and Industrial School. *See* Florida Agricultural and Mechanical College
State Normal School for Colored Students. *See* Florida Agricultural and Mechanical College
State Normal School for White Students, 6, 22, 30, 34, 92, 120
State University of New York, 187n1
State University System of Florida: post–World War II, 173–74; creation of chancellor's office, 177–78
Stetson University, 15, 23, 91; its appeal to out-of-state students, 84–85, 195n12
Stockbridge, Horace E., 48–51, 82
Storrs, R. W., 92, 120
Stoutamire, Frank, 155
Stoutamire, Ralph, 117, 138, 164–65
St. Petersburg Normal and Industrial School, 7, 72, 94, 120
Summerlin Institute, 192n18
Summer School Act of 1913, 116–17
Summer schools, 20, 115–17
Sutton, John B., 141, 143, 203n26

222 · Index

Taliaferro, Thomas Hardy, 49–56, 94; conflict with faculty at university, 57–60; conflict with Horace Stockbridge, 50–51
Tallahassee Democrat, 103
Tampa Tribune, 86, 104
Teacher certification, 19–20, 116
Tench, John, 80
Thackston, Jonathan, 115–17
The Ringling, 183
Thomas, Homer, 155
Thomas, William R., 80–81, 83, 95, 104–5
Thrasher, John, 179
Tigert, John James, 173, 194n1
Trammel, Park, 102, 113, 122, 124, 203n24
True, Alfred Charles, 44
Tucker, Thomas DeSaille, 28–30
Tuskegee Institute, 29–30, 157

United Negro College Fund, 157
University of Florida: admission requirements, 65, 97, 201n15; athletics, 36, 59, 65, 194n29, 203n26; Board of Trustees, 182–83; building construction, 162, 171–72; capital campaign, 162, 207n3; coeducation, 173–74; College of Engineering, 143–44, 204n31; College of Pharmacy, 161; desegregation, 176; enrollment, 97, 135–36, 161, 145, 161, 173; faculty, 63–65, 139–41, 144; Florida Legislative Investigation Committee, 176–77; normal school, 72, 74, 91–92, 103–4, 120–22, 124–30; opening of Gainesville campus, 95–97; preparatory department, 66; rankings, 174, 185; school colors, 96; Summer schools, 116–17; Teachers College, 120–27, 201n4; University Council, 139–40
University of Florida Alumni Association, 117, 138, 164–71
University of Georgia, 65, 74, 76, 97, 100
University of South Florida, 174, 185

Vals, Fred, 170
Van Hise, Charles, 110–11, 165
Veblen, Thorstein, 165
Vestel, E. D., 156–57

Walker, Stanton, 169
Wartmann, Edgar Lawrence, 113, 133, 142, 152, 155, 157–59
Washington, Booker T., 15, 24, 30, 65, 148
Watson, John, 170
Wattenbarger, James L., 174–75
Weaver, W. L., 155
West Florida Seminary, 22, 38, 120; conflict with University of Florida over coeducation, 52; creation of college department, 32; development of, 31–36; enrollment, 35; expansion of normal department, 34; Florida University, 31–32; football, 36; governance of, 14, 23–24; high school, 35, 194n30; origin of, 3–4; renamed Florida State College, 35, 52; Westcott Estate, 35
Wetherell, Thomas Kent (T. K.), 184
Wilson, George, 44, 83, 86
Winn, John, 181, 185
Wisconsin Idea, 111–12, 200n7
Wolfe, J. Emmett, 25

YMCA, 162
Yocum, Wilbur F., 43–44, 48–49, 62
Yonge, Philip Keyes (P. K.), 80, 176; attitude toward Florida A&M, 151–58, 204–5n9; on budgets, 143–44, 163, 167; as chair of the Florida Board of Control, 110, 113, 128, 132, 141; on normal schools, 122–27; Sledd resignation, 101, 103; vote on university site selection, 89–90
Yonge, Philip Keyes, grandson of P. K. Yonge, 176
York, E. Travis, 178, 180–84
Young, Charles (Chuck), 181–82
Young, Nathan Benjamin, 158–59; appointment as president of the State Normal and Industrial School, 29, 93; conflict with state officials, 151–54; at Lincoln University, 155; political involvement, 150; relationship with William Sheats, 148, 153; tenure at Florida A&M, 29–30, 146–48

Carl Van Ness is university librarian emeritus at the George A. Smathers Libraries at the University of Florida. A native Floridian, he served as an archivist in the libraries' special collections unit for thirty-eight years. In 2006, he was appointed as university historian by UF President Bernie Machen. As historian, Van Ness lectured and wrote frequently on subjects related to the university's past. He retired in 2022.